DEVOTIONS FROM PROVERBS

DEVOTIONS
from PROVERBS

LEARNING TO GROW IN YOUR WALK WITH
GOD THROUGH THE BOOK OF PROVERBS

*Read a chapter of Proverbs every day for 31 days
and watch what God does in your life!*

BRIAN J. RECHTEN

Xulon Press
2301 Lucien Way #415
Maitland, FL 32751
407.339.4217
www.xulonpress.com

Scripture quotations taken from the Holy Bible, New International
Version (NIV). Copyright © 1984 by Biblica, Inc.™. Used by permission.
All rights reserved.

Book cover design by Xulon Press.

Printed in the United States of America.

ISBN-13: 9781545614402

What others are saying about 'Devotions from Proverbs':

"The Proverbs instruct us in how to avoid foolishness and nurture wisdom. The Proverbs promote a diligent work ethic and point out the danger and the damage of laziness. They are candid about the benefits and hazards of money, sex, and power. The Proverbs bring uncommon insight to common sense and illumine ordinary life with extraordinary light. Anybody living in the real world will immediately see themselves in the pages of the Proverbs. Brian lives in the real world and the Proverbs have been his daily bread from God. As a businessman, Brian is well aware of the need to avoid foolishness and nurture wisdom, to walk in harmony with God and people, to develop a diligent work ethic, and is well aware of the benefits and hazards of money, sex, and power. His passion for the Proverbs and their power to keep a person on the right path shines out brightly in this volume of devotional writings. Allow Brian to take you on a guided tour of how God has used the book of Proverbs to guide, protect, and inspire his life."

- Tim Brown – Senior Pastor –
Calvary Chapel of Fremont, CA

"As Brian's first pastor, I witnessed his total surrender and compassionate love for his Savior. From day one he lived and showed his faith with boldness and without compromise. The insights he has gained in his journey are reflected in this book which will bless and challenge your life."

- Elmer Vogelsang: BA, MA, M DIV - Retired Minister,
Director of Missions, SBC

"Not having a mom and dad growing up, the book of Proverbs became my parents. Even before I became a Christian, I drank deeply from this wellspring of wisdom. As a follower of Christ, a husband, father and pastor for over 35 years, I greatly appreciate my good friend Brian's heartfelt devotional. This is practical, powerful, and sound advice from his years of pondering these proverbs and a remarkably helpful tool for reflecting and applying these truths to real life."

- Lloyd Pulley – Senior Pastor –
Calvary Chapel of Old Bridge, NJ

"Here is a book that can fill a deep need in Christian literature. When have you seen a daily devotional guide on Proverbs that involves a creative dialogue with the text? A proverb is not a promise. It is a very practical guide for the choices that shape our lives. A strength of this book is that our author looks at these ancient and God-inspired texts through the lens of Jesus, making it an effective tool for evangelism. I feel the push of the Spirit to begin my own journey through Proverbs as a result of this book."

- Ed Vanderhey - Retired Pastor -
First Baptist Church, Red Bank, NJ

"In reading 'Devotions from Proverbs' penned by you I can say unequiv-ocally that from the day you began sending them out to me it was my own daily and personal time with you and the Lord. The words spoke to me as I heard your heart and your struggles, and they became mine. I, along with untold others will be blessed by your insight and wisdom on how to make the unreal become real. 'God Bless' as you always say! Your brother in Christ."

- Dick Modzeleski – Founder & President,
Rainbow Funding & Real Estate

Reading this book is like having a conversation with a friend whose name is Jesus. Full of personal stories from his life experience, Brian reveals how God's infinite wisdom has personally instructed and guided him as he travels his own spiritual journey. These lessons will strengthen and encourage you in your faith walk. Clear, compelling, and written with con-viction, Brian plumbs the depths of God's Word.

- Pastor Tom Crenshaw,
New Monmouth Baptist Church

Table of Contents

Page

Introduction xi
Chapter 1. 1
Chapter 2. 13
Chapter 3. 24
Chapter 4. 36
Chapter 5. 46
Chapter 6. 55
Chapter 7. 65
Chapter 8. 73
Chapter 9. 84
Chapter 10. 95
Chapter 11. 106
Chapter 12. , , ...116
Chapter 13. 126
Chapter 14. 135
Chapter 15. 144
Chapter 16. 154
Chapter 17. 166
Chapter 18. 175
Chapter 19. 185
Chapter 20. 194
Chapter 21. 203
Chapter 22. , ... 213
Chapter 23. 224
Chapter 24. 236
Chapter 25. 248
Chapter 26. 257
Chapter 27. 268
Chapter 28. 279
Chapter 29. 289
Chapter 30. 296
Chapter 31. 305

Introduction

*S*everal years ago a dear friend and brother in Christ made a suggestion that has had a profound impact on my life. The suggestion? A simple one. He reminded me that the Book of Proverbs has 31 chapters, and that most months have 31 days. He gave me a challenge; to read a chapter of Proverbs every day for 31 days and see what happens. I took him up on the challenge. That was about 15 years ago! The result? It would take too long to tell you the impact this daily discipline has had on my personal walk with God and on my marriage, work and relationships.

The Book of Proverbs deals with just about every issue one faces in life. By the time you get through chapter 31, you will have been confronted with topics including, but not limited to, wisdom, justice, finances, purity, morality, honor, love, fairness, worship, relationships, honesty, business principles and righteous living. This has proven very helpful to me as a follower of Christ, and as a husband, father and grandfather.

Even as I write these words, I am reminded of how different my life could have been. I'm one of four siblings. My father left our mom when I was just three years old. My younger brother was just 18 months old. When I look at my own children and grandchildren, I wonder in amazement how a father can abandon those so young and in need of a Dad.

My childhood was not a good one. My mother did the best she could with us, but because she was always working to provide for us, we basically raised ourselves. Stating the obvious . . . it is never a good idea for kids to raise themselves! I started drinking alcohol at a very young age. And I experimented with drugs in my early to late teens. I barely made it through high school - not because of poor grades – but because I never did more than just enough to pass. The reason they weren't going to give me my high school diploma was due to absenteeism. You see, I missed

186 days of school over four years, the equivalent of an entire school year! My mom had to convince the district superintendent that nothing would be gained by failing me. I would just end up a statistic of another failed education. After high school, the only thing that kept me out of jail or death was my entrepreneurial desires. I missed all those school days . . . to work! Yep! I liked to work. I liked being productive, and I liked earning money. I had odd jobs starting at 10 years of age. I delivered newspapers, shined shoes, pumped gas and mowed lawns, to name a few. At 11 years old I won a bicycle by gaining the highest number of new subscribers to my paper route! In my late teens I sold vacuum cleaners and quickly became a top salesman! That led me to a career in paper and packaging sales (*I sold a vacuum cleaner to the owner of the paper company, and he hired me on the spot!*)

I kept real busy because I didn't want to think about my personal life and the heartache I always felt from my father's abandonment. I was 21 years old when someone had the courage to talk to me about a God who loved me and had a wonderful plan for my life. I needed a father desperately, and God seemed a good choice. I gave my heart and soul to my Lord and Savior Jesus Christ, and never looked back . . . and never regretted that decision. I began a life that no longer had regrets and no longer needed to be consumed by drugs and alcohol. My love for business and sales grew and grew, and at 26 I started my own company that I sold 25 years later. In all that time, I have felt God's love and presence in my life. As of this writing I have been a Christian for just over 40 years. Reading the Bible daily, as well as a chapter of the Book of Proverbs has helped mold me and make me into the man I have become. It is because of the life lessons learned from reading the Bible that I started writing these short devotionals from the Book of Proverbs to pass on to friends, family and co-workers. And now these devotionals have been compiled into the book you now hold! My hope and prayer is that by reading some of my thoughts gleaned from this amazing book . . . that you too will begin a daily discipline of reading a chapter of Proverbs each day.

My pastor back east has often stated that all the temptations you and I face today are the same that Adam and Eve faced; the lust of the eyes, the lust of the flesh and the pride of life. He has further stated that these temptations rule more supremely in various decades of life. For instance in our decade of the 20s, we tend to be ruled by the lust of the flesh. We're consumed with pleasure. We fantasize, we lust and we live life with a distinct emphasis on self. The trinity of stupidity; me, myself and I.

The decade of the 30s is the lust of the eyes. We want to start gaining things! A car, a better job, a house, a bigger house, a spouse, a bigger car, for some . . . a new spouse! We enlarge our bank account, our wardrobe and even our waistlines!

The decade of the 40s is the pride of life. We have arrived. We now know a lot about everything. We're smarter than most (or so we think). We look at our stuff with pride over all we have gained in this life. We are happy, or so we think.

By the time we get to our 50s, most of us will look back at the 20s, 30s and 40s and realize how immature, selfish and arrogant we were.

The 60s teach us that we still have so much to learn, just when we begin to realize we are running out of time. We sense a need to 'make a difference' in this world. We want to leave a legacy. We want our lives to have counted. If you are still under 50 . . . all is not lost! Some of the wisest advice I have ever received was from men and women in their 60s, 70s and 80s. Perhaps my ruminations will help you get started on a better path a little earlier in life! If this happens to just one person, I will consider this book a success!

This is where this book, and more importantly, the Book of Proverbs, can help you! On the following pages, I start with Chapter 1 of Proverbs, followed by several devotionals from a verse or group of verses from that chapter. I do this for all 31 chapters of Proverbs. You can choose to read one or more of the devotionals each day of the month. Don't feel any pressure. There's little value if you start reading Proverbs as a daily ritual that 'must' be done. Better to read when able, even if only once every few days or few weeks. Start journaling thoughts as you read. I've left a blank page at the end of each chapter for that very purpose. Should you get through all of them, you will have read over 200 devotionals!

You can wait and start reading at the start of the next month, or you can start with today's date and go from there. You could refer to this book more as a journal . . . or even a workbook as you start jotting down your own thoughts and ideas from each chapter. Spend some time reading *my* thoughts, but spend more time journaling *your* thoughts on the verses that have the most meaning to you. Commit to paper the thoughts that God puts on your mind and heart as you read.

I hope this proves helpful in your journey to a closer walk with God.

Brian J. Rechten, MAS, CRSM – September, 2017

Proverbs 1

Always start by reading the entire chapter of Proverbs 1 from your favorite Bible translation! I really look forward to the 1ˢᵗ day of the month… because I get to start over again in the Book of Proverbs. Solomon makes it real easy for us by telling us exactly why he wrote so many proverbs. The reason for his writing can be found in the first six verses of Proverbs 1.

I have written seven devotionals from Proverbs 1. I hope you find them to be beneficial in your personal walk with God. Remember to add some notes as you read them! After several months you will be amazed at the insights you will gain each time you re-read Proverbs 1-31.

Today's devotional thought from Proverbs 1:1-6

¹ The proverbs of Solomon son of David, king of Israel:

² for attaining wisdom and discipline;
for understanding words of insight;

³ for acquiring a disciplined and prudent life,
doing what is right and just and fair;

⁴ for giving prudence to the simple,
knowledge and discretion to the young-

⁵ let the wise listen and add to their learning,
and let the discerning get guidance-

⁶ for understanding proverbs and parables,
the sayings and riddles of the wise.

Solomon starts by stating very clearly why he penned these Proverbs. I often refer to this book as being loaded with the ingredients necessary in a recipe for a godly life. Remember that this is the same Solomon given a double portion of wisdom from God. Proverbs has been contrasted with Psalms in this way: Psalms is man writing to God and Proverbs is man writing to man. Proverbs is written to be a very practical guide to daily living. *(It is loaded with probabilities but not necessarily promises.)* I want to pass on the same recommendation that was made to me by a friend a dozen or more years ago, and that is to get into the habit of reading a chapter of Proverbs every day. I liked that suggestion and I have been doing it ever since.

So let's look at the application for us today. Why read Proverbs? For wisdom, for discipline and for insight as a start. Friends, I want these things in my daily life more and more. I read this quote awhile back:

"Men do not decide their future…they decide their habits…and their habits decide their future."

I think this states it well. Make reading Proverbs a part of your daily life and you will see a future loaded with wise choices . . . a disciplined life . . . a keener understanding of God's plan, a purpose for you . . . and a brighter future! Why else should we read Proverbs? Verse 3 shows us that we will learn how to make better choices, doing what is right and just and fair. We will actually develop better discernment in our decision making. I want that in my life. There are really only two types of decisions for every situation. There are moral decisions; those between right and wrong and there are priority decisions, those between right and right, but circumstances make one a better choice over the other. Example: "I'm going to cheat on my taxes." This is a wrong moral decision. Period. "I need a new car, so I may buy a brand new luxury car, or I may buy a late model used car with low mileage so I can take my family on a small vacation and still have money for a new washer and dryer that my wife says we need." This is a priority decision, and every person or family would have to determine which priority decision is the right one for them. These verses promise us we will learn how to make both types of decisions better when we have invested the time to develop discernment. Verses 1-3 show the personal benefits of reading Proverbs, but Verse 4 introduces the idea of giving or teaching or passing on this wisdom to others. Your life will take on new meaning and purpose as you learn and then pass on to others what you have learned. How cool is that? Verses

5 and 6 tell us that the wise will become wiser and the more we understand the better our counsel will be to others.

Friends, I want this in my life! I want to learn more and more about the wisdom of God. I want more and more to pass that wisdom on to those that God chooses to bring into my path. So I encourage you to take the challenge. Read a chapter of Proverbs every day. Do it for a month and I think you will find that you won't want to stop.

Think about these things – keep studying the Bible – and have a blessed day!

Today's devotional thought from Proverbs 1:7.

[7] The fear of the LORD is the beginning of knowledge,
but fools despise wisdom and discipline.

Solomon offers us a fundamental law of morality . . . and that is . . . our need to serve and worship God. This connection of a reverence for God and our moral compass is not immediately apparent. The word *fools* used here in Verse 7 is defined as one who is morally deficient. What's the point? We need to understand that faith in God is what gives meaning, purpose and direction to all other aspects of life. I may be preaching to the choir here and you may be thinking, *"Well of course Brian, everyone knows that!"* Well, I'm not so sure. We teach morals and ethics when we should be teaching the Word of God. Without our hearts yielded to God, our instincts are more natural and base, like an animal. Our main thoughts in life become survival, food and sex. If we're not showing someone their need for God then we will naturally gravitate away from wisdom and discipline. Listen to the words of Jesus in John 7:16-18:

Jesus answered, "My teaching is not my own. It comes from him who sent me. If anyone chooses to do God's will, he will find out whether my teaching comes from God or whether I speak on my own. He who speaks on his own does so to gain honor for himself, but he who works for the honor of the one who sent him is a man of truth; there is nothing false about him.

We live in a fallen world and the temptations of this world are far too great for anyone who is not anchored securely in Jesus. We need to be bolder than ever before in telling others of the hope that is within us. The obligation falls to those who have trusted in Jesus. God revealed Himself to us and gave us His Holy Spirit. What a wonderful gift, and worthy to be shared with all we come in contact with. 1 Corinthians 2:9-10 states:

However, as it is written:
 "No eye has seen
   no ear has heard,
   no mind has conceived
   what God has prepared for those who love him"— but God has revealed it
   to us by his Spirit.

The fear of the LORD is the beginning of knowledge and it all starts with a heart of repentance and a heart yielded to the Savior. Tell someone today of this glorious hope. May God give all of us a reminder of what our lives were like before we met Jesus. May we imagine what a Christless eternity would be like and may that image overshadow any fears of ridicule or rejection that might come from telling others about Him.

Think about these things – keep studying the Bible – and have a blessed day!

Today's devotional thought from Proverbs 1:8-9.

Listen, my son, to your father's instruction
   and do not forsake your mother's teaching.

They will be a garland to grace your head
   and a chain to adorn your neck.

I like these two verses a lot because the principles behind this wise counsel is universal, it applies to all of us, even those that received little or no wise counsel from their parents. My father left our home when I was three years old. My mother worked very hard to raise four children by herself, so she was rarely home. During my early years I was pretty much on my own to figure things out. As a result, I was undisciplined and got into trouble often. My turning point came when someone cared enough about my soul to tell me that there was a God who loved me and that this same God had a wonderful plan for my life. I welcomed my Heavenly Father into my life!

The point being made in today's verses is the importance of remembering our teaching, those good and godly truths we learn early in life or early in our walk with Jesus, regardless of who we learn them from. For me, the point of these verses is to remind me to always *'wear'* godly teaching and counsel wherever I go. In my 40 years as a Christian, I find myself getting into trouble when I forget *'the basics'* of living the Christian life. I get into trouble when I decide I've got this 'Christian thing' wired. The basic and practical principles of life are the ones we always have to come back to and this is true in so many areas of life.

A recent round of golf reminded me of this great spiritual truth. I was hitting from the 18th tee, having played a better than average round of golf, at least up to this point! I hit a horrible shot and left myself in an impossible situation. Now for a golfer, that part happens all too often. It's what happened next that taught me a spiritual analogy that I want to share with you today. What I did next was to ignore every 'basic principle' I have ever learned about golf. I tried to 'solve' my problem using my principles instead of golf principles. After my third attempt at getting back into the game, I realized I was abandoning those 'basic golf principles' I had learned. I went 'back to basics' and focused on the principles I was forgetting and got back into the game.

I have counseled many people over the years that have gotten themselves into one mess after another. They often forget that they got themselves into the mess in the first place. And some mess-ups have long and painful consequences! They do what I did on the 18th tee! Just as I 'forgot' that it was my poor shot that got me in trouble on the golf course, we forget that we usually have only ourselves to blame for the various messes we find ourselves in. We want to blame everyone else but ourselves! It's always someone else's fault and rarely our own. So what's the application for you and me today? Well first it's the reminder from these two verses, to listen and remember what we have learned. To put that knowledge into action 'before' we make the wrong choice.

Think about the circumstances you have found yourself in, then ask yourself this simple question: Did you know better? Did you abandon godly teaching and counsel? Did you 'remove' in a spiritual sense your godly clothing, those spiritual principles that were learned early in your Christian walk? If so, then make a decision today to go back to basics. Seek God daily, pray early and pray often. Read God's Word and apply what you learn to your daily life.

Think about these things – keep studying the Bible – and have a blessed day!

Today's devotional thought from Proverbs 1:10.

My son, if sinners entice you,
do not give in to them.

Here, Solomon offers another general rule to young people. Those of you reading this that are in your teens or 20s may not want to believe this yet, but you do have a lot to learn. I can say this without hesitation because I've lived more than a half-century . . . and I'm *still* learning. And I *still* have so much more to learn. Therefore this verse has application for all of us, no matter our age. The verses that follow Verse 10 outline a scenario whereby others get around this young man and start suggesting things for him to do that he would NEVER consider doing on his own. And here's the critical point, others *WILL* try to steer you into trouble. Misery does love company. Temptation is real! The challenge for each of us is to have the spiritual maturity to 'see it coming'. Even more important than that is to limit the opportunities for temptation. Friends, let's be honest. We all too often allow ourselves to go places and befriend people that we know are wrong for us. We might rationalize that we can handle it. After all, we're not going to let others steer us down a path we don't want to travel. Well that is easier said than done! We are not as mentally or spiritually strong as we think we are. That's why in Acts 2 Peter ended his appeal for repentance by warning his audience to

". . . save yourselves from this corrupt generation".

You see, there really isn't anything new under the sun. Over 2000 years later and the current generation is still trying to corrupt you and me. Watch TV for more than an hour and you'll see what I mean. Friends, sinners love company when they sin! With clever flattery and speech, they hook you with whatever bait they have available, like lambs to the slaughter, and then you spend the next weeks and months trying to repair the damage you've done to your testimony! You might even have someone in your life right now that is working overtime to cause you to stumble. Don't give in to them. Hold fast! Ask God to help you!

James 4:7 states: *Submit to God, resist the devil and he will flee from you.*

Take Solomon's advice on this matter. You will be glad you did!

Think about these things – keep studying the Bible – and have a blessed day!

Today's devotional thought from Proverbs 1:20-21.

[20] *Wisdom calls aloud in the street,*
she raises her voice in the public squares;

²¹ at the head of the noisy streets she cries out
  in the gateways of the city she makes her speech:

For the sake of space, I'm listing these two verses, but the theme of verses 20 through the end of the chapter deal with the dangers of rejecting wisdom. There is a right way, and that's the way of wisdom, found only in a life yielded to Christ. I love the way these verses state this: Wisdom calls aloud, she raises her voice above the noise and confusion of man's feeble attempts to answer life's questions.

We read here that through all the distractions of life, if we really listen, we'll hear the call of God on our lives. Scripture confirms over and over that God's Spirit is always speaking to man's heart. He loves all of His creation . . . He wants none to perish but all to have everlasting life. I thank God that He loved me enough to speak to my heart through all the foolish distractions of my own life, showing loving patience toward me. I love the verse in Isaiah 30:21 that states:

²¹ Whether you turn to the right or to the left, your ears will hear a voice behind you, saying, "This is the way; walk in it."

In fact, it's these words that caused me to yield my life to Jesus. I recall that day 40 plus years ago leading up to surrendering my life to Christ. I actually sensed God telling me "This is the way; walk in it." How about you? This is God raising His voice above all of life's distractions, and He's speaking to YOU! You are one of God's creations. He is speaking to you through His Spirit saying 'This is the way; walk in it." Why not yield your heart to Him right now? I've never known anyone that has ever regretted coming to Christ. Yet I've known many that have regretted that they didn't listen to His call and delayed for too many years the day they stood before God and admitted they were a sinner in need of a Savior.

Isaiah 1:18 states:

¹⁸ "Come now, let us reason together,"
  says the LORD. "
  Though your sins are like scarlet,
  they shall be as white as snow;
  though they are red as crimson,
  they shall be like wool.

Why not make today your day of Salvation? Pray right now. Confess you're a sinner in need of a Savior and ask Jesus to come into your life. You'll remember this day for the rest of your life and you'll spend eternity with God in Heaven.

Think about these things – keep studying the Bible – and have a blessed day!

Today's devotional thought from Proverbs 1:28-31.

²⁸ *"Then they will call to me but I will not answer;*
they will look for me but will not find me.

²⁹ *Since they hated knowledge*
and did not choose to fear the LORD,

³⁰ *since they would not accept my advice*
and spurned my rebuke,

³¹ *they will eat the fruit of their ways*
and be filled with the fruit of their schemes.

These four verses speak to the consequences of rejecting wisdom. The complete text can be found in Verses 20 thru 33. These verses capture the sad ending to a life of rejecting the Lord. Let me say first and foremost that if you are alive and hearing these words and have *not* given your heart to Jesus Christ, it's *not* too late. However, these verses do speak of a time when it will be too late. Since you don't have control over your next breath I urge you to cry out to God in repentance.

Isaiah 55:6 states:

Seek the LORD while he may be found;
call on him while he is near.

Jesus Himself states:

Behold…I stand at the door and knock. If anyone hears my voice and opens the door, I will come in and eat with him, and he with me. Revelation 3:20

In Luke 16 Jesus tells a parable about a rich man who died in his sin. It shows very clearly that once we die we have lost our opportunity to repent. I encourage you to read this parable. What about those of us who have trusted in Christ and have confessed our sins and have the assurance of eternity? I think we need to throw caution to the wind and become bold witnesses for Jesus. We should be doing this anyway, but now more than ever. The signs are clear. Time is running out. We need to have hearts that are broken for those dying into a Christless eternity. We need to get a picture of what it would be like. If we know the truth

. . . shouldn't we do whatever it takes to make sure others understand the eternal consequences of rejecting Christ? I will be forever grateful for the couple that told me about Jesus. They were more concerned for my eternity than whether or not I would mock their faith or reject their friendship. Keep in mind, there are only three responses you can get from sharing your faith.

1 – The person can accept the Lord!

2 – You get to plant a seed that God will water!

3 – You get rejected! And Jesus Himself states in Luke 6:22 that we are blessed when we are rejected because of our faith. So, there are only three ways a person can respond and all three are good! I say go for it! Let's start together in sharing our faith more boldly and let's see what God does!

Think about these things – keep studying the Bible – and have a blessed day!

Today's devotional thought from Proverbs 1:32–33.

³² *For the waywardness of the simple will kill them,*
and the complacency of fools will destroy them;

³³ *but whoever listens to me will live in safety*
and be at ease, without fear of harm."

These verses complete a broader thought on the overall topic regarding rejecting wisdom. The broader text begins at Verse 20, which you can read on your own. Let's start with the observation that the word 'simple' in this context describes a person that lacks moral direction and has a heart that is inclined toward evil. Solomon adds the word 'fool' which is an even stronger word, one that describes a morally deficient person who believes there is no God. Combine this with the words 'waywardness' and 'complacency' and we begin to see the real dangers of finding ourselves in this mindset. This verse points to a person that goes through life without a moral compass. One who slowly turns away from all godly influence and is drawn to a godless view of life.

For the Christian who knows where they will spend eternity, this paints the picture of a tragic end for this individual. The good news in this? God adds the word 'but'! This little word brings hope back into the picture! But

9

. . . whoever listens to Me will live in safety and be at ease without fear of harm! Brothers and sisters . . . God loves you! He wants you in Heaven! He has provided us a way, and that way is through Jesus! Eternal security! Security that comes from knowing and understanding that Jesus will never leave us or forsake us. The security that comes from knowing that God gives us His Holy Spirit to guide us and direct us if we would simply yield our lives to Him.

So . . . what's the application for you and me? Are we listening? The verse states: "but whoever listens." It seems simple, but it's so easy to miss. Are you and I taking the time to listen to God? Are we spending quiet time with Him each day? Or are we racing through life, operating in our own strength instead of His strength? Friend, His arms are not too short to carry each of us through this life. I have wasted far too much time striving in my own strength. I want my remaining time on earth to be effective for the kingdom. I want to have a heart that breaks for the simple and foolish person, remembering that this was me before some friends risked their friendship by telling me about Jesus. I pray you join me on this journey!

Think about these things – keep studying the Bible – and have a blessed day!

Proverbs 1 NOTES

Proverbs 1 NOTES

Proverbs 2

*S*olomon penned Chapter 2 with two thoughts on his mind: wisdom and morality. Both are essential traits in the life of a follower of Jesus. Both are skills that can be developed when we have hearts inclined toward God and a sincere desire to live for him.

Proverbs 2 remains a favorite chapter of mine. I suspect the same may hold true for you!

One can have lots of worldly wisdom and still be very foolish about the things of God. Solomon offers us godly wisdom in this chapter. Thinking morally comes over time as you develop a Biblical vs. secular worldview. Ask God to help you! David asked for wisdom and God gladly gave it to him . . . and more! I penned six devotionals from Proverbs 2. I hope you find them beneficial as you journey through this amazing book of the Bible. Don't forget to pause and write some personal thoughts as to what these verses mean to you. And always read the entire chapter before reading any of the devotionals. Let the word of God speak to you before the thoughts of any man!

Today's devotional thought from Proverbs 2:1-5.

[1] *My son, if you **accept** my words*
 *and **store** up my commands within you,*

[2] ***turning your ear** to wisdom*
 *and **applying** your heart to understanding,*

[3] *and if you **call out** for insight*
 *and **cry aloud** for understanding,*

*⁴ and if you **look** for It as for silver*
    *and **search** for it as for hidden treasure,*

I'll save Verse 5 for later. What can we observe from these verses? Well the first thing Verse 1 reminds me of each month is the need for you and me to accept God's teaching. We need to exercise faith! God has taken the first step, so the next step is ours. For me, it was only after accepting Christ that the cobwebs began to disappear. I had a lot of crazy questions before trusting in Christ. Yet, I remember how quickly many were answered after trusting in Christ. Until we take that step of faith, we remain much more vulnerable to the pull this world has on us. Now note the next few action words like 'storing up', 'applying', 'calling out', 'looking' and 'searching'. Our faith must be an active faith. I've known too many Christians that have tasted and seen that the Lord is good, but that's it. They stop pursuing their new relationship. God's word tells us we need to search for wisdom and knowledge the way we would search for hidden treasure. If I told you there was a million dollars buried in your backyard and you were guaranteed to find it, how long would it take you to start digging? Well, brothers and sisters there's far more than a million dollars buried in God's word. There is an abundant and fulfilling life waiting for you. Let's get back to the application for you and me.

If we do all these things, then we have the promise found in Verse 5:

⁵ then you will understand the fear of the LORD
    and find the knowledge of God.

I don't know about you but I want what God wants for me! I want to find the knowledge of God. His ways are far better than my ways could ever be. I want to encourage you to become a student of God's word, the Bible. Make knowing Him and His wonderful plan for your life a priority. I assure you that the outcome will be worth far more than silver or gold.

Think about these things – keep studying the Bible – and have a blessed day!

Today's devotional thought from Proverbs 2:1-9.

¹ My son, if you accept my words
    and store up my commands within you,

² turning your ear to wisdom
    and applying your heart to understanding,

³ *and if you call out for insight*
and cry aloud for understanding,

⁴ *and if you look for it as for silver*
and search for it as for hidden treasure,

⁵ *then you will understand the fear of the LORD*
and find the knowledge of God.

⁶ *For the LORD gives wisdom,*
and from his mouth come knowledge and understanding.

⁷ *He holds victory in store for the upright,*
he is a shield to those whose walk is blameless,

⁸ *for he guards the course of the just*
and protects the way of his faithful ones.

⁹ *Then you will understand what is right and just*
and fair—every good path.

I love the richness of God's Word and the simplicity of its message! Here we learn where wisdom can be found, and not just any form of wisdom, not worldly wisdom but wisdom from God. Where do we find it? In His Word, the Bible! Notice in Verse 2 the action steps required· turning our ears and applying our hearts! This tells me that understanding this wisdom requires some effort on our part. We read in Verse 4 that we need to look for and search for it the way one would search for hidden treasure. Do you read your Bible like you're searching for gold? Are you even reading your Bible? Sadly, too many churches today just toy with the Word of God. They pick a verse here and a verse there, instead of teaching the whole book cover-to-cover. Yet, these verses assure us that the only way we're ever going to find the knowledge of God is to study His Word - all of it! The Bible is God's love letter to His children! It's how God speaks to us! Friend, I urge you to make His Word a daily part of your life. Approximately 20 years ago I was challenged by my pastor to develop a daily habit of reading my Bible. He said to start in Genesis and end in Revelation. I've done this every year since. I've also encouraged many others over the years to do the same. Along the way I added the daily discipline of reading a chapter of Proverbs each day of the month. The Book of Proverbs is loaded with so many practical principles for daily living. Let me end by looking again at Verse 9:

Then you will understand what is right and just
and fair—every good path.

This verse gives us the likely outcome of living a life focused on God's plans and purposes. We see here that we'll come to understand what is right and just and fair. Wisdom, my friend, is the key to the Christian life. James 1:5 states:

If any of you lacks wisdom, he should ask God, who gives generously to all without finding fault, and it will be given to him.

Think about these things – keep studying the Bible – and have a blessed day!

Today's devotional thought from Proverbs 2:6-8.

[6] *For the LORD gives wisdom,*
    and from his mouth come knowledge and understanding.

[7] *He holds victory in store for the upright,*
    he is a shield to those whose walk is blameless,

[8] *for he guards the course of the just*
    and protects the way of his faithful ones.

What a great comfort can be had from reading these precious verses. Brothers and sisters, look at what comes to those who have put their faith and trust in Jesus Christ! First we get wisdom from the Lord! I don't know about you, but I need all the wisdom I can get just to navigate through life in this fallen world. We also have God's word that gives us knowledge and understanding. This is why reading the Bible is so critical for the Christian. The Bible is one of the key methods that God uses to talk to us! God also speaks through His Holy Spirit, and through other believers that He brings into our lives along life's journey. Solomon is writing this proverb to remind us that there is much to glean from the routine study of God's word . . . knowing that all wisdom comes from God.

Let's face it, beloved, we're sinners under construction! We face daily temptations and ungodly thoughts that are part of our sinful nature. But God has provided a way for us to live in this world and participate fully in it, even while going through this process called sanctification. From the day we accept Christ as our Savior, He is molding us and making us into the men and women He wants us to be. To be sanctified is to be set apart, or consecrated.

Look at what is available to us along the way! Verse 7 states that He is our shield as we walk through this difficult minefield we call life. We will never know on this side of Heaven all that He has actually shielded us from. Have you ever stopped to think about how many times you change your plans in the course of a week? Is He in those changed plans? Did God help you avoid a temptation that He knew you would be vulnerable to? Have you ever come upon a roadblock or detour or made a wrong turn? You get frustrated at the delay, but maybe it was God changing your path to avoid an accident.

He is our Guard, keeping watch over us day and night. And finally, He is our Protector. His Holy Spirit watches over His faithful ones. We so desperately need all that God makes available to us. How do we know all He has for us? By knowing Him intimately. We need to know His Word, the Bible. There is more to be learned and understood and experienced with each passing day. I want *all* He has for me. I want to understand His plan for my life more fully every day. How about you? If you haven't done so already, please read the entire chapter of Proverbs 2. This chapter talks a lot about paths, and how to choose them. So my question for you today is this: What path are you taking? I want to encourage you today. Choose God! He will lead you to the path of a life far more abundant than anything we can even begin to imagine!

Think about these things – keep studying the Bible – and have a blessed day!

Today's devotional thought from Proverbs 2:9-15.

If I were to title this devotional, it would be: *What path are you on?* In Verses 1-8 Solomon gives us a wonderful action plan for attaining wisdom. And the result of wisdom is always two-fold: what you gain and what you avoid!

Let's start by looking at Verses 9 through 11.

9 *Then (having gained wisdom) you will understand what is right and just and fair—every good path.*

10 *For wisdom will enter your heart,*
and knowledge will be pleasant to your soul.

11 *Discretion will protect you,*
and understanding will guard you.

So let me go ahead and ask the question. What path are you on? God's path or the world's path? Each day offers us many choices! This idea of daily choices is captured well in the classic book called Pilgrim's Progress by John Bunyan. He creates a brilliant word picture and story of the choices we have EACH DAY of which path we can choose to take. The main character in Pilgrim's Progress is called Christian and he sets out on a pilgrimage to the Celestial City and along his journey he meets all types of people. People with GOOD intent and people with BAD intent. It's a classic story and one I hope you will make a point to read. Friends, victory in this life and for eternity rests in our willingness to choose the better path.

I'll wrap up today's devotional with Verses 12 through 15:

12 *Wisdom will save you from the ways of wicked men,*
  from men whose words are perverse,

13 *who leave the straight paths*
  to walk in dark ways,

14 *who delight in doing wrong*
  and rejoice in the perverseness of evil,

15 *whose paths are crooked*
  and who are devious in their ways.

These verses give us a glimpse of what we avoid by making right choices. Have you ever heard the expression: "misery loves company?" It's true you know, and these verses describe men and women that are intent on bringing you and me down. Here we learn the dangers of leaving the straight path for the crooked path. Brothers and sisters, be very careful. These dark ways can be very dark. Madison Avenue paints a very attractive picture of this crooked path. Yet, I've had six decades to see what this path looks like 'up close and personal'. Friends, this life can be very dark when lived outside of God's plan and purpose for our lives.

Here's another thing life has shown me (contrary to the world's view) and that is the simple fact that I'm not miserable! I'm not unhappy and I don't feel like my path as a Christian has caused me to miss anything! I met the woman of my dreams, and she married me. I started a business that turned into a 25 year career. We have traveled the world. We have two children and as of this writing, two beautiful grandsons. We have great friends, great hobbies and great fun in this life! I can't even imagine a richer, more fulfilling life than the one I live today in Christ. Madison Avenue has it all wrong! I've walked the crooked path and I've walked the straight path offered to everyone who trusts in Jesus! I choose Jesus! He is the Way and the Truth and the Life! How about you? Are you trusting in Jesus

Christ alone for your salvation? He has a wonderful plan and purpose for your life. Why not pray right now and ask Him to be your Lord and Savior.

Think about these things – keep studying the Bible – and have a blessed day!

Today's devotional thought from Proverbs 2:12-15.

12 *Wisdom will save you from the ways of wicked men,*
    from men whose words are perverse,

13 *who leave the straight paths*
    to walk in dark ways,

14 *who delight in doing wrong*
    and rejoice in the perverseness of evil,

15 *whose paths are crooked*
    and who are devious in their ways.

Well, I've mentioned in past devotionals that Proverbs 2 is one of my favorite chapters in the book. There is so much practical advice and principles for godly living to be found in these verses, and today's verses are no exception. Wisdom, my friend, is the key to the Christian life. I've known a lot of very knowledgeable people that don't show much wisdom. You see knowledge is the totality of what we know but wisdom is how we apply what we know. There's a big difference. There are people in this world that have a clear desire to lead you down the wrong path, and they have no interest in your desire to live for God. And this is where wisdom comes into play. You see, there will always be situations in our life where we have choices in what path we choose to take. Let's assume for the sake of this discussion that both paths are acceptable, meaning we're not talking about a morally wrong path vs. a morally right path. Let's assume both paths are morally pure but based on knowledge that we have learned, we begin to apply wisdom that shows one path to be better than another. Let me try a real specific example. Suppose you need to buy a home. You get pre-approved for a mortgage for a certain amount of money. A realtor has now presented you with two homes in two different towns that both fit all your criteria. Knowledge would effectively cause you to consider the age of the furnace and when you will need to replace the shingles on the roof. Wisdom would cause you to commit the choice to prayer.

Wisdom would lead you to talk to people that know the area. You would also look into the crime rate in one town compared to the other. And finally, if you're a Christian, you would want to investigate churches in the two towns and make sure a solid Bible-believing and Bible-teaching church can be found. I hope this example helps to explain the difference between knowledge and wisdom. So what's the application for me and you? One thing I've learned about a life lived in service to Jesus Christ is that whatever path you're taking, if it's a good path then keep walking it. The danger in the Christian life is when we stop somewhere along the path and decide that we can put our Christian walk on hold. Brothers and sisters, when you stop moving forward in your relationship with God you will inevitably start going backward. So until God calls you heavenward, continue to walk with Him, live for Him and tell others about Him.

Think about these things – keep studying the Bible – and have a blessed day!

Today's devotional thought from Proverbs 2: The entire chapter!

Let me summarize the chapter by stating right from the start that it's my favorite of all 31 Proverbs. We can title this devotional: Moral Benefits of Wisdom. Verses 1-4 identify action steps we need to take in our search for wisdom.

*1 My son, if you **accept** my words*
    *and **store** up my commands within you,*

2 turning your ear to wisdom
    *and **apply**ing your heart to understanding,*

*3 and if you **call out** for insight*
    *and **cry aloud** for understanding,*

*4 and if you **look** for it as for silver*
    *and **search** for it as for **hidden treasure**,*

I get excited when I read these rich 'action' words. It's a reminder to me that wisdom isn't sitting on a shelf. It's not a charm we can wear on a bracelet. Wisdom is pursued diligently and purposefully! Have you ever watched a program like Animal Planet, when they describe how an animal pursues its prey? Some animals may track their prey for several days over hundreds of miles and risk their own safety in the process. That's how I picture wisdom! It's there but I need to be as diligent as a hunter to search for it. The rewards are worth it as stated in verse 5:

5 then you will understand the fear of the LORD
    and find the knowledge of God.

You'll really need to read the entire chapter on your own to fully understand all it has for you. Verses 1-11 outline what you get if you pursue wisdom. Verses 12-19 gives a great picture of what you avoid by pursuing wisdom. And Verses 20-22 highlight the better way of wisdom! On the few occasions that I've taught on Proverbs 2, I will usually ask my audience this question: What path are you taking??? Sadly, I run into too many people that don't have a good answer to that question. It's a risky business to not have a plan and purpose for your life. It's been said that it's hard to hit the bulls-eye if you don't have a target. So what's the application for me and you? Every day is a choice. We can choose to live for God and people or we can live for ourselves. My experience and what I've seen and learned in over 60 years of life and 40 years as a Christian is a simple truth. The path of God is a path to life and the path of selfishness leads to death and misery. Brothers and sisters, this world offers very little. It's all a façade! Remember the scene in the Wizard of Oz when the little dog pulls back the curtain to reveal the phoniness of the great OZ? The end result of every pursuit of riches and fame from this world often ends in misery. I want to encourage you to pursue life, pursue others and pursue God! Give your heart completely to Jesus and hold nothing back.

Think about these things – keep studying the Bible – and have a blessed day!

Proverbs 2 NOTES

Proverbs 2 NOTES

Proverbs 3

*S*tart today by reading all of Proverbs 3. This chapter offers additional insight and benefits to gaining wisdom in your walk with God. Keep reading Proverbs and wisdom will surely follow. By the way . . . Chapter 3 is my favorite chapter in the entire Book of Proverbs! The following pages offer seven devotionals from this awesome chapter!

Today's devotional thought from Proverbs 3:1-2.

1 My son, do not forget my teaching,
but keep my commands in your heart,

2 for they will prolong your life many years
and bring you prosperity.

There is much controversy in many circles on the topic of health and wealth. You may hear terms like 'Name it and Claim it'; or the 'Health & Wealth Gospel' and similar terms like it. For the purposes of today's devotional I prefer to focus on the simple truths of these two verses and view them in proper order. Please note Verse 1 states 'do not forget my teaching, but keep my commands in your heart'. What is being stated here?

It seems to me that if we learn God's word and His purposes for our life, then there is a strong probability that we will live a long, happy and *'heart'* healthy life. Why? Well to me it's obvious and in fact statistics do show, that people of faith live longer, healthier and happier lives. If we are living for Christ and following the teachings of His word, then we will most likely be living a balanced life.

What do I mean? We will not be out drinking and drugging. Many of us will either never smoke cigarettes or quit smoking. We will not be exposed to sexually transmitted diseases that have devastating effects on health and cuts too many lives short each year. We will have a balanced view of wealth and financial gain; hence we will not work ourselves to death chasing after money.

1 Timothy 6:6-9 states:

But godliness with contentment is great gain. For we brought nothing into the world, and we can take nothing out of it. But if we have food and clothing, we will be content with that. People who want to get rich fall into temptation and a trap and into many foolish and harmful desires that plunge men into ruin and destruction.

If we are not out partying every night or doing a lot of other meaningless things with our money then we are more likely to have a few extra dollars to invest for the future. So it's totally reasonable to expect that a Christian, living for God and following His word will, in fact, be much more likely to live longer and have sound financial principles.

Is this a guarantee? No. And anyone that says otherwise is misinformed and is being misleading. Scripture and church history are full of stories of godly men and women that have died young, lived with disease or hand-icaps and others that lived their entire lives without even the promise of a paycheck, yet were happy, fulfilled and content.

I was given good advice many years ago that I'll pass on to you. The percentages I mention are not meant to be specific or legalistic, but to be a practical guide to living. Learn to live on approximately 80% of your income. Live on 80%, give 10% away and save 10%. If you were inclined to follow this simple life principle, not too many years from now, you will more than likely be living a comfortable life, with quite a few dollars in the bank and a legacy of giving that will have an impact for eternity.

Think about these things – keep studying the Bible – and have a blessed day!

Today's devotional thought from Proverbs 3:3-4.

3 *Let love and faithfulness never leave you;*
    bind them around your neck,
    write them on the tablet of your heart.

4 Then you will win favor and a good name
in the sight of God and man.

Today's verses make me think of my precious wife. On a recent night, she was out having coffee with a girlfriend from church who needed some encouragement. Later that evening, she called me in a panic. It seemed her car wouldn't start and she needed me to come and rescue her. By the time I got there, three men had come to the aide of my wife and her friend. They were trying to jumpstart her car, but nothing was happening. As soon as I looked under the hood I immediately knew what the problem was. Her car battery happens to have plastic caps over the battery posts. I guess they're designed to help eliminate corrosion build-up. The problem is, these caps don't look like plastic. They look like metal. I had to learn the hard way myself several years prior when I had to jumpstart her car for the first time. It took me quite awhile to realize I was trying to make a connection, but the plastic caps were preventing it! Okay, by now you're asking yourself what this has to do with today's devotional. Well, there are two points that I think have direct application. The first point is that my wife modeled faithfulness. When I pulled up, she immediately had a peace about the situation and she understood that this 'dead battery' was an opportunity in disguise. Remember the three men that had come to her rescue? They were still there when I arrived, so I was able to point out that it only looked like they were 'connected' to the battery. My wife saw the spiritual principle being unfolded right before her eyes. If we're not 'connected' to Jesus each day, in prayer and Bible study and fellowship, we can't possibly receive the power available to us to live our lives for him! The second point was that my wife modeled love for these men. She wasted no time going to her purse and pulling out three Bible tracts to give to these kind men. She explained that there are no accidents in life, and they came to help her for a reason greater than they knew. She asked them if they would promise to read the tracts and they assured her they would. So, what's the application for me and you? Let love and faithfulness never leave you. Live an 'others' focused life, and watch what God will do!

Think about these things – keep studying the Bible – and have a blessed day!

Today's devotional thought from Proverbs 3:5.

5 *Trust in the LORD with all your heart*
and lean not on your own understanding;

This one verse catches my attention each time I read it! By nature, we tend to err on the side of leaning on our own understanding - I know I do. I often catch myself, sometimes several hours into a challenging situation only to realize that I haven't even thought of 'praying about it'. I guess I'm as guilty as the next person of having what I refer to as 'I' disease'. Not the eye that we see with, the other 'I' referring to ME . . . MYSELF . . . and I!

I can fix this. I know how. I have the answer. I, I, I!!! Instead it should be: God can fix this. God knows how. God has the answer. God, God, God!!! I've lived a lot of years leaning on my own understanding and, friends, the results weren't pretty! I have made every mistake in the book. It wasn't until I surrendered my heart to my Lord and Savior, Jesus, that I was able to see my life for what it was. We tend to go through life with blinders on. Then one day, God in His abundant mercy, allows us to see Him. The blinders come off, and the things that just the day before seemed so normal and right and okay come into clear view and we see what we've been missing. Even after this, we often manage to sneak back up onto the throne of our own lives and start leaning once again on our own understanding.

We have short memories and we somehow forget the mess we made of things when we were living outside the will of God. What's the application for you and me? Two thoughts come to mind. First, God has a wonderful plan for our lives. We need to trust Him. He will never leave us and He will never forsake us. He has given us His Holy Spirit that lives within us and to guide us, if we will simply yield our hearts to Him. Second, be patient with those around you that haven't come to this point of surrender to God. I often pray that God will remind me of how my mind thought before I came to Christ. It helps me avoid the tendency to think how foolish the world thinks, forgetting that this was me for a long period of time. My wife and I recently spent the evening at one of the large Jersey shore board-walks, just walking and praying and asking God for a few divine opportu-nities to talk with people about Jesus. We had wonderful conversations. God gave us a number of people that we sat with on a bench and had lengthy discussions about where they would go when they die. We didn't drive home that night. We floated home! It was so amazing to see how God orchestrated so many divine opportunities to tell others about Him.

Think about these things – keep studying the Bible – and have a blessed day!

Today's devotional thought from Proverbs 3:9-10.

9 *Honor the LORD with your wealth,*
with the first fruits of all your crops;

10 *then your barns will be filled to overflowing,*
and your vats will brim over with new wine.

In these two verses we have words that cover a multitude of great topics. The topics mentioned are productivity, faith, giving, honor and God's promises to His people. There are a lot of directions this devotional can go in, but for today I want to focus on productivity. I'm reminded of an agricultural analogy and the importance of putting our hand to the plow. If you're not familiar with this term, it means we have to *'work'* at whatever we are doing. The plow doesn't move by itself. The fields will not produce an abundant harvest without hard work! I interpret this to mean that God wants to bless us, but we have our part to play in this process. He is not going to bless laziness. We all have gifts and abilities that are meant to be used. These abilities can be used to provide for our needs, and they can be used to honor God in all we do. And by giving back from our *'first fruits'* we are participating in Kingdom work.

Malachi 3:10 is a familiar passage on this subject:

10 Bring the whole tithe into the storehouse, that there may be food in my house. Test me in this," says the LORD Almighty, "and see if I will not throw open the floodgates of heaven and pour out so much blessing that you will not have room enough for it.

The important thing to remember is to read God's Word in context. This is *not* to be interpreted as some kind of guarantee of prosperity for every Christian. We often forget the part about honoring God with our entire lives, putting Him first, and not with an attitude of *'what's in it for me'*. I'm reminded of the parable in Luke 12 of the rich fool whose land produced an abundant harvest. There's nothing wrong with the abundant harvest, but what the rich fool thought of the abundant harvest. He thought it was *his* accomplishment! He never acknowledged God, or thanked Him for the great crop! He was trusting in his own talent and newfound riches. He decided that he would tear down his barns and build bigger ones, never knowing his life would end that day and all he had would become someone else's.

So what's the application for me and you? It's simple! God has a wonderful plan and purpose for our lives. If we honor him with all aspects of our lives, then He is faithful and He will guide and provide for all our needs. We make a mistake when we turn this promise into dollar signs. I've known too many people of great wealth that are miserable and I've witnessed first-hand that money is *not* the solution to everything. Sufficiency should be your goal. My advice is to just be faithful to our Lord Jesus and watch and see what God does in your life! I'm confident that you will look back and see His hand of blessing all around you! In fact, you have His word on it!

Think about these things – keep studying the Bible – and have a blessed day!

Today's devotional thought from Proverbs 3:13-20.

13 *Blessed is the man who finds wisdom,*
  the man who gains understanding,

14 *for she is more profitable than silver*
  and yields better returns than gold.

15 *She is more precious than rubies;*
  nothing you desire can compare with her.

16 *Long life is in her right hand;*
  in her left hand are riches and honor.

17 *Her ways are pleasant ways,*
  and all her paths are peace.

18 *She is a tree of life to those who embrace her;*
  those who lay hold of her will be blessed.

19 *By wisdom the LORD laid the earth's foundations,*
  by understanding he set the heavens in place;

20 *by his knowledge the deeps were divided,*
  and the clouds let drop the dew.

What a clever question arises from these verses. Solomon urges us to seek diligently for wisdom. But the question becomes, what shall we get from wisdom once we've found it? I find it interesting how the pursuit of wisdom in these verses is contrasted with riches and honor! I have to think that God is giving us a chance here to really consider what it is that we're after in this life. God isn't saying that gold and rubies and honor are bad, but He is showing us that godly wisdom is far more valuable. He's telling us through these verses that we should want wisdom from God the way many want fame and fortune! In fact, He makes it very clear by contrasting the two that wisdom is a far better pursuit. I think we know this intuitively, but we still seem to want fame and fortune, often at any price! If we read a newspaper or watch even an hour of television we are sure to hear about another rich or famous person that is getting their third or fourth divorce or has died of a drug overdose or is checking into rehab or has committed suicide or any number of other tragic stories of the rich and famous.

Don't misunderstand me brothers and sisters. I'm not condemning wealth or fame! I'm just reading God's Word and asking myself if I'm pursuing the next step to be found in God's plan for my life in the same way an entrepreneur might be pursuing the next business opportunity? Am I as diligent to pass on what I've learned from God's Word as I am to offer business advice to someone who asks?

Wisdom from God is described this way by Jesus in Matthew 13, which reads:

"Again, the kingdom of heaven is like a merchant looking for fine pearls. [46]When he found one of great value, he went away and sold everything he had and bought it.

So friends, what's the application for me and you? It's this question: What are we doing TODAY . . . for Kingdom's sake? What are we reading, what are we watching, and what are we studying that will make God's plan for our lives clearer?

Let me close with the words of Jesus in Matthew 6:19-21:

Do not store up for yourselves treasures on earth, where moth and rust destroy, and where thieves break in and steal. [20]But store up for yourselves treasures in heaven, where moth and rust do not destroy, and where thieves do not break in and steal. [21]For where your treasure is, there your heart will be also.

Where are you storing your treasure?

Think about these things – keep studying the Bible – and have a blessed day!

Today's devotional thought from Proverbs 3:21-23.

My son, do not let wisdom and understanding out of your sight,
preserve sound judgment and discretion;
22 they will be life for you,
an ornament to grace your neck.
23 Then you will go on your way in safety,
and your foot will not stumble.

I don't know about you, but I can't be reminded enough about the peace and safety and spiritual wisdom available to me as a child of God. It's available, but it's not in pill form. You can't just take two of these a day and be spiritually healthy. Attributes like wisdom, knowledge, peace, patience, kindness - these are gifts available to us, but we have to develop them. The more we study God's word, the more we will understand and apply these gifts. Proverbs 2 tells us we need to search for wisdom like we would search for hidden treasure. So here's a question I ask myself often. Am I diligently seeking the Lord every day? Is my prayer life strong? Am I in His word the Bible, reading, learning and applying it to my daily life? My own pastor mentions to his flock regularly that if we're relying on 'just' church for our spiritual growth, we're in big trouble, because that's just not enough.

In addition to your own personal devotions and time reading God's word, another great idea is to seek out a spiritual mentor. We should all have someone in our lives that we give permission to ask us any question and tell us anything they're observing in our lives that could be a sign of trouble. It's not easy to find a good mentor/accountability partner, but it's worth the effort. Friend, God has a wonderful plan for your life . . . much greater than we can imagine.

Jeremiah 29:11 states:

[11] For I know the plans I have for you," declares the LORD, "plans to prosper you and not to harm you, plans to give you hope and a future.

Here's another precious promise from Matthew 7:7:

[7] "Ask and it will be given to you; seek and you will find; knock and the door will be opened to you. [8] For everyone who asks receives; he who seeks finds; and to him who knocks, the door will be opened.

So friends . . . God's word is full of amazing truths and life principles that will keep you from stumbling. Seek Him today like never before and watch what He will do!

Think about these things – keep studying the Bible – and have a blessed day!

Today's devotional thought from Proverbs 3:21-26.

Note: I wrote this devotional on the 10th anniversary of the 9/11 disaster.

21 *My son, preserve sound judgment and discernment,*
do not let them out of your sight;

22 *they will be life for you,*
an ornament to grace your neck.

23 *Then you will go on your way in safety,*
and your foot will not stumble;

24 *when you lie down, you will not be afraid;*
when you lie down, your sleep will be sweet.

25 *Have no fear of sudden disaster*
or of the ruin that overtakes the wicked,

26 *for the LORD will be your confidence*
and will keep your foot from being snared.

Have no fear of sudden disaster! Sudden disaster describes well what happened on 9/11, yet God is telling us to have no fear in these trying times! Our hope, confidence and peace must rest in the Lord. While groups and factions fight, and even so-called Christian groups hold public Quran-burnings, we miss the mark by a country mile! This is a time to be about the business of telling others about the peace, hope and eternal life that comes through faith in Jesus Christ.

We all need that gentle reminder that we're not in control of any of this. We can't control our next breath! Friend, there will always be great causes, great political battles, and ideological battles we can and should be a part of but never at the cost of alienating the very souls for whom Chris died. The challenge for me and you is to love our enemies and pray for those who persecute us. Jesus gave us the model for daily living in the Sermon on the Mount, so let me end with the blessed words from Matthew 5:3-12:

3 *"Blessed are the poor in spirit,*
  or theirs is the kingdom of heaven.
4 *Blessed are those who mourn,*
  for they will be comforted.
5 *Blessed are the meek,*
  for they will inherit the earth.
6 *Blessed are those who hunger and thirst for righteousness,*
  for they will be filled.
7 *Blessed are the merciful,*
  for they will be shown mercy.
8 *Blessed are the pure in heart,*
  for they will see God.
9 *Blessed are the peacemakers,*
  for they will be called sons of God.
10 *Blessed are those who are persecuted because of righteousness,*
  for theirs is the kingdom of heaven.

11"Blessed are you when people insult you,
  persecute you and falsely say all kinds of evil against you because of me.

12 *Rejoice and be glad, because great is your reward in heaven,*
  for in the same way they persecuted the prophets who were before you.

Think about these things – keep studying the Bible – and have a blessed day!

Proverbs 3 NOTES

Proverbs 3 NOTES

Proverbs 4

*R*ead Proverbs 4 with the thought of gaining wisdom at any cost! It should no longer be a mystery to my readers that wisdom is critical if the believer wishes to walk in the ways of the Lord. Chapter 4 offers more and more sound advice on how to gain wisdom. This may require some changes in your life . . . changes in priorities and changes in relationships. You need to ask yourself an important question: Are my friendships drawing me closer to God? Who is doing the influencing in the friendship? You or them? Ponder these thoughts as you read one or more of the following devotionals!

Today's devotional thought from Proverbs 4:11-12.

11 *I guide you in the way of wisdom*
and lead you along straight paths.

12 *When you walk, your steps will not be hampered;*
when you run, you will not stumble.

I confess I like analogies that include themes about 'straight paths'. I think it's because, as mentioned previously, my fondness for the classic book 'Pilgrim's Progress'. Every time the main character deviated from the straight path on his pilgrimage to the Celestial City, he would end up in trouble. Whenever he stayed on the straight path, things went well for him. We learn from Proverbs 4:11-12 that wisdom will help you stay on the straight path. We learn that this path aids us in our walk, and even when running, we will not stumble. The picture I want you to have in your mind right now is a clear, level path that's had all potential obstacles cleared out of the way. This is in contrast to a rough, overgrown path that has rocks and tree limbs and trash making walking or running very dangerous. The thought here is whether we are walking or running or whatever we are doing, make sure we are doing it with God at the center of it. Otherwise, like Christian, the main character in Pilgrim's Progress, you will find yourself in trouble and that trouble might be far worse than anyone can imagine.

I was reminded recently just how easy it is to get 'off the straight path'. I had a conversation with someone who has allowed themselves to drift far from God. Now they feel that they need to clean up their life before crying out to God. That's just a ploy from the devil. Satan wants you to believe you are not worthy . . . that you are too far gone to be used by God. Don't believe the lie!!! I shared with him something that I had just heard a radio preacher state. Here's how he put it:

"Don't wait to clean up your life before you cry out to Jesus…cry out to Jesus… and let Him clean up your life!"

So, what's the application for you and me? If you're walking the straight path with Jesus . . . praise God. I want to encourage you. Right living is a choice. Saying **no** to the things of this world is not always easy. God delights in your desire to live a godly life before Him. And remember, your life is being observed by others. And God is using your godly life to draw others to him. If however, you feel you've drifted from the straight path, don't wait to get right with Jesus! Every day you delay makes it harder to cry out to him. Every day you delay could lead to a regret that could have life-long consequences. Cry out to Him 'right now'. Confess your failure and He will help you get back on the right path. You have His word on it!

Think about these things – keep studying the Bible – and have a blessed day!

Today's devotional thought from Proverbs 4:18.

18 The path of the righteous is like the first gleam of dawn,
 shining ever brighter till the full light of day.

I'm giddy with excitement to share my thoughts with you about this verse. Oh, that we would live an 'others' focused life. Oh, that we would walk through each day knowing and believing that Jesus is the ONLY answer for every question about life on this earth! Oh that we would be the light reflectors that God wants us to be.

Listen to the words of Jesus in Matthew 5:14-16:

[14] "You are the light of the world. A town built on a hill cannot be hidden. [15] Neither do people light a lamp and put it under a bowl. Instead they put it on its stand, and it gives light to everyone in the house. [16] In the same way, let your light shine before others, that they may see your good deeds and glorify your Father in heaven.

Friends, these few verses are why we are here! If we've trusted in Christ for our salvation then we exist in this world to tell others about Him. I've learned firsthand in recent years that most people we meet are desperate for what we have. I spent far too many years as a Christian talking myself out of telling others about Jesus, listening to the lies of the enemy, that they will only mock me, or that there's a better time to talk to them, but not now! We need to boldly and confidently tell others about Jesus with no fear, doubts or hesitancy. If not me and you, then who?

Here's something that has helped me immensely in sharing my faith. And that is to just be faithful with my part. Be a link in the chain! You don't have to be the whole chain, and most often you won't be because God has someone lined up to be the next link, and another the next link until that person sees their need for a Savior. Here's one practical example. My wife and I try not to ever leave the house without a pocket full of Bible tracts. If one of us engages someone for more than a minute, we just automatically assume that to be a 'divine opportunity' to give them a tract and tell them about how God has changed our lives for the better. That's one simple thing you can start doing. And when you leave the house, pray that God will bring people into your path . . . and He will! Friend, your light will shine brighter and brighter each time you share with someone the hope that is within you. I can't encourage you enough to live radiantly for God today. Start focusing your time and energy on others and be the light that they need in order to see more clearly the face of our Savior!

Think about these things – keep studying the Bible – and have a blessed day!

Today's devotional thought from Proverbs 4:18-19.

*18 The path of the righteous is like the first gleam of dawn,
    shining ever brighter till the full light of day.*

19 But the way of the wicked is like deep darkness;
they do not know what makes them stumble.

The theme of Proverbs 4 is focused almost exclusively on *wisdom*. Verse 18 is such a wonderful statement of what we can expect if we seek wisdom with all our heart. The result of this pursuit is likely to be a path that will lead to a much happier and healthier life for those that are yielding their lives to God.

I love the sound of the words being used in this verse; *"the first gleam of dawn."* We may not want to be awake for the first gleam of dawn, but on those occasions that you have caught a sunrise, you know the feeling that comes from watching it.

I recall a trip to the Grand Canyon a number of years ago. My wife and I got up very early and walked out to the edge of the canyon. Just the two of us and our Bibles, and God, and His sunrise! It was truly spectacular! I love the way this verse continues; *"shining ever brighter till the full light of day."* I believe the key to the Christian walk can be found right here in these words found in Verse 18. The Christian walk requires us to choose to walk the right path! Proverbs are not promises, but they are probabilities, if we choose the right path. By choosing the path of righteousness, with each passing day, week, month and year, the light *(which represents Jesus)* will become brighter and brighter in our lives. Oh, what a possibility this verse offers those who choose this path!

Verse 19 gives us fair warning of the dangers of choosing the wrong path. When reading this verse, our tendency may be to see this verse as describing someone else, but certainly not you or me! Heaven forbid! Perhaps a better way to read this verse is more of a reminder of what could easily describe you or me, if we don't pursue righteousness. What is the end result of the Christian life that is never fully developed? I think it's a life that will be filled with great difficulty and many challenges. This is not to say that challenges can't come to the Christian, too. Even the Apostle Paul gives us a laundry list of challenges in 2 Corinthians 11:24-26:

24 Five times I received from the Jews the forty lashes minus one. 25 Three times I was beaten with rods, once I was pelted with stones, three times I was shipwrecked, I spent a night and a day in the open sea, 26 I have been constantly on the move. I have been in danger from rivers, in danger from bandits, in danger from my fellow Jews, in danger from Gentiles; in danger in the city, in danger in the country, in danger at sea; and in danger from false believers.

The difference though, is that for the follower of Christ, those challenges can be met with these other words from the Apostle Paul in Philippians 4:13:

"I can do all this through him (Jesus) who gives me strength."

The non-believer faces darkness differently than the believer. How I pray that when those dark times come, that those who have not given their hearts to Jesus, cry out to Him! What is darkness? Darkness is the absence of light! Have you ever been in a room or somewhere that was pitch black? Take a moment to picture what total darkness feels like. I'm talking about *total* darkness! Now imagine that you are required to walk an obstacle course in *total* darkness. There would be no possible way to avoid stumbling, tripping and falling many times over. Now imagine just a little bit of light becoming available, and what a difference just a little bit of light would make. Now, add more light! And a little more, and a little more! That picture you now have is the picture of the Christian that chooses a godly path. Brothers and sisters, I urge you to pursue Jesus with all your heart, soul, mind and strength. Don't settle for mediocrity in your Christian walk. You should want to be a bright beacon of light and hope to all you come in contact with. Be a light reflector for Jesus! You have His assurance that He will shine ever brighter in your life until the full light of day!

Think about these things – keep studying the Bible – and have a blessed day!

Today's devotional thought from Proverbs 4:20-22.

20 *My son, pay attention to what I say;*
    listen closely to my words.

21 *Do not let them out of your sight,*
    keep them within your heart;

22 *for they are life to those who find them*
    and health to a man's whole body.

These verses cover so many important topics but today I'd like to focus on the aspect of being teachable. Because Verse 20 starts with the words, 'my son', we might mistakenly limit the counsel given here to that of a father to a son when we should really interpret 'son' as anyone that has ears to hear, because Solomon's advice is universal to all that would heed his wise counsel. Whether a son or daughter, another relative, a co-worker or friend, if we've been walking with God for a number of years it's only natural to want to see those younger than us avoid some of the mistakes we may have made when we were younger.

It comes down to how teachable we are. Are we open to advice from those that have gone before us? Take Solomon for instance. He is called the wisest man that ever lived. He was given a supernatural gift of wisdom by God, so we sit at his feet the way we should? Do we read Proverbs daily as a rich source of practical advice on daily life? Do we see that these words are inspiration directly from the creator of the universe? Do we read God's word, the Bible, daily? Do we read godly writings of men like Charles Spurgeon, E.M. Bounds, John Stott, Ravi Zacharias and Alan Redpath?

If we're teachable, there are many ways to avoid some of the trappings of this world. These verses go on to show us that if we search for wisdom, and apply it to our hearts then there's a probability of health and happiness. Well isn't that a good thing? I've mentioned this in the past that research has shown that those that believe in God and pray regularly actually live longer and healthier lives. These verses are a fresh reminder of the richness of God's word and the way God's word has daily application for our lives. Verse 22 states 'for they', meaning the words of God, are life to those who find them. As Christians, we know that when this life ends we will spend eternity in Heaven. Of course, this applies to those that receive the free gift of salvation available to each of us when we call out to Jesus and confess we are sinners and ask for His forgiveness. He is faithful and just, to forgive our sins and cleanse us of all unrighteousness.

Think about these things – keep studying the Bible – and have a blessed day!

Today's devotional thought from Proverbs 4:23-27.

23 *Above all else, guard your heart, f*
   or it is the wellspring of life.

24 *Put away perversity from your mouth;*
   keep corrupt talk far from your lips.

25 *Let your eyes look straight ahead,*
   fix your gaze directly before you.

26 *Make level paths for your feet*
    and take only ways that are firm.

27 *Do not swerve to the right or the left;*
    keep your foot from evil.

There are hundreds of verses in the Bible that deal with various aspects of the heart but it is often noted that the very first reference to the heart in Genesis 6:5 is referred to in the negative. We have to know that our natural inclination of the heart is bent toward evil. We learn here in Verse 23 that out of the heart comes the issues of life. All that we are is based on what is in our heart. A cold, dead heart means our physical life is over. This is true spiritually, as well. In Psalm 139:3 David states:

3 *Search me, O God, and know my heart; test me and know my anxious thoughts.*

Spiritually speaking, are you 'heart' healthy? As we continue reading in Verses 24 thru 27 we will see some very practical advice for living out our lives. We learn in these verses that we're defiled by what we say (the mouth) what we see (the eyes) and by what we do (the feet). Solomon starts with our hearts and then uses our very bodies as a practical teaching tool. We are to be careful with what we say. Our words are important and we should choose our words wisely especially with the knowledge that others are always listening. We are to keep our eyes focused on God. This idea of keeping our eyes 'fixed' carries with it the sense that this is a pre-determined mindset. Before our feet hit the floor upon waking, we need to have determined in our hearts that we will not allow our eyes to distract us from what God has planned for our day.

And finally, we need to choose paths that are safe. One practical example I have used and heard many times states *"if you have a problem with alcohol, you shouldn't hang out in bars"*. Yet how often can we find ourselves on paths that we know are leading us in the wrong direction. Speaking of paths, if you have never read the book 'Pilgrim's Progress', I recommend you read it. This idea of paths and where we walk and the idea of keeping our eyes fixed on our ultimate destination are the themes of the wonderful story in Pilgrim's Progress. The main character, Christian, sets out to find the celestial city and each day of his journey he has to deal with the many distractions that he encounters along the way, including people, places and things. And it's interesting to note that these distractions include everything our verses for today deal with: i.e. what is said, what is seen and what is done. Brothers and sisters, there are many things and many people that will come into our lives that will be a constant source of distraction if we allow it. These verses remind us of the importance of starting each day on our knees, figuratively and maybe even literally before our God, seeking His divine guidance and pre-determined to live with eternity in mind.

Think about these things – keep studying the Bible – and have a blessed day!

Proverbs 4 NOTES

Proverbs 4 NOTES

Proverbs 5

*T*he topic changes dramatically in Proverbs 5. Take a moment to pray prior to reading this important chapter. This is the first of several chapters that Solomon devotes to the topic of adultery. This sin has clearly done great damage over the centuries. There is much that you and I can learn about avoiding this severely damaging sin.

Today's devotional thought from Proverbs 5:1-6.

1 *My son, pay attention to my wisdom,*
   listen well to my words of insight,

2 *that you may maintain discretion*
   and your lips may preserve knowledge.

3 *For the lips of an adulteress drip honey,*
   and her speech is smoother than oil;

4 *but in the end she is bitter as gall,*
   sharp as a double-edged sword.

5 *Her feet go down to death;*
   her steps lead straight to the grave.

6 *She gives no thought to the way of life;*
   her paths are crooked, but she knows it not.

Well, our topic is pretty clear today. We'll be discussing biblical warnings against adultery. Solomon does something very important before turning his attention to the topic at hand. He reminds his son one more time to pursue wisdom and to become a very good listener. You see it is so important to never stop seeking wisdom and knowledge. The day will never come when you 'get it'! In fact, the day you start thinking you 'get it', is the day you become vulnerable to the very temptation we'll talk about today. I've known several men that have been involved in adultery and in every instance, they always stated that they didn't wake up one morning and say "I think I'll become an adulterer today". On the contrary . . . nearly every instance involved men that were convinced that they could never fall into this sin. What should this show us? That none of us can assume invulnerability. Yet for the grace of God go I. I should mention that this sin is definitely NOT limited to men. Women are just as susceptible to this sin as men and in fact more and more women are falling into this sin. To the believer, I would caution you to avoid situations where you are alone with a member of the opposite sex that is *not* your spouse. Avoid conversations that would have you listening to the opposite sex talking to you about struggles in their marriage. Married men, if a woman starts showing interest in you, tell your wife. Then take steps to avoid being alone with this woman. When you start hearing yourself saying that you think you can help her, you're already in trouble. Women need to do the same thing. Always encourage someone struggling in their relationship to seek pastoral counsel. The sooner they seek help the sooner they can begin the healing and restoration process in their marriage. God is more than able to intercede. I have seen some of the most hopeless marriages find help and healing. It's a lie of the devil that your marriage is going to fail. Only the enemy wants that. God's arm is not too short for this. Philippians 4:13 is a great reminder that you can *". . . do all things through Christ who strengthens you."*

Think about these things – keep studying the Bible – and have a blessed day!

Today's devotional thought from Proverbs 5:7-10.

7 Now then, my sons, listen to me;
    do not turn aside from what I say.

8 Keep to a path far from her,
    do not go near the door of her house,

9 *lest you give your best strength to others*
   and your years to one who is cruel,

10 *lest strangers feast on your wealth*
   and your toil enrich another man's house.

We can easily observe that these verses deal with adultery, but as we look deeper and begin to interpret what God is showing us, we begin to see more than just the need to avoid adultery. We see an awesome picture of the steps we can take to avoid this sin and many other sins by applying these principles to our lives. You will often hear teachers of the Bible speak about the need for 'hedges'. These aren't the hedges that separate your yard from your neighbors, but the idea is similar. Verse 8 speaks about keeping on a path far away from this particular temptation. It teaches us much more! It teaches us how to avoid adultery and how to avoid any temptation that is one you know yourself to be vulnerable to. For example, if you're a man and your temptation is to lust after women, then you may be wise to not choose lifeguarding as a profession. If your temptation is to buy too many clothes and jewelry, you may not want a job in a department store. You get the idea. God is showing us the importance of removing ourselves from the proximity of the temptation. We shouldn't go anywhere near a place of temptation! It seems obvious, yet I've known many people who put themselves in the wrong place all the time and then wonder why they mess up!!! Have you ever heard the statement; "that's an accident waiting to happen?" If you want to be kept from harm then you need to keep out of harm's way! If you work in a fireworks factory it's best not to play with matches! Verses 9 and 10 drive the point home well. Your flirtation with sin will cause you to fall or cause you to waste precious time that could be used in a godlier manner. So what's the application for me and you? Don't be overconfident of your own strength to overcome sin. The reality is that any one of us can be on the brink of falling into sin, especially if we're foolishly putting ourselves on a path that can lead right to the temptation. In the words of the Clint Eastwood character Dirty Harry: *"a man has to know his limitations."* There's more theology in that statement than was ever intended but the advice is as biblical as it gets!

Think about these things – keep studying the Bible – and have a blessed day!

Today's devotional thought from Proverbs 5:11–14.

11 *At the end of your life you will groan,*
   when your flesh and body are spent.

12 *You will say, "How I hated discipline!*
How my heart spurned correction!

13 *I would not obey my teachers*
or listen to my instructors.

14 *I have come to the brink of utter ruin i*
n the midst of the whole assembly."

Proverbs 5 deals primarily with the sin of adultery. We will look more closely at this issue in other devotionals, but today I want to offer a thought or two regarding these first four verses. My heart's heavy as I ponder these verses. The remorse that one would feel if these words express one's true feelings would be agonizing. It causes me to ask myself if I know anyone in my sphere of influence that feels this way. Am I sensitive enough to those around me to know? Do I care enough to want to find out? Am I willing to risk a relationship to tell someone about the hope available through Jesus Christ?

There are several ways to view these verses. The first would be to view these verses through the eyes of one who has never given their heart to Jesus. What a sad commentary on a life that the Bible tells us will be spent in a Christless eternity. Now we know as Christians that it is never too late to repent, to confess that we are a sinner in need of salvation. These words in Verse 11 imply that this person is at the brink of eternity. But we know from reading about the thief on the cross that even moments before death, one can come to the saving knowledge of Jesus Christ. 2 Peter 3: 9 assures us that God doesn't want anyone to perish, but everyone to come to repentance. But what if these verses could be spoken by a Christian at the end of his or her life? Is it possible that a Christian could find themselves in this situation? Sadly, I believe the answer to be yes! If you're a Christian, you have everything you need to live a godly life. 1 Timothy 6:6 states that *'godliness with contentment is great gain.'*

However . . . even as Christians we can hate discipline and spurn correction. We can choose to ignore our instructors. Isaiah 53:6 states in part that: *'we all, like sheep, have gone astray, each of us has turned to his own way.'*

Proverbs 5 is a reminder to me as I read it each month, that no temptation is beyond me, and I can easily throw my entire life away, through adultery, or through any sin that could cause me to state these words at the end of my life.

Lord, I want to abide in you. Lord, I want to be open to receive correction. Lord, I want to remain teachable. How about you? Is there anything in your life keeping you from godliness and contentment? We are never more than a prayer of repentance away from a closer walk with God.

Think about these things – keep studying the Bible – and have a blessed day!

Today's devotional thought from Proverbs 5:15-23.

15 *Drink water from your own cistern,*
   running water from your own well.

16 *Should your springs overflow in the streets,*
   your streams of water in the public squares?

17 *Let them be yours alone,*
   never to be shared with strangers.

18 *May your fountain be blessed,*
   and may you rejoice in the wife of your youth.

19 *A loving doe, a graceful deer—*
   may her breasts satisfy you always,
   may you ever be captivated by her love.

20 *Why be captivated, my son, by an adulteress?*
   Why embrace the bosom of another man's wife?

21 *For a man's ways are in full view of the LORD,*
   and he examines all his paths.

22 *The evil deeds of a wicked man ensnare him;*
   the cords of his sin hold him fast.

23 *He will die for lack of discipline,*
   led astray by his own great folly.

The first 14 verses of Proverbs 5 give us a great warning about the sinfulness of adultery as well as the consequences of succumbing to this temptation. Here in Verses 15-23 we get a lesson in how to avoid falling this way. These verses outline the better way, God's perfect plan for your life regarding intimacy in marriage. Solomon writes such beautiful words here as he describes intimacy between a husband and wife. Let me note, too, that these words were to *husbands and wives*, not to men and women. Physical intimacy expressed here and elsewhere in Scripture is so crystal clear in this regard. God designed intimacy in the context of marriage and marriage only!

Once again, the first 14 verses of Proverbs 5 deal directly with warnings against adultery. What is adultery? Any verbal or physical intimacy between a man and a woman that is *not* your spouse. I include 'verbal adultery' because I think someone can easily fall into the sin of adultery without ever touching someone. You can become flirtatious, or communicate in an improper way via phone or email. In God's eyes, this would be just as wrong. It would also have a direct and negative impact on your feelings for your spouse. The only place a married couple should seek intimacy at any level is with each other! In Verses 18 and 19 Solomon describes marriage in the most beautiful of terms!

18 *May your fountain be blessed,*
and may you rejoice in the wife of your youth.

19 *A loving doe, a graceful deer—*
may her breasts satisfy you always,
may you ever be captivated by her love.

And I would be remiss in not mentioning that as a married man for over 40 years, I'm still very much captivated by my wife! I'm *'head over heels'* in love with her! But I think these verses have application for more than just married couples, because the final two verses of this chapter give a warning that everyone listening to me today should heed and apply. In Verse 22, Solomon uses the term, *'the cords of sin.'* I really had to pause and let those words sink in when I was preparing this devotional. You see, sin does ensnare us, and a good word picture for you and me right now might be to picture a hangman's noose, because that's what sin is! And as the last verse states, the man or woman ensnared by sin of any kind will die for lack of discipline! Friends, we don't have to become slaves to sin, or be led astray by sin! Jesus is the ultimate sin bearer, and He is ready, willing and able to cleanse us from our sins! Jesus promises us in John 8:34 that ". . . if the Son sets you free, you will be free indeed."

Think about these things – keep studying the Bible – and have a blessed day!

Today's devotional thought from Proverbs 5:22-23.

22 *The evil deeds of the wicked ensnare them;*
the cords of their sins hold them fast.

*23 For lack of discipline they will die,
    led astray by their own great folly.*

If you're like me, you read these verses and immediately think about, other people! Those evil and wicked people that will get their due in the end. For some, this bad end is exactly what awaits them, but it doesn't have to be. If they would just give their hearts to Jesus all would be fine. Well, two thoughts come to mind. First, isn't it better that we pray for those that seem to be living a life of rebellion to God? Do we come to faith in Christ and quickly take an 'us versus them' attitude toward those still living in sin? Aren't we all guilty of being like the man in Luke 18:10-11? You know the story . . .

The Parable of the Pharisee and the Tax Collector

10 "Two men went up to the temple to pray, one a Pharisee and the other a tax collector. 11 The Pharisee stood up and prayed about himself: 'God, I thank you that I am not like other men—robbers, evildoers, adulterers—or even like this tax collector.

We seem to forget so quickly what we were like before coming to faith in Christ. Shouldn't our hearts be broken when we see people in bondage to their sin? That's God's heart, and that should be ours. Second, I think we too quickly assume these verses apply to the unrepentant person and never to me and you! Heaven forbid! But why couldn't they apply to you and me? Don't we experience times where we lack spiritual discipline? Don't we have times when we knowingly take a wrong path? The Bible reminds us often that even after we trust in Christ, our hearts are bent toward wickedness. We live in a fallen world, and until we get to Heaven we'll be prone to give in to our wicked hearts. But here's the Good News! Though our hearts are prone to sin, when we are quick to see our failures, and repent, God is quick to forgive! God delights in a repentant heart! He promises to forgive our sin as far as the east is from the west. Anything and everything is possible with God if we approach Him with a broken spirit. Hebrews 11:6 reminds us that God rewards those who earnestly seek Him! Brothers and sisters, remember, you and I are always just a prayer of repentance away from a closer walk with God.

Think about these things – keep studying the Bible – and have a blessed day!

Proverbs 5 NOTES

Proverbs 5 NOTES

Proverbs 6

*N*o sense in pulling any punches when it comes to Proverbs 6. Solomon warns us about . . . stupidity! Yes! Stupidity! Wrong choices! Misplaced priorities! Foolishness. There are many ways to say it . . . but they all mean the same thing . . . stupid decisions are going to get you in trouble. Actions have consequences. If we heed the advice of this chapter we will avoid a lot of heartache! Always read the entire chapter before reading any devotionals. Don't forget to add your own notes on the blank pages at the end of each chapter.

Today's devotional thought from Proverbs 6:1-5.

1 *My son, if you have put up security for your neighbor,*
   if you have struck hands in pledge for another,

2 *if you have been trapped by what you said,*
   ensnared by the words of your mouth,

3 *then do this, my son, to free yourself,*
   since you have fallen into your neighbor's hands:
   Go and humble yourself;
   press your plea with your neighbor!

4 *Allow no sleep to your eyes,*
   no slumber to your eyelids.

5 *Free yourself, like a gazelle from the hand of the hunter,*
   like a bird from the snare of the fowler.

The amazing thing about the Word of God and the Book of Proverbs in particular is the ability to take these verses that were written thousands of years ago and be able to make direct and practical application to our lives today. As we read the Book of Proverbs, and once again I encourage you to make a chapter a day your routine and you will receive instruction in the areas of wisdom, justice, finances, purity, morality, business principles and righteous living. Here we have timely advice on the dangers of making a poor financial decision. Given the difficult financial times that come and go, we all need a good reminder of the need to be very careful in the financial decisions we make. It is very tempting in hard times to make 'risky' choices in an attempt to make up for losses or downturns in other areas.

I've made these mistakes in my own life and I can look back in hindsight and see how a bit more prayer or wise counsel from others, or even just waiting 24 hours on a significant financial decision would have spared me a few very hard lessons. I've stated this in the past, and if you read enough of my devotionals, you'll learn about every mistake I've ever made, and I've made my fair share of them! The important thing is to keep seeking God and the wise counsel of others in any important area of life.

Proverbs 15:22 states: *Plans fail for lack of counsel, but with many advisers they succeed.*

This idea in Verse 1 of "striking hands in pledge" can be taken as anything you co-sign for someone. They may be buying a car or a home or applying for a personal loan. Use wisdom in these situations. Use wisdom in all your financial decisions. You have to make these decisions allowing for the unexpected downturn or job loss or other financial setback. It's too easy to fall into the temptation to assume things will 'always work out'. So now more than ever, make wise choices in all areas of your financial life. A conservative approach will always win in the end.

Think about these things – keep studying the Bible – and have a blessed day!

Today's devotional thought from Proverbs 6:6-11.

6 *Go to the ant, you sluggard;*
    consider its ways and be wise!

7 *It has no commander,*
    no overseer or ruler,

8 yet it stores its provisions in summer
    and gathers its food at harvest.

9 How long will you lie there, you sluggard?
    When will you get up from your sleep?

10 A little sleep, a little slumber,
    a little folding of the hands to rest-

11 and poverty will come on you like a bandit
    and scarcity like an armed man.

I hope you're enjoying our journey together through the Book of Proverbs. It offers us such great insights into living as Christians in this fallen world. As a business owner for nearly 25 years I always found myself drawn to chapters in Proverbs that deal with business principles. These verses have broader applications than just business for people, but I have to admit a fondness for this industrious little ant. We learn here that this little creature has the ability to plan ahead for the future. Many of us have heard some of the interesting facts about ants. For instance, they can lift 20 times their body weight. To put this in human terms, it would be like a 200 lb. man being able to lift 4000 lbs. They spend their entire 45-60 day lifespan working, planning and preparing for the future benefit of their colony.

In business, as in life in general, proper planning makes all the difference. Contrast the ant with the image of a lazy individual that makes no provision for tomorrow or even for today. Solomon writes in the book of Ecclesiastes 10:18: *"If a man is lazy, the rafters sag; if his hands are idle, the house leaks."* Yet it is often this same person that is completely surprised when his or her business fails or he or she loses their home. The godly principle for us to glean today is to be diligent in all our undertakings, and to seek God in all our plans, in business and in life. If we take seriously the great commission then there really is no room for laziness in the life of a Christian.

Which brings me to my closing thought for today. We need to know what the Bible says about how we're to live our lives. The only way to know God's plan and purpose for our lives is to read His word and seek Him through prayer. The Bible offers a blueprint for all aspects of our life. The next time you're tempted to buy a self-help book, consider first the Word of God. Whatever your circumstances, whatever your need, the Bible has the answer.

Think about these things – keep studying the Bible – and have a blessed day!

Today's devotional thought from Proverbs 6:12-19.

12 A scoundrel and villain,
who goes about with a corrupt mouth,

13 who winks with his eye,
signals with his feet
and motions with his fingers,

14 who plots evil with deceit in his heart—
he always stirs up dissension.

15 Therefore disaster will overtake him in an instant;
he will suddenly be destroyed—without remedy.

16 There are six things the LORD hates,
seven that are detestable to him:

17 haughty eyes,
a lying tongue,
hands that shed innocent blood,

18 a heart that devises wicked schemes,
feet that are quick to rush into evil,

19 a false witness who pours out lies
and a man who stirs up dissension among brothers.

You'll note that the first four verses are devoted to a discussion about a devious man, a scoundrel and villain that must have been clearly known by Solomon. And God inspired him to write this as a reminder and warning to the coming generations that there will always be those who are bent on our destruction. This isn't reserved for just the devil! There are many miserable, heartless and evil people that want nothing more than to bring misery into your life and mine. It's interesting to note that Verse 16 states there are six things God hates, even seven, and worded in a way to bring additional attention to the last one, or the seventh thing detestable to God and here we see it as the man who sows dissension among brothers, the same man or type of man described in Verses 12-15. I know I've mentioned this in the past, but it's worth repeating. When God takes the time in His word to emphasize a point as strongly as He does here, it must be important! But let's not neglect a discussion on the list of things God hates. First, we should note the strong use of the word hate.

If God takes the time to tell us in advance that He hates these things, we would be wise to note what they are. So here we go:

Haughty eyes –

A lying tongue –

Hands that shed innocent blood –

A deceitful heart –

Feet bent toward evil –

False witnesses (obviously emphasizing hatred for liars)

And lastly, scoundrels and villains, or stated another way, people of ill repute! Friends, the application for us is to read these verses with humility and ask God to break us in any of these areas we may struggle with. We need to take this wonderful opportunity to humbly ask God to show us any wicked way within us. The quicker we come to Him with confession on our lips, the more He is able to use us for the great work He has for us on this earth. Call out to Him right now, whether in praise or confession. He is waiting patiently and He wants to use us in bigger and greater ways!

Think about these things – keep studying the Bible – and have a blessed day!

Today's devotional thought from Proverbs 6:27.

27 *Can a man scoop fire into his lap*
    without his clothes being burned?

The original context of this verse deals with the sin of adultery, but the application for you and I is much broader. If I were to retitle this verse for the modern day reader, I'd call it:

Too smart for your own good!!!

This idea of scooping fire into our laps . . . will obviously result in us getting burned. In the same way, the longer we walk with Jesus, there is a very strong possibility that we can become STUPID! Let me explain . . .

I've been a Christian for 40 years. I've learned a lot, seen a lot and heard a lot. I've built a sizeable storehouse of knowledge and wisdom from God. And that's why I'm at a greater risk! The Bible is loaded with examples of great men and women of God who did amazing things with their yielded lives . . . but all too often we read that later in life . . . they messed up. It would seem that the opposite should happen. Look at this example; if I want to get really good at golf, I would take lessons, go to the driving range, spend many hours honing my skills . . . and the end result would most likely be that many years later . . . this discipline would result in a better golf game. Well, as already observed, there are numerous biblical examples of men that spent many years sitting at the feet of God, studying His word, applying the truths of scripture . . . even teaching others effectively . . . only to mess up their own lives by taking their eyes off the Lord! How does this happen? Well, that's why I titled this devotion *"Too smart for your own good"*

You see, we tend to become complacent in our walk with God. We figure we've got this *'God thing'* all figured out. We've read the book cover to cover for years, we've logged thousands of church services . . . we've even taught Sunday school! So watch out world! I'm a super Christian! And therein lies the problem . . . you and I are at a far greater risk when we think we've got it all figured out.

At the risk of personal embarrassment, I can't begin to tell you how many times I will be fretting about something with my wife . . . and she listens attentively . . . and then quietly asks: "Have you prayed about it?"

OUCH!!! (Too often the answer is no!)

How easy it is to fall into the trap of thinking we can tell God: "It's okay, God, I'll take care of this one. I'll call You if I need You." You don't literally say these words, but your actions show that this is exactly what you're doing. I think you get the point. Walking with Jesus is a life-long journey. Our goal should always be to FINISH WELL!

Perhaps you need to do what I just did. Pray! Ask God to forgive you for routinely taking over. Put God back on the throne of your life . . . and watch what He will do with it!

Think about these things – keep studying the Bible – and have a blessed day!

Today's devotional thought from Proverbs 6:27-29.

Can a man scoop fire into his lap
without his clothes being burned?

Can a man walk on hot coals
without his feet being scorched?

So is he who sleeps with another man's wife;
no one who touches her will go unpunished.

These verses deal specifically with the sin of adultery. I'm reviewing just a few of the verses for the sake of brevity but I think these verses capture the point well. And that point SHOUTS out to us from these verses that you are *'out of your mind'* if you consider touching a man or woman that is not your spouse. Brothers and sisters, if you have even thought about such a thing, you're already in danger of being burned. You need to stop and count the cost. There are MANY lives that will be damaged, perhaps permanently, if you continue down this path. All sin is wrong in God's eyes and all sin is destructive but the sin of adultery is almost guaranteed to end in ruin for many years and many lives. I've talked with men and women who have succumbed to this sin. In every instance that I'm aware of, the decision was not a spontaneous one. The individuals *'toyed'* with the possibility, never actually believing that they would go through with it. The way of this particular sin is downhill and downhill fast! It's a deep pit and to even stand near its edge is foolishness. So if you're reading this and are contemplating this sin, then you still have time to repent. I would go immediately to God and confess even the thought of adultery. Then tell a trusted friend so you have some accountability. Then cut off any communication with the individual and never allow yourself to be alone with them again. Remember Joseph, when he was tempted by Potiphar's wife? He fled from her as fast as he could. You would be wise to do the same! Here's the good news! We have an awesome promise from God's Word.

1 Corinthians 10:13 states:

No temptation has seized you except what is common to man. And God is faithful;
he will not let you be tempted beyond what you can bear. But when you are
tempted, he will also provide a way out so that you can stand up under it.

Finally, take it to God in prayer! Real, fervent, direct, specific and heartfelt prayer. We have another amazing promise in Ephesians 3:20:

Now to him who is able to do immeasurably more than all we ask or imagine, according to his power that is at work within us,

God is able to help you have victory in this area, and you have His word on it!

Think about these things – keep studying the Bible – and have a blessed day!

Proverbs 6 NOTES

Proverbs 6 NOTES

Proverbs 7

As you read through this chapter from your Bible, you will quickly note that this is another chapter devoted to the dangers of adultery. In this chapter we see a description of a young man in the wrong part of town, with the wrong motives. Solomon says he is like a lamb being led to the slaughter. An apt description of the ruined life after falling into this temptation. I hope the following devotionals will help you make a commitment to never fall into this sin.

Today's devotional thought from Proverbs 7:1-5.

The entire chapter deals with a warning to guard against the adulteress. Yet, I believe the application applies to all of us for every circumstance of life.

Let's start by reading verses 1 thru 5 . . .

1 *My son, keep my words*
  and store up my commands within you.

2 *Keep my commands and you will live;*
  guard my teachings as the apple of your eye.

3 *Bind them on your fingers;*
  write them on the tablet of your heart.

4 *Say to wisdom, "You are my sister,"*
  and call understanding your kinsman;

5 they will keep you from the adulteress,
    from the wayward wife with her seductive words.

Because I want to focus on the first four verses let me sum up the rest of the chapter. Verses 6 thru the end of the chapter tell a story of a young man led astray by a female seductress. She pulls out every trick in the book to lead this young and vulnerable man into her bed. Verse 22 sums up the story well: 'All at once he followed her like an ox being led to the slaughter house'. Here's what I get out of this chapter - whether you are a man or woman, young or old, black or white, there are devious people in this world that will attempt to ruin your life. They won't look devious and in fact they usually look and sound quite appealing. That's one of the devil's favorite tricks. He always wears camouflage. He's never what he appears to be. So what's the solution? It's found in Verses 1 through 4. What does it mean to 'store up' or to 'treasure' something? Solomon is reminding us of the importance of already knowing how we will deal with various circumstances and temptations before they happen!

The animal doesn't wait for winter and then realize "Oh, I need food for winter." By then the ground is frozen and it's too late. Instead it stores up, or treasures a food supply in the fall so it has what it needs for the winter. It's no different for us with spiritual food, which is God's Word. We need to store up the knowledge and wisdom of God's Word so that when the adulteress or any temptation comes our way, we have a ready rebuke. If we find ourselves saying 'now what do I do?' you are already in trouble! The young man in today's devotional was vulnerable because he was unprepared! When I read words like 'store up' or 'treasure' and to 'keep' and to 'guard' and to 'bind' even to 'love God's wisdom' the way I love my spouse or family member, I'm reminded of how critical it is to be prepared for the traps being set for me by the enemy.

So, are you going to heed this warning that Solomon offers us? I want to encourage you to study God's word on your own. Do it in a small group Bible study. Do it in church. Do it with a friend, or maybe all the above. Wherever, whenever, however, make God's Word a priority!

Think about these things – keep studying the Bible – and have a blessed day!

Today's Devotional thought from Proverbs 7:5.

5 they will keep you from the adulteress,
    from the wayward wife with her seductive words.

Proverbs 7 deals almost exclusively with the topic of adultery. If you haven't already done so, please read the entire chapter. Verses 1-4 encourage the reader to seek God's Word and commandments . . . to know God's will in any given situation. It's this idea I want to focus on today. To say adultery is wrong would be the understatement of the century. Everyone knows how wrong it is . . . yet we see it rampant in society. Solomon must have had his own father David's sin on his mind when he penned this. And he clearly had his own struggles with lust.

My observations in this area are that most men and women are not steeped deeply enough in God's Word to be ready when this sin or temptation crouches at their doorstep. If you don't have a ready response to this temptation before it comes your way, then you're already in trouble, because you're already too vulnerable. This particular sin is often progressive, meaning one doesn't wake up on a given morning and decide they're going to commit adultery that day. It's usually more of a process of putting themselves in a setting that could lead to this sin. Therefore the decision to avoid this temptation MUST come much earlier in the process.

I had my own business for over 25 years . . . and during that time I had many out-of-state business trips. I would inevitably be invited to a night out with the 'guys'. I never accepted these invitations. I was 'predetermined' to not put myself in a situation where I could be tempted to indulge my fleshly lusts and weaknesses. The mistake is usually made at this earlier stage and then a gradual set of circumstances leads to the sin of adultery.

A man accepts an innocent invitation to lunch with a female co-worker. A woman starts having daily conversations with her neighbor who happens to be a stay-at-home dad . . . you get the idea. It nearly always starts out innocently. Here's a simple point to consider - if you never put yourself in a situation where you're totally alone with a member of the opposite sex that isn't your spouse, the chances of you ever falling into the sin of adultery drops dramatically.

You need to know God's Word on this topic and apply it to your heart. Let me close with this final thought. Adultery hurts many people. Restitution for adultery is difficult. Adultery is never forgotten and it never goes away. Steal someone's possessions and you can return them. Steal money and you can pay it back . . . with interest! Commit adultery and watch all the lives that are damaged, perhaps permanently. Have a ready response to this temptation, before it comes your way!

Think about these things – keep studying the Bible – and have a blessed day!

Today's devotional thought from Proverbs 7:7-9.

7 *I saw among the simple,*
I noticed among the young men,
a youth who lacked judgment.

8 *He was going down the street near her corner,*
walking along in the direction of her house

9 *at twilight, as the day was fading,*
as the dark of night set in.

The fact that Proverbs deals with the subject of adultery as often as it does should give us pause. God doesn't repeat Himself unnecessarily. I have seen too many good and godly men and women fall into this temptation to think that it can't happen to them. Having said that, this verse touches on a few other elements worth highlighting. The first is that these verses mention a young man, a youth who lacked judgment. Now for those of you that are reading this that are under 35 and since I have a son that old, it makes anyone under 35 'officially young' - at least in my mind. And like my son and my daughter and like me when I was young, I realize that no one really likes to take advice from their elders because young people think they know it all already! I'm reminded of the well-known quote from Mark Twain:

"When I was a boy of fourteen, my father was so ignorant I could hardly stand to have the old man around. But when I got to be twenty-one, I was astonished at how much he had learned in seven years."

Well, I'm not suggesting you take my advice or even the advice of Mark Twain. But I am strongly recommending you take advice from your Creator. I'm suggesting you heed the advice God gives you and me here in Proverbs 7. I mentioned that there are a few specific points being made beyond the obvious topic of adultery. The first dealt with being young and a younger person's hesitancy to take advice from those older and wiser. The second and third have to do with idleness and darkness. Too much idle time is a great danger. If you find yourself with too much idle time on your hands then get busy with something, because the enemy of your soul will quickly find something to occupy your time. Idleness will lead to temptation so you'd be wise to heed this advice. The other problem has to do with darkness or the thought of doing things that can't be seen. Even Judas chose the darkness of night to betray Jesus! First let me give you a gentle reminder. God sees it all!

Numbers 32:23 states:

23 *"But if you fail to do this, you will be sinning against the LORD; and you may be sure that your sin will find you out.*

This verse should be a comfort as much as a warning. Getting caught in a besetting sin will end up being the best thing that could happen to you.

Think about these things – keep studying the Bible – and have a blessed day!

Today's devotional thought from Proverbs 7:22-27.

The seventh chapter of Proverbs is all about adultery. The text describes a young man who finds himself in the wrong place at the wrong time, which is usually the first step in falling into many types of sin. I encourage you to take the time to read the entire chapter on your own. The text infers that the youth was not ignorant of his surroundings and he was on a street presumably in an area where one might find a prostitute. He went there when it was getting dark, suggesting what he was doing was meant to be in secret. The next point worth mentioning has to do with the woman mentioned in Verse 10. It states; *"Then out came a woman to meet him, dressed like a prostitute and with crafty intent."* It would seem her clothing and then her words that followed were part of a purposeful plan to draw this young man into sin. The first lesson for us today is to understand that there are those we meet that are intent on bringing us down and often it is intentionally *because* we take a stand for Christ. So let's pick up the story at the point where she successfully captures her prey:

22 *All at once he followed her*
like an ox going to the slaughter,
like a deer stepping into a noose

23 *till an arrow pierces his liver,*
like a bird darting into a snare,
little knowing it will cost him his life.

24 *Now then, my sons, listen to me;*
pay attention to what I say.

25 *Do not let your heart turn to her ways*
or stray into her paths.

26 *Many are the victims she has brought down;*
   her slain are a mighty throng.

27 *Her house is a highway to the grave,*
   leading down to the chambers of death.

Listen to the words the writer uses to describe the setting: An ox to the slaughter, a deer stepping into a noose and a bird into a snare! These are all examples of traps! Would someone actually try to trap us into sinning? You better believe it. There are those that delight in doing wrong and they want nothing more than to bring others down with them. Misery really does love company! How do you and I avoid straying into her path? Simply choose a different path! Because the path being described here is a path that leads to sure death, spiritually speaking! There are no shortcuts to any place worth going.

Matthew 7:14 states: *"But small is the gate and narrow the road that leads to life"*

Stay on the narrow path and keep your eyes focused squarely on Jesus.

Think about these things – keep studying the Bible – and have a blessed day!

Proverbs 7 NOTES

Proverbs 7 NOTES

Proverbs 8

*H*ere's another great chapter that deals primarily with the topic of wisdom. At this point, we should be noting that Solomon repeats topics. It's safe to say this is intentional . . . because we're like balloons . . . we leak! We sometimes hear these very wise and practical pieces of advice, and the thought goes in one ear and out the other! It's a hard lesson to learn, but here's the bottom line on this. Right living is a choice! I pray that a thoughtful review of this chapter will bring you victory in this area of your life. Take some extra time to journal your thoughts on the blank pages provided at the end of each chapter.

Today's devotional thought from Proverbs 8:1-3.

I always look forward to the eighth day of the month because I love reading Proverbs 8. Chapter 8 can be referred to as a Messianic Proverb because it's all about Jesus! In fact, every time you read the word 'wisdom' you can exchange it for Jesus and this will help you understand what I mean.

1 Does not wisdom call out?
    Does not understanding raise her voice?

2 On the heights along the way,
    where the paths meet, she takes her stand;

3 beside the gates leading into the city,
    at the entrances, she cries aloud:

Let's focus on a few key words the writer uses to help us understand why seeking wisdom needs to be proactive not passive. Note first the fact that wisdom, or Jesus, is always calling out to us. Then we see words that remind us that we need to be observing opportunities to seek wisdom wherever we find ourselves. Note that we can find wisdom on the heights and on various paths and beside gates and entrances. Basically, we are being shown the importance of looking for wisdom everywhere. Why all these constant reminders to actively pursue wisdom? Could it be because we are basically knuckleheads that are very slow learners? We do need to seek God daily! None of us can rely on yesterday's manna. We need to seek God every day.

God's word tells us His mercies are new every morning! Verse 10 of this chapter says we need to choose God's instruction. Brothers and sisters, right living is a choice and one I urge you to make! Verse 11 tells us that right living is worth far more than gold, silver and gems. We foolishly think money will help us when in fact it often hurts us. No friends, it's not riches and prosperity that will matter for eternity, its God and people.

I read recently about an island off the coast of Georgia called Jekyll Island. In the early 1900's this island was owned by a very small group of American Industrialists. This small group of men controlled 1/6 of the nation's entire wealth. Members had names like Rockefeller and Getty and Morgan and Vanderbilt. Today, other than a few restored buildings for tourists, the island is overgrown and ignored. And the former members? They're long gone. I like to read Christian history . . . and I often read about Christian men and women from past generations who had little or no wealth, but they had Jesus! And their legacy is all about a life dedicated to God! That's the legacy I want to leave! How about you?

Think about these things – keep studying the Bible – and have a blessed day!

Today's devotional thought from Proverbs 8:1-11.

1 *Does not wisdom call out?*
    Does not understanding raise her voice?

2 *On the heights along the way,*
    where the paths meet, she takes her stand;

3 *beside the gates leading into the city,*
    at the entrances, she cries aloud:

4 *"To you, O men, I call out;*
I raise my voice to all mankind.

5 *You who are simple, gain prudence;*
you who are foolish, gain understanding.

6 *Listen, for I have worthy things to say;*
I open my lips to speak what is right.

7 *My mouth speaks what is true,*
for my lips detest wickedness.

8 *All the words of my mouth are just;*
none of them is crooked or perverse.

9 *To the discerning all of them are right;*
they are faultless to those who have knowledge.

10 *Choose my instruction instead of silver,*
knowledge rather than choice gold,

11 *for wisdom is more precious than rubies,*
and nothing you desire can compare with her.

These verses can be summed up to say that God's Word makes godly living a far easier process than we make it out to be. The ingredients required for gaining godly wisdom and learning godly living are clear and available to all who seek them. Wisdom is proclaimed from pulpits all around us. Wisdom is proclaimed from on high through God's love letter to us . . . the Bible.

We have access to Bible studies and home groups and devotionals and books on godly living. We have never had more educational tools available to us since the beginning. These verses are reminding us that godly living is a choice that we make or don't make but there's no excuse.

1 Corinthians 1:30 states: *It is because of him that you are in Christ Jesus, who has become for us wisdom from God—that is, our righteousness, holiness and redemption.*

Jesus Himself states in Matthew 11:15: *He who has ears, let him hear.*

God's word is our guide. It outlines a path to follow for godly living. It provides a path that leads us directly to Jesus . . . and our salvation! Wisdom can only truly be found in Jesus . . . and He tells us through these verses that He has worthy things to tell us…things that are right and true! If you haven't done so already . . . choose Jesus! He is far more precious than silver, gold or precious gems. If you're reading this and you know that you've drifted from God, then seize this moment to rededicate your life to Him right now. He is ready, willing and able to forgive and restore. He just wants you to ask!

Think about these things – keep studying the Bible – and have a blessed day!

Today's devotional thought from Proverbs 8.

Normally I would select a few verses and speak from just those verses but today I want to comment on all of Proverbs 8. This Proverb is all about Jesus and in fact it could easily be described as a Messianic Proverb. You'll see this quite clearly through this devotional. So what are you going to do with Jesus? I'm reminded of all the pithy statements I've heard over the years, such as "He's either Lord of all or not at all." And my personal favorite:"Ninety-five percent devotion to Christ is still five percent short!" So what's the point? It's really simple. A fully devoted walk with Jesus needs to be our priority. Jesus can't be just an important part of your life. He needs to be the center of your life. Thirty seven years as a Christian has given me more than enough time to see good people struggle in many aspects of their life simply because they wanted part of Jesus, not all of Jesus. This has been true in my own life. As soon as I think I've 'arrived', the minute I get comfortable and relax my relationship with the Lord and as soon as I think I can 'check in' with my Savior 'when I have a few extra minutes', I'm already in trouble. Let me be clear about something. I'm not talking about good works here. God already tells us in Isaiah that good works are like filthy rags. An intimate relationship with the Lord is for our benefit, not His. God **'wants'** our devotion to Him to be voluntary. He doesn't **'demand'** it. In fact, the more **'things'** we do to show external devotion without inward conviction is detestable to Him. Make a note to read Isaiah 1: 11-14 for an insight into God's disdain for outward expressions without a heart that beats for God. So, what are you going to do with Jesus? If you're reading this and you know **'about'** Jesus but don't **'know'** Jesus, then I urge you to settle this matter today, right now! If you are not trusting in Jesus Christ **'alone'** for your salvation than speak to Him right now and ask Him to come into your life. Confess you're a sinner in need of salvation. If you mean it in your heart, He will come into your life before you can even finish the prayer. If you know Jesus and you know you're a Christian, but have allowed Jesus to become just a part of your life and not the center of your life, you too are only a prayer of repentance away from a right relationship with the

Savior of the world. I encourage you today to make Jesus your all-in-all. He's standing there, right outside the door of your heart. He won't barge in because He's a gentleman; He will wait patiently for an invitation. Can you hear Him knocking?

Think about these things – keep studying the Bible – and have a blessed day!

Today's devotional thought from Proverbs 8:22-31.

22 *"The LORD brought me forth as the first of his works,*
before his deeds of old;

23 *I was appointed from eternity,*
from the beginning, before the world began.

24 *When there were no oceans, I was given birth,*
when there were no springs abounding with water;

25 *before the mountains were settled in place,*
before the hills, I was given birth,

26 *before he made the earth or its fields*
or any of the dust of the world.

27 *I was there when he set the heavens in place,*
when he marked out the horizon on the face of the deep,

28 *when he established the clouds above*
and fixed securely the fountains of the deep,

29 *when he gave the sea its boundary*
so the waters would not overstep his command,
and when he marked out the foundations of the earth.

30 *Then I was the craftsman at his side.*
I was filled with delight day after day,
rejoicing always in his presence,

31 *rejoicing in his whole world*
and delighting in mankind.

These words that were penned some 1000 years before the birth of Christ describe Him in such a compelling way. Consider the words just read in light of these words in John 1:1-2:

¹In the beginning was the Word, and the Word was with God, and the Word was God. ²He was with God in the beginning.

Now read again Proverbs 8:22-23:

22 *"The LORD brought me forth as the first of his works,*
before his deeds of old;

23 *I was appointed from eternity,*
from the beginning, before the world began.

Now read what Jesus states in His own words from John 17:5:

⁵And now, Father, glorify me in your presence with the glory I had with you before the world began.

We just read John 1:1-2. Now read verses 3-4:

³Through him all things were made; without him nothing was made that has been made. ⁴In him was life, and that life was the light of men.

If someone wanted to try to stretch every conceivable realm of reason to suggest that Jesus could have manipulated his own three-year public ministry, there is NO way He could have predicted His own parents, or the timing of His birth, or where He would be born, nor the circumstances of His birth and all the fulfilled prophecies that resulted from these events. Nor the circumstances of His death and the dozens of fulfilled prophecies regarding His burial, nor are there any credible ways to deny the many miracles that occurred in the 40 days after His resurrection! Friends, Jesus is who He said He is! Your friends and relatives that believe differently or have another faith or no faith, no matter how sincere, are sincerely wrong.

Jesus Himself states in John 14:6:

"I am the way and the truth and the life. No one comes to the Father except through me.

Brothers and sisters, don't let anyone cause you to doubt these truths! As for your unbelieving friends and family, just keep loving them and gently leading them to Christ!

Think about these things – keep studying the Bible – and have a blessed day!

Today's devotional thought from Proverbs 8:32-36.

32 *"Now then, my sons, listen to me;*
   blessed are those who keep my ways.

33 *Listen to my instruction and be wise;*
   do not ignore it.

34 *Blessed is the man who listens to me,*
   watching daily at my doors,
   waiting at my doorway.

35 *For whoever finds me finds life*
   and receives favor from the LORD.

36 *But whoever fails to find me harms himself;*
   all who hate me love death."

There are so many strong points in these verses, and we could focus in on any number of topics but the one I want to speak on today is the idea of knowing and discerning the voice of Christ. I've heard it said that you could put several shepherds together with hundreds of sheep, all in the same place, mix them all up and then have the shepherds call out to the sheep and suddenly you would see all the sheep move from where they were to where their shepherd is standing. Why? Because they know their shepherds voice! It reminds me of the importance of knowing God's voice. There's always some group that comes along with the latest and greatest Christian teaching and those that don't know God's voice can easily be drawn into the latest Christian fad. We need to be centered on the Word of God! That's why it's so important to be spending time DAILY in God's Word. Verse 34 states 'watching daily' at my doors! Brothers and sisters, we err when we allow our study to just be Sunday at church and then our Bibles are put away until the next Sunday. We need to be in prayer and in the Bible 'daily'. It's the only way we're going to learn to discern truth from lies.

Ephesians 4:14 states it well in describing one who is growing deep roots in Christ:

14 *Then we will no longer be infants, tossed back and forth by the waves, and blown here and there by every wind of teaching and by the cunning and craftiness of men in their deceitful scheming.*

Now I realize I'm writing to a very diverse audience from many different churches and denominations and one church might have an emphasis in ministering to the homeless and another focuses on another godly expression of their faith but at the end of the day we as individuals need to have our eyes and hearts set squarely on Jesus and His love letter to us, the Bible! I was reading up on some early church history and came upon a story of a man named Richard Baxter. Most of us have never heard of this godly preacher who lived in the 17th century, but he coined a phrase that is still used today:

"In essentials unity, in non-essentials liberty and in both charity."

The thought so eloquently expressed in these words is the allowance for diverse opinions on many aspects of our faith except the essentials. Where the unprepared Christian is vulnerable, is when even essentials are taught falsely and one lacks the wisdom to discern it. Our verses for today speak clearly to these points. We need to listen to instruction and be wise and if we fail in this area we bring harm to ourselves and risk passing on harmful teaching to others.

Friends, our freedom in Christ is what allows us to have unity in the midst of diversity and I thank God for that! It's quite apparent to me that God loves diversity. But that in no way negates our need for personal and 'daily' time with our Leader and Lord. I know, you're very busy. So am I. But I still urge you to find time and to spend time with the one who made time!

Think about these things – keep studying the Bible – and have a blessed day!

Today's devotional thought from Proverbs 8:35.

35 *For whoever finds me finds life and receives favor from the LORD.*

I always try to be open about my faith in Christ. I work at sharing my faith with those I meet. I just share about the hope within me and I leave the rest with the Holy Spirit. I try to be faithful with my part. A friend once shared with me the idea that we are to be a "link in the chain" that leads someone to Christ!

You and I need to pray daily for opportunities to tell others about Christ. Lost people are dying without hope in Jesus. This verse in Proverbs needs to be taped to our bathroom mirrors! Whoever finds Jesus finds life . . . now and forever! Lost people matter to God . . . so they should matter to us.

If we tell someone about Jesus, we are either going to pray with them to receive Christ, plant a seed or be told 'not interested'. In all instances, the witness was effective. Even those who say 'not interested' are still hearing the truth and a seed has been planted. God has someone else that will share again with that person down the road! The Bible tells us in Luke 15:10 that the angels in heaven rejoice over every sinner who repents.

A number of years ago I was on a flight from Newark to Cleveland and a gentleman sat down next to me. He settled into his seat, book in hand, ready to start reading, which is the international symbol for "leave me alone"! Fortunately, I ignored the fact that he wanted to read, because God put such a clear sense on my heart to tell him about Jesus! To make a long story short, before we landed in Cleveland, Bob was praying the sinner's prayer and asking Jesus to come into his heart! It was really exciting to see that this man had a 'divine appointment' with the Creator of the universe that day and God wanted me to handle the introduction! Bob and I remain friends and he is doing great.

So what's the application for you and me? I'll never fully understand why, but God has chosen you and me to tell others about Him. It's not always easy or convenient but it's always the right thing to do. I'm reminded of the couple that talked to me about Jesus over 40 years ago. I thank God that they were willing to risk a negative response so that I could learn about the love of Jesus. Why not decide today to keep the angels in heaven rejoicing without a break! Tell someone today about Jesus and His love for them!

Think about these things – keep studying the Bible – and have a blessed day!

Proverbs 8 NOTES

Proverbs 8 NOTES

Proverbs 9

$\mathcal{S}$olomon uses Chapter 9 to contrast wisdom with folly. It will be easy to pick up this theme as you read through this chapter in your own Bible. One thought that resonates when I read this chapter, and that's the importance of remaining teachable. The Christian life is a marathon, not a sprint. Take a minute to pray. Ask God to reveal areas of your life that need work. God is able! I hope you enjoy the following seven devotionals. Don't forget to journal some thoughts at the end of the chapter.

Today's devotional thought from Proverbs 9:1.

1 *Wisdom has built her house;*
    she has hewn out its seven pillars.

Here we have a beautiful picture of all that is awaiting those that put their faith and trust in Jesus. Note this word picture. This *house* is built strong and firm as identified by its seven pillars. This reminds us that we have a strong and mighty Savior that can carry us through every storm of life.

Listen to the words of Jesus in Matthew 7:24-27:

[24]*"Therefore everyone who hears these words of mine and puts them into practice is like a wise man who built his house on the rock.* [25]*The rain came down, the streams rose, and the winds blew and beat against that house; yet it did not fall, because it had its foundation on the rock.* [26]*But everyone who hears these words of mine and does not put them into practice is like a foolish man who built*

his house on sand. ²⁷ The rain came down, the streams rose, and the winds blew and beat against that house, and it fell with a great crash."

Are you building your house on the Rock? Do you have a sure foundation? Are you trusting in Jesus Christ alone for your salvation? We need no further description of Jesus than this, He is the ROCK of our salvation.

1 Peter 2:4-5 states:

4 As you come to him, the living Stone—rejected by men but chosen by God and precious to him— 5you also, like living stones, are being built into a spiritual house to be a holy priesthood, offering spiritual sacrifices acceptable to God through Jesus Christ.

Jesus sits right now at the right hand of God. He has prepared a place for those that have put their faith and trust in His saving grace. This eternal home can be your home and my home forever because of what Jesus did on the cross. Our part is to recognize our desperate need for a Savior. We need to confess we are sinners and we need forgiveness for our sins. We need to recognize that there is nothing we can do, except to believe in what Jesus has already done.

Here's an analogy that might be helpful. It was shared with me many years ago and has helped me to see so clearly what God has done for us. Religion can be spelled D-O, because religion is all about what we think we need to do to earn our salvation. The problem with *doing* is that you could never do enough because all have sinned and fall short of the glory of God. Relationship can be spelled D-O-N-E because a personal relationship with Christ is all about what He has already *done* for us. If it's all been done already than our part is to just recognize that He's *done* it all. Our part is to accept the free gift of salvation.

Romans 6:23 states:

23 For the wages of sin is death, but the gift of God is eternal life in Christ Jesus our Lord.

If you've not done it yet, accept the free gift of salvation today!

Think about these things – keep studying the Bible – and have a blessed day!

Today's devotional thought from Proverbs 9:6.

6 *Leave your simple ways and you will live;*
walk in the way of understanding.

This is a plain and simple reminder to live life the right way, God's way. Why is this message that sounds so logical such a stumbling block for us? I think stubbornness and pride have much to do with it. I lived a long time with the attitude that *"no one was going to tell me how to live my life."* I really had an incomplete view of God and His wonderful plan for my life. I always looked at a life lived for God as an impossible task, even a burden. The problem became all too clear. I was trying to live a godly life through my own abilities. I fell far short. That was my error, trying in my own abilities! We aren't meant to live life in Christ when we are still on the throne. It's when we relinquish our control and let God lead us that we find the victory! It's only through Him and the strength He can provide through His Holy Spirit that the impossible becomes possible.

There's a story told of a Christian man who was sharing his faith with a friend. The friend started his list of all the *'good'* things he had done in his life. His friend started to give a point value to all the man's *'good deeds'* telling him that the goal was to get to 100 points. So his friend started his list; *"I have been faithful to my wife"*. Wonderful, says the friend, that's a half point. His friend added, *"I once saved a boy from drowning"*. Great, that's worth a whole point. *"I was employee of the month three times last year"* That's great, that's another ¼ point! The man went on for many more minutes, and when he seemed exhausted with his list of good deeds, he was only at 15 points.

Then the Christian man asked, *"Have you ever lied"?* That's minus one point. Have you ever stolen anything, even a candy bar from a store when you were a kid? That's another point lost!" Well at this point the friend said. *"Then it's impossible, only by the grace and mercy of God could I ever hope to get into heaven!!!"* His friend stated enthusiastically, *"Exactly!"* He then went on to explain the wonderful gift of Salvation that comes through faith in Jesus Christ alone. This little story gets us to a simple yet profound truth! Salvation is free, we can't earn it, and if we try, we will fail. Romans 6:23 states:

For the wages of sin is death, but the gift of God is eternal life in Christ Jesus our Lord.

My struggles in life come when I try to live the Christian life in my own strength, and that's the mistake most of us routinely make. Jesus states in Matthew 11:28-30:

[28] *"Come to me, all you who are weary and burdened, and I will give you rest.* [29]*Take my yoke upon you and learn from me, for I am gentle and humble in heart, and you will find rest for your souls.* [30]*For my yoke is easy and my burden is light."*

So what's the application for you and me? God does offer a better way! He has a wonderful plan for our lives, we just need to trust Him, and yield our hearts and our total self to Him!

Think about these things – keep studying the Bible – and have a blessed day!

Today's devotional thought from Proverbs 9:10.

"The fear of the LORD is the beginning of wisdom,
and knowledge of the Holy One is understanding.

When we read "fear of the LORD" it conjures up thoughts of an angry taskmaster that demands we follow him or he'll zap us into oblivion. There is a holy wrath that exists but God is a loving and patient God and any basic understanding of the Bible would convince you of this. I prefer to think of this fear of God as a majestic awe of who He is and what He has done for me. If you're living in an ungodly way, if you are not married, but living with someone in sexual union, then you're not fearing the Lord. If you're abusing drugs or alcohol, you're not fearing the Lord. If you're sitting on the throne of your life and living a self-directed life, you're not fearing the Lord. There are many references in scripture that deal with the fear of the Lord. This fear should be thought of as a holy reverence of God. It's a simple recognition that our very next breath is by His divine will. Try holding your breath for a minute or two for a quick reminder of how little control we have over our lives. But let's look at what this verse means to us. It states that the fear of God is the beginning of wisdom. It's where it all starts and once we begin to understand God's plan for our lives then things seem to start falling into place. Brothers and sisters, there is a wonderful life available to you and me if we would simply 'let go and let God'. His ways are far better than our ways.

So what's the application for us today? We need to seek God with all our heart, soul, mind and strength. We need to seek wisdom and knowledge and understanding. Then your life and mine will make more sense. Our lives will have more purpose. We'll have a stronger desire to see others come to Christ. We'll more easily love our neighbor as ourself.

I want ALL that God has for me. How about you?

Think about these things – keep studying the Bible – and have a blessed day!

Today's devotional thought from Proverbs 9:8-10.

8 *Do not rebuke a mocker or he will hate you;*
   rebuke a wise man and he will love you.

9 *Instruct a wise man and he will be wiser still;*
   teach a righteous man and he will add to his learning.

10 *"The fear of the LORD is the beginning of wisdom,*
   and knowledge of the Holy One is understanding.

If you study Proverbs for any length of time, you realize that wisdom is a theme that runs throughout many of the chapters. The great thing about Proverbs is that the applications apply equally to all of us, young or old, man or woman, married or single . . . we can all benefit from regular reading of Proverbs.

These verses actually make me laugh at myself, because I can look back at 40 years as a Christian and see that there were many circumstances when I fit very nicely into the definition of a mocker or scorner. . . one completely unwilling to receive wise council from others. I still have to guard myself from believing that I have everything figured out.

A mocker that receives a rebuke is immediately on the defensive. They don't even really hear what was said but instead go directly into a defense of their position. They will dislike or even hate someone that has the audacity to point out a character flaw in them. We often make the mistake of relying on knowledge rather than wisdom at times like this. Knowledge is the sum total of what we know. Someone can be extremely knowledge-able about many things or even be brilliant, but still be a fool. And what is a fool? The Bible teaches us that a fool is someone who says there is no God. The fool thinks he knows it all! To be wise is to be willing to add to our learning. It's the realization that we still have much to learn.

A wise individual sees everything as an opportunity, a chance to gain wisdom and understanding. Even if they receive correction that they are not sure is deserving, they will still take time to ponder the thought. A wise person remains teachable in all circumstances. I want to be willing to ask God: Is this You speaking thru this individual? Am I really this way? Do I really overreact on occasion? Regularly? Often? Oh Lord . . . forgive me!

Verse 10 states:

"The fear of the LORD is the beginning of wisdom,
and knowledge of the Holy One is understanding.

Do you know God? That's where it has to start. Praise God if you do! Not sure? Settle it today . . . right now! Ask Jesus to come into your life. Confess that you are a sinner in need of salvation. You have God's promise that He will come into the life of a repentant sinner.

Think about these things – keep studying the Bible – and have a blessed day!

Today's devotional thought from Proverbs 9:17.

17 *"Stolen water is sweet;*
food eaten in secret is delicious!"

We all have a sin nature handed down to us from Adam. Just as there was a need to eat from the one and only tree that Adam and Eve were told to stay away from, it is our fallen nature to want what isn't ours or isn't what is right or isn't what is best for us. We're still prone to the same three sins that caused Adam's fall. What are those three sins? The lust of the eyes, the lust of the flesh and the pride of life! These are areas that will always cause us to be tempted. But here's the good news, and something we lose sight of, as well. Temptation isn't a sin. One more time so it sinks in. Temptation isn't a sin! Yet, if you're anything like me, you find yourself feeling condemned . . . just for a temptation! This is nothing more than a trick of Satan because there is no sin in the temptation. The sin is in giving into the temptation! Friend, this is a huge distinction. Satan wants us to feel defeated by the temptation so that we give in to it more easily.

Food eaten is secret has the same connotation! We delude ourselves into thinking that if no one sees our sin, then it hasn't hurt anyone. Let me first state the obvious, nothing we ever do is in secret because God sees it all. But more importantly, we never truly know who's watching us! Choose to do well in every situation. I can't begin to tell you how many times I've done the simplest of things for another person, like giving up my seat on a train to a woman when men closer to her ignored her, only to end up in a spiritual conversation that would have been far less meaningful if I hadn't performed this simple act of kindness.

I'm sure you can come up with your own examples, even before the end of this day. So what's the application of Proverbs 9:17 for me and you today? Sin in the form of things we view as sweet or delicious are nothing more than the bait of Satan. It's only when you take the bait that you have sinned. Remember what's written in 1 John 4:4, which states "greater is He that is in you than he that is in the world." There's nothing sweeter or more delicious than the words we hope to hear when we stand before our Maker: "Well done thou good and faithful servant!"

Think about these things – keep studying the Bible – and have a blessed day!

Today's devotional thought from Proverbs 9:13-15.

13 *The woman Folly is loud;*
she is undisciplined and without knowledge.

14 *She sits at the door of her house,*
on a seat at the highest point of the city,

15 *calling out to those who pass by,*
who go straight on their way.

Here are a few verses that remind us that there are always those that want to cause us to fail in our Christian walk. You can read Verses 13 thru the end of the chapter for the full context, but I want to focus today on this idea of a straight path. Let's start by observing the word 'folly'. Folly is defined as foolishness. A complete lack of understanding and good sense. Sadly, we all know people that fit this definition. Some wear their lack of good sense on their sleeves and it's very apparent to see. Others are much more subtle in their foolishness, and their real goal is to bring others into their way of life. These verses capture this thought when we see this woman literally watching, waiting and verbally encouraging others to enter her foolish world. Here's the interesting application for me and you. Unlike the young man in Proverbs 7 who actually pursues a path that will lead to ungodliness, here we have a picture of someone who is choosing the straight path. Their desire is to walk through life in a godly way.

We see here someone that is trying to make godly choices in what they do, say and see . . . yet there are still those that will make it their mission in life to tempt and tease and cajole someone into sin. The expression 'misery loves company' comes to mind. So how do you and I guard ourselves against tempters? Ephesians 6 comes to mind. Verse 12 reminds us that our fight is not against flesh and blood alone, but against spiritual forces of evil. Verse 14 reminds us of our need to stand firm and then provides us with a reminder of the importance of being spiritually prepared. I encourage you to read Ephesians 6:14-18 on your own. You may want to consider taping these verses to your car dashboard or bathroom mirror for a few weeks, until you have them memorized! The best way to cause the tempter to flee is to quote God's word. It's a great way of reminding yourself, and those trying to lead you astray, that you are God's and that you are determined to live for Him!

Think about these things – keep studying the Bible – and have a blessed day!

Today's devotional thought from Proverbs 9:13-18.

13 The woman Folly is loud;
she is undisciplined and without knowledge.

14 She sits at the door of her house,
on a seat at the highest point of the city,

15 calling out to those who pass by,
who go straight on their way.

16 "Let all who are simple come in here!"
she says to those who lack judgment.

17 "Stolen water is sweet;
food eaten in secret is delicious!"

18 But little do they know that the dead are there,
that her guests are in the depths of the grave.

Let me start with a critical reminder to all of us that name Jesus as our Savior. We have an enemy of our souls and he is the Satan. 1 Peter 5:8 states that: *"Your enemy the devil prowls around like a roaring lion looking for someone to devour."* Please brothers and sisters, never underestimate the subtle and seductive ways he tries to destroy us. In these verses we see the tempter described as a 'foolish woman'. Folly is the total opposite of wisdom. Folly has no wisdom and folly is ignorant of the things of God. Folly wants only immediate gratification with no thought regarding actions or consequences. Who among us are most vulnerable to folly? Well, all of us, but especially our children. Those brought up knowing the things of God. The danger for those of high school and college age is that they have been sheltered from the world to a great degree. They are often unprepared for the subtle ways the seducer tries to bring them down.

Verses 14 and 15 show us that even the person that is determined to walk right past a temptation is still vulnerable because the tempter will literally follow the unsuspecting young person and will lay snares and use every cunning trick in the book to cause one to fall. We see in Verses 17 and 18 that we are prone to want what is forbidden and this applies to all of us no matter how well equipped we are spiritually. Wasn't the fruit the one thing in the garden that God said Adam and Eve couldn't have and didn't that become the one thing they most wanted?

That's why we need to always be on guard against the attacks of the enemy. He'll watch and wait until he thinks he sees an opening and then he'll strike! But here's the good news! God has a remedy! It's called Repentance! You and I are never more than a prayer away from being right with God. Sinners and saints have the same opportunity. If we've trusted in Christ for our salvation then we have the Holy Spirit, our advocate and our intercessor who is by our side and ready to forgive us and help us after we sincerely repent. We may fall down, but thanks to God, we can get up!

Think about these things – keep studying the Bible – and have a blessed day!

Proverbs 9 NOTES

Proverbs 9 NOTES

Proverbs 10

*M*ore wisdom from Solomon. There are so many great verses in Chapter 10. It's certainly one of my favorite chapters. Most of us have heard the term; "Idle hands are the Devils workshop". Verse 5 is often attributed to the origin of this saying, as are other verses in the Bible. Have fun reading! Here's an idea that has proven helpful to me. When reading Proverbs, I put a letter 'T' next to verses that deal with the tongue, mouth or words. I have 11 verses marked with a 'T'. How many have you found? Don't forget to journal some thoughts on the blank page at the end of the chapter!

Today's devotional thought from Proverbs 10:1

A wise son brings joy to his father,
but a foolish son grief to his mother.

If you're a parent then it's only natural to want to see your children grow up to be wise, and to do well by others. For Christians, we long to see our children come to their own decision to follow Jesus as their Leader and Lord. When this doesn't happen it's only natural to grieve the poor decisions of our children and especially grieve if they reject Jesus as their Leader and Lord. Now, having said that, parents that are reading this fall into one of these two categories. For parents that have children that are walking with the Lord, there really is no greater joy. Seeing your children yielding their lives to God, living for Him and making decisions based on a biblical worldview has to be the ultimate joy in your life. I want to encourage you to never stop praying for them and feeding them with

the wisdom and knowledge you have learned from your walk with God.
If you have children that have not accepted Jesus as their Savior, or like
in my case, you have children that have made professions of faith, but as
of this writing show little or no evidence of a life yielded to Him, I understand all too well the feelings that come with that. Let me start by saying
that God isn't finished with them yet *(or us!)*. It really is critical that you
and I understand that God is in control. He always was and always will
be. Nothing ever catches Him off-guard. God really does love our children
more than we do. He hasn't given up on them and we shouldn't either!

In looking back on how my two children were raised, it becomes very
obvious that how we raise our children matters in who they become as
adults, their values, their manners, their ethics, their morals, their atti-
tudes and such. But, how we raise our children does *not* determine their
faith. Faith in Jesus Christ is an individual decision. Everyone alive has to
answer to the question; *"What will you do with Jesus"*, and everyone has
to answer it on their own. You are not born into Christianity! Becoming
a Christian occurs when an individual makes a personal decision to put
their faith and trust in Jesus Christ *alone* for their salvation.

So what's the application for me and you? Love your children, and pray
for them! Whether they are walking with God or not or once were, nothing
changes. You keep loving them and you keep praying for them. I know
it's hard to watch our children grow up and make mistakes. And I know
it's extremely hard if we see them make painfully wrong choices with their
lives. Salvation is a choice that comes with eternal consequences. But
remember this, God has watched all of us make wrong choices since
the beginning of creation. But guess what? He still loves us! He always
will! He isn't done with us as long as we live. And He loves you and He
loves your children *(and nieces, nephews, parents, neighbors, friends
and co-workers too!)* and He wants them to spend eternity with Him in
Paradise. Your part is to love them and keep leading them to Jesus!

Think about these things – keep studying the Bible – and have a blessed day!

Today's devotional thought from Proverbs 10:2-3.

2 *Ill-gotten treasures are of no value,
    but righteousness delivers from death.*

3 *The LORD does not let the righteous go hungry
    but he thwarts the craving of the wicked.*

These two verses are a reminder that we're not to worry or wonder about the person that gets rich by wicked means. I know how tempting it is to focus on this injustice. But these verses tell me that I'm wasting time and energy on things that I have no control over and more importantly, God knows all about! Listen to what the Gospel writer says in Matthew 16:26:

What good will it be for a man if he gains the whole world, yet forfeits his soul? Or what can a man give in exchange for his soul?

We really need to have our eyes fixed on Heaven and leave everything else to God! Friends, if we've given our hearts to Jesus and we are trusting in Him for salvation, then we must remember that we're just passing through this life. Our ultimate destination is eternity in Heaven with God! At the end of our lives it will be too late to worry about what we accumulated in our 401K, but many of us will come to the end of our lives regretting the times wasted on earthly pursuits when there was so much work that could have been accomplished that had eternal value. Friends, none of this is meant to beat you up. It's just a reality that the longer we walk with God the more we'll realize that only what we do for Jesus is what counts for eternity. Today's devotional presents all of us with a blessed reminder to make sure that we're starting our day with Jesus and telling others about Him whenever possible!

Are we seeking His plan and purpose for our lives? Are we seizing the opportunities that come our way to tell others about the hope within us? Let's not forget that there is a world of humanity dying to a Christless eternity. We have the remedy for eternal death, and it's Jesus, our only hope for everlasting life. We need to introduce Him to those God sends our way. This devotional will take you three to four minutes to read. A person dies in this world every 4 seconds, which means 45-60 people will die in the time it takes me to share this Proverb with you!

How many of those people knew Jesus? It's safe to say not all. Hopefully some but prayerfully, many. But friends this is not that complex! God's people are everywhere! He only wants you to be faithful with those He puts in your sphere of influence. He just wants you to be faithful with your part of His eternal plan! You may be the only person that someone will listen to about these matters. This is a gentle reminder for me and you to keep our eyes, ears and hearts open to those we come in contact with. I believe that many are ready, willing and desirous to hear our testimony. We just need to start the conversation! Will you today?

Think about these things – keep studying the Bible – and have a blessed day!

Today's devotional thought from Proverbs 10:4.

4 _Lazy hands make a man poor,_
     but diligent hands bring wealth.

It's interesting to note that laziness is a recurring theme in the book of Proverbs. I recall my pastor back east mentioning on numerous occasions that when God's Word repeats itself, it's usually for a very good reason. If laziness is mentioned often then we're very likely prone to it. There are a number of thoughts that come to mind when we talk about lazy hands. This has implications regarding actual physical work, or how we use our time and resources. I have to admit that all too often I can be careless with my time. When we think of our hands as the sum total of what we're called to do as Christians in this world, we gain a bigger picture of how 'idle hands' really are the Devil's workshop. We need to be diligent with all aspects of our life. The results are promising since the latter part of Verse 4 states that diligent hands bring wealth. Here again, I think the implication is far greater than monetary wealth. A life lived for Christ brings a wealth of many sorts, such as:

A wealth of purpose

A wealth of opportunity

A wealth of contentment

A wealth of friendships

A wealth of testimonies

A wealth of souls that will live in Heaven forever!

Financial wealth may have its advantages but a life lived in vibrant service to our Lord and Savior brings far more reward! What can be more fulfilling in this life than richness of our faith and richness in service to others? I can't think of anything, can you? So what's the application for you and me? Laziness has many potential risks and diligence has many potential rewards. We need to be seeking opportunities to serve God and serve others. A friend recently sent me a clever little poem that I think fits today's Proverb teaching well:

God won't ask what kind of car you drove. He'll
  ask how many people you drove who didn't have transportation.

God won't ask about the clothes you had in your closet,
  He'll ask how many you helped to clothe.

God won't ask how many friends you had. He'll ask
  how many people to whom you were a friend.

God won't ask in what neighborhood you lived,
  He'll ask how you treated your neighbors.

An others focused life will mean a happier and a healthier life! And that's a promise you can take to the bank!

Think about these things – keep studying the Bible – and have a blessed day!

Today's devotional thought from Proverbs 10:5.

5 *He who gathers crops in summer is a wise son,*
  but he who sleeps during harvest is a disgraceful son.

Here's some very practical advice and this advice applies equally to both body and soul! First, the body. I spent most of my adult life in sales of one sort or another. The first thing I realized very early on was the critical need to be extremely disciplined in my need to 'gather crops' when times were good. I had to learn to stay out in the field and to keep cultivating the next customer. I couldn't make assumptions on where or when the next sale would come from. Like Nehemiah, I needed to pray but then I needed to put feet to my prayers. We have a moral and biblical obligation to give 100% to our employers, since ultimately all we do in life and work is really for God. And God is not going to let you sit back and wait upon Him for blessings. He's not going to treat you like a rich uncle that flowers you with gifts even when undeserved. If we're Christians, we should be the best employees any company has because we represent the creator of the universe!

This is where the 'soul' or spiritual application comes in. In the same way we need to be diligent in our careers always working diligently in the work God has placed us in, we need to be equipping ourselves spiritually as well. We need to be students of God's Word and always learning and maturing so that we are able, when the time is right, to pass on what we've learned to others. Here's the thing that becomes so very clear to me the older I get. I know very little! I mean it! I'm not using false humility here. The longer I live and walk and serve God the more I come to realize that I haven't even scratched the surface of all that God wants to teach me. There is so much wonderful learning to be had and I want all that God has for me. I want to learn so I can pour what I've learned into others, including my wife, my children, my staff and anyone God puts in my life.

At the end of my life, which by the way could be any day, I want to leave a legacy. I can't assume I have 10, 20, or 30 years or more. I need to be learning and passing on what I've learned today! How about you? Let's decide today, like the farmer in today's verse, to be that wise son or daughter and to make each day count for eternity. Let's leave a legacy!

Think about these things – keep studying the Bible – and have a blessed day!

Today's devotional thought from Proverbs 10:7.

7 *The memory of the righteous will be a blessing,*
   but the name of the wicked will rot.

I ponder this verse each time I read it. It causes me to look ahead into the future and I try to picture myself 10, 20 or even 30 years from now, should the Lord tarry and should I live that long. I often think about the end of my life. Not about my death because I have no fear or concerns regarding that. I rest in God's word and I have trusted in Christ alone for my salvation, so when absent from this body I will be present with the Lord. The thing I ponder most is what my legacy will be after I'm gone? The righteous and the wicked have this in common, all will die and face judgment. I try not to think selfishly about things like who will cry at my funeral. It's much more than that. I ponder what impact my life will have made on people still living. Will I finish well? Will what I do and what I say and how I live my life make a difference? Will my life have mattered for eternal purposes or will I have lived selfishly with just 'me' in mind?

These are some of the questions I found myself asking in 2007, the year before selling my company, with the thought of going into some form of full-time Christian ministry. I'm not saying that anyone listening should sell their companies or quit their jobs. That's between you and God, but for me, these were thoughts that I couldn't escape. I make no attempt at false humility here. I had serious questions in my own mind about my ability to represent the Kingdom well if I went into ministry. But I also had and still have, a burning desire to make a difference for the Kingdom and I sincerely desire to finish well.

The wicked person mentioned in this verse is clearly someone that lived and died without the security of salvation through Jesus Christ. This person's name will never be remembered, or worse, will be remembered forever in infamy, like Hitler or Stalin. But would it be any better if I live my life selfishly, for me, myself and I? With no lasting legacy that impacts eternity, or if I were to end badly, walk away from God, be unfaithful to my wife or in some way dishonor the name of God, will my legacy be any different than any of the wicked? What's the application for me and you? Are we living each day with eternity in mind? Are we living each day with a deep and sincere concern for those dying to a Christless eternity? Are we living each day putting God first, others second and ourselves third?

Think about these things – keep studying the Bible – and have a blessed day!

Today's devotional thought from Proverbs 10:13.

13 *Wisdom is found on the lips of the discerning,*
     but a rod is for the back of him who lacks judgment.

Wisdom. What a helpful aspect of life wisdom can be. Can wisdom be developed? With God's help, absolutely! We sometimes confuse wisdom with knowledge and this is a mistake. You might be thinking, well I've never been that bright and I always struggled in school. Well, I assure you that I've known brilliant people, rocket scientist types, that weren't terribly wise in how they lived their lives. Wisdom is very different from knowledge though God is limitless in His ability to give you more of both! Wisdom is likened more to discernment than to book knowledge. And wisdom is something God can develop in someone with an open heart. Note that wisdom is found on the lips. This shows that a wise person responds with wisdom. To have God's wisdom on our lips, we need to be studying God's word to find the rich advice He offers us. Let's look at the words of Paul when writing to Timothy in 2 Timothy 3:17-17 about the importance of studying the scriptures:

[16]*All Scripture is God-breathed and is useful for teaching, rebuking, correcting and training in righteousness,* [17]*so that the man of God may be thoroughly equipped for every good work.*

101

The mistake you and I make all too often is to rely on our own wisdom instead of the wisdom from God. Listen to the words of the prophet in Jeremiah 9:23-24:

23 *This is what the LORD says:*
   "Let not the wise man boast of his wisdom
   or the strong man boast of his strength
   or the rich man boast of his riches,

24 *but let him who boasts boast about this:*
   that he understands and knows me,
   that I am the LORD, who exercises kindness,
   justice and righteousness on earth,
   for in these I delight," declares the LORD.

When we pursue our own way we foolishly and willfully prepare rods for our own backs. Folly will follow us wherever we go. Brothers and sisters, God has a far better plan and purpose for our lives than we can even imagine. Our challenge is the need to die daily to our wills and to follow God's plan and purpose for our lives. Why not pause right now and pray and ask God to take His rightful place on the throne of your life? I think you'll be amazed at what happens.

Think about these things – keep studying the Bible – and have a blessed day!

Today's devotional thought from Proverbs 10:19.

19 *When words are many, sin is not absent,*
   but he who holds his tongue is wise.

I must confess, I'm often guilty of loving to hear myself speak. I don't say this lightly because it's not a good habit. The more talking done, the more chance for idle words to be spoken and then words get spoken that we wish we could recall. If you're like me you've had at least a few occasions where you cupped your mouth right after saying something that you wish had never left your lips. God has such a great way of reminding me of my desperate need for His guiding hand in this area of my life. I read this chapter and verse the day after spending an afternoon with my son. I had to call him right after reading this verse to ask him to forgive me for something stupid I said to him. He was gracious in accepting my apology and didn't think much about what I said but the fact that he recalled what I was apologizing for told me that it hurt him, at least a little.

I find myself in trouble when I'm attempting to be funny. All too often humor leads t sarcasm and someone I respect has told me that sarcasm is never funny. But what's the larger point this verse is making? What's the real application for you and me? It's the second part of the verse which reminds us that it's far wiser to hold our tongues! This idea of choosing our words more wisely is a great lesson for me. I've mentioned in the past the advice my mother always gave, that God gave us two ears and one mouth so we would listen twice as much as we speak. Sometimes I think I'd have been better off with three ears . . . and no mouth!

For further application, I'd like to add one more aspect that we can glean from this verse. The implication is that by choosing our words more carefully, we are also inclined to seize more opportunities to choose words that encourage and build up rather than saying things that tear down. Even in circumstances that require discipline or correction we have an obligation as Christians to say things in love. Our Heavenly Father offers the best example When He corrects us, He always does it in love. In my apology to my son I was able to express a much more heartfelt thought because in my apology I chose my words more carefully and I could tell it had a very positive effect. I thank God for the lesson I learned and I will renew my commitment to choose carefully the words I speak. Here's a creative way to remember this lesson of Proverbs 10:19; by being prayerful with our words we can learn to speak less but actually say more! You and I can learn to be more focused on the content of our words, rather than the quantity of our words.

Think about these things – keep studying the Bible – and have a blessed day!

Proverbs 10 NOTES

Proverbs 10 NOTES

Proverbs 11

*H*ere's another chapter loaded with individual thoughts that I find myself quoting often. (Usually to myself!) Verse 1 is a business principal I tried to live by for the 25 years that I owned my own business. Verse 14 is another great business (and life) principle. I can think of a lot of decisions that would have gone in a better direction, had I sought more advice before moving forward! There are a total of 31 separate thoughts within this chapter. How many will become favorites of yours?

Today's devotional thought from Proverbs 11:1.

*1 The LORD abhors dishonest scales,
    but accurate weights are his delight.*

These words are about as strong as one can express. Other translations state that dishonest scales are an abomination to God. In the time of Solomon, it was not uncommon for dishonest merchants to use dishonest scales. One typically purchased products by weight...whether it was meat or bread or produce. An honest merchant would weigh the food being purchased using accurate measuring bowls. The dishonest merchant would use techniques such as false bottoms in their measuring bowls. This would make it seem like one was purchasing a pound of meat, when in fact the bowl was designed to give the buyer far less than what it seemed they were buying! This term for scales in today's jargon would mean any dishonest action on our part.

I've mentioned in the past that I spent 25 years running my own business. There were many times in those years when the temptation to use *'dishonest scales'* was very great. As a Christian business owner I needed to be honest and trust the Lord for the outcome. There were many times when it would have been *'convenient'* to lie and rationalize that it *'wouldn't hurt anyone'*. Situations like this present themselves to us all the time. Have you ever been given too much change during a transaction? This is when it's important to remind ourselves that God delights in accurate weights! I say let the chips fall where they may. Do the right thing and be honest and trust God for the outcome, however minor or large the financial impact. God delights in us when we choose to be honest. I want to please God. I really want to do the right thing even when it's not convenient! Even when it hurts.

I've often been reminded by brothers in the Lord that a good measure of my true heart is what I do with my time, money and thoughts . . . when no one else is watching! This is good practical advice and can help us in moments of temptation, but we also need to remind ourselves that there is always someone watching, and that's our Creator. I want to live my life in a way that pleases my Creator! I need to know my Creator in order to know what pleases Him. This requires me to learn from Him. And how do I accomplish this? By being a student of His word! How about you! Will you make Him a priority in your life today? Why not start today with a renewed commitment to reading your Bible daily. One great idea would be to start reading a chapter of Proverbs each day! It's pretty easy. On the first day of the month you read Proverbs 1 and continue right through to the end of the month. Then start over again! I can promise you that if you do it for a month, you'll do it for a lifetime, because you'll find it quite helpful in your daily walk with God.

Think about these things – keep studying the Bible – and have a blessed day!

Today's devotional thought from Proverbs 11:2.

2 *When pride comes, then comes disgrace,*
  but with humility comes wisdom.

Friends, you would be amazed at how long I stared at a blank sheet of paper and prayed before being able to prepare this devotional. Just when I think I'm getting better at this 'pride' thing, God begins to show me all the areas where I still struggle with it! If you're like me it's uncanny how many times in a week the 'other' person is the problem, but never me! Well, truth be told, there's still an awful lot of me in me! And when it's me then it's not Jesus leading and guiding me. I've often heard it said that Jesus is a gentleman so He's never going to push Himself onto the throne of our lives. He waits patiently, like a gentleman, until we're ready to offer Him the seat! Oh Lord, how I want to gain victory in this area of my life! Note in these verses the connection that humility has with wisdom. The more pride that fills our chests, the less opportunity to learn all that God has for us. Listen to how God describes His servant Moses in Numbers 12:3:

Now Moses was a very humble man, more humble than anyone else on the face of the earth.

We often remember how wise Moses was and how his wisdom is seen throughout the first five books of the Old Testament, but I think we forget this verse. This little verse helps us understand all the rest! This verse identifies the source of his wisdom and how he was able to receive it. You see, he had a humble heart and therefore he was able to receive what God had for him. His pride wasn't in the way! Proverbs 3:34 states that *"God mocks proud mockers but gives grace to the humble."* James and Peter repeat this same admonishment and many more verses throughout the Old and New Testament are there to show us how pride destroys us and others. Paul states in Romans 12:16:

Live in harmony with one another. Do not be proud, but be willing to associate with people of low position. Do not be conceited.

Brothers and sisters, God has a wonderful plan and purpose for our lives. Our challenge is to love Him and trust Him and get our own selves out of the way. Join me today in a prayer of repentance. Confess the sin of pride and watch what God will do in your life and mine!

Think about these things – keep studying the Bible – and have a blessed day!

Today's devotional thought from Proverbs 11:5-6.

5 *The righteousness of the blameless makes a straight way for them,*
    but the wicked are brought down by their own wickedness.

6 *The righteousness of the upright delivers them,*
    but the unfaithful are trapped by evil desires.

Both of these verses contain nearly identical meanings. The comment regarding the righteous should be of great encouragement to those that have put their trust in Christ. Through Salvation we have all we need! 2 Peter 1:3 states:

His divine power has given us everything we need for life and godliness through our knowledge of him who called us by his own glory and goodness.

This should be an amazing comfort for the Christian. However, it's what we do with what we've been given that matters. It's not enough to have the basic ingredients if we don't do anything with them. I can take out 30 ingredients to make a gourmet meal but unless I know what to do with them, they will remain 30 separate ingredients. And the ingredients will only result in a gourmet meal if I follow the directions! So what's the recipe for living a righteous life? We have to start with the recipe book, which is God's Word! Brothers and sisters, the Bible is God's instruction book for our lives. We talk to God through prayer and He talks to us through His love letter to us, the Bible. Our best chance at living an upright life will come from following the biblical directions!

Most of us and hopefully all of us have a time each day for Bible reading and prayer. It's important for our spiritual nourishment the same way a good breakfast gives physical nourishment. In the past I've had periods in my life where I was very good at reading someone else's books about what God wanted to teach me, but I wasn't reading God's book to learn what He wanted to teach me. What's the point I'm trying to make here? It's great if you're reading each day from one or two devotional books and I would never suggest you stop, but please make sure your reading includes *the book*, the Bible. A surefire way to fall as a Christian is to be under-equipped for the challenges of life. We are reminded about trials and tribulations in this life directly by Jesus in John 16:33:

"I have told you these things, so that in me you may have peace. In this world you will have trouble. But take heart! I have overcome the world."

The way to navigate through this life, and the challenges that come with it are found by regular study of the Bible. A great help would be to join a small group where the Bible is being studied. A place where you can ask questions and learn how to live the Christian life, and to live it abundantly.

Friends, I want to encourage you to make daily Bible reading a priority. There are many ways to read the Bible. You can read about 25 minutes a day and read the entire Bible in a year, Genesis to Revelation. You can find reading schedules online that have you read a portion of the Old and New Testaments plus a chapter of Psalms and Proverbs. You can add a chapter of Proverbs each day like I do. The important thing is to develop the daily habit. If you're not already doing it then start today. You'll be glad you did!

Think about these things – keep studying the Bible – and have a blessed day!

Today's devotional thought from Proverbs 11:7.

7 When a wicked man dies, his hope perishes;
all he expected from his power comes to nothing.

What a privilege it is for me to be able to share some thoughts with you from the Book of Proverbs. If you've made it this far into the book, then perhaps it's been beneficial. I pray it has! Brothers and sisters . . . this verse reminds us of the need to be ever vigilant in pursuing prayerful opportunities to tell others about Jesus. This verse encompasses all the sadness that is the result of one who dies to a Christless eternity. I'm reminded of the parable in Luke 12 of the rich fool whose land produced an abundant harvest. There's nothing wrong with the abundant harvest, it's what the rich fool thought of the abundant harvest. He thought it was his accomplishment. You see he never acknowledged God in it. He was trusting in his riches alone. He determined he would tear down his barns and build bigger ones, never knowing his life would end that day and all he had would become someone else's. This verse implies this was a man of great wealth and power.

I've been in homes of men with great wealth. Very recently I was with a man of significant wealth. This man, however, was a Christian. He held his possessions loosely in his hands. He understood that it is all God's, and he uses his wealth to further Kingdom work. I've also been in homes of wealthy men that don't know Christ. At the end of their lives their hopes and dreams and aspirations will be dashed to pieces, if they continue to trust in their riches and never acknowledge God.

Friends, the person who dies outside of Christ is doomed. We need periodic reminders of what a Christless eternity will be like. I know for some of us, sharing the hope that comes from knowing Jesus is not always an easy thing to do, but let me encourage you. The more you share your faith, the easier it gets. More importantly, you are sharing hope and salvation that lasts for all of eternity. I'd like to recommend a book by Mark Cahill titled "The one thing you can't do in Heaven." It's a clever title! The one thing you can't do in Heaven is tell someone about Jesus! If you're in Heaven, then your opportunities to tell others is over. The book is a tremendous encouragement and offers very practical advice on how to share your faith with others. There really is no downside to telling others about Jesus.

What can happen if you boldly share your faith?

1 – They can accept Jesus! And the angels in Heaven will rejoice with you.

2 – They can reject Jesus!

3 – Or you can plant a seed that God will water and He'll have someone else pick up where you left off. If they accept Jesus or you plant a seed, it's all good. But even if they reject Jesus, Luke 6:22 states: *"Blessed are you when people hate you, when they exclude you and insult you and reject your name as evil, because of the Son of Man."* God just wants us to be faithful to tell others about Him, and if we do, it's a win, win, win. There is no downside.

I encourage you to go to www.markcahill.org and order his book and start sharing Jesus with others today!

Think about these things – keep studying the Bible – and have a blessed day!

Today's devotional thought from Proverbs 11:14.

14 *For lack of guidance a nation falls,*
but many advisers make victory sure.

What a great life principle we see stated here. This idea of seeking wise counsel and seeking it from multiple sources is extremely practical! Whether a nation, a business, a church, a ministry or an individual, the application is the same. We need to make decisions wisely. What's implied in this verse is the idea that the higher our level of authority and power to make decisions, the more important it is to seek counsel. The problem with this is that this is often the levels where the most problems occur. Human nature being what it is, the more power or influence one gains, the less likely they are to get advice from others! I guess it's the thought that since they have all this decision-making authority, they're going to use it. The wise leader will recognize the need for many advisors. They will find it to their advantage to share their idea with others. If they agree in their advice then the decision will become clearer. If they differ in their thoughts, then there is opportunity to hear more from all sides and possibly end up with a different determination. We need to avoid putting ourselves in situations, especially those that have long term consequences affecting ourselves and others, without seeking wise counsel.

I've made this mistake too many times to not implore you to be careful in this area of decision-making. We all have some areas of expertise but none of us have expertise in all areas. Seek wise counsel from others that have knowledge about things in which you have limited understanding. It's been said that two eyes see more than one and this is a good principle when it comes to decisions, especially those that affect others. I realize that one cannot necessarily include others in every decision that you make but I think it's safe to say that all of us could include others more often than we do now. I can also speculate that most of us can think of a decision or two that we wish we hadn't made or that with a bit more counsel may have caused us to make a different decision, with a decidedly different outcome! Here's what it boils down to, are we humble enough to realize we don't have all the answers? Or will we allow our pride to once again get in the way of wise decision-making?

Think about these things – keep studying the Bible – and have a blessed day!

Today's devotional thought from Proverbs 11:25.

A generous man will prosper; he who refreshes others will himself be refreshed

I like this Proverb a lot! At first glance I think we immediately see the use of the word 'prosper' as being financial in nature. Maybe it's just me but as I prayed and pondered this simple proverb, I began to see what an awesome thing it would be if I were to walk through life in this world with an 'others focused' mentality. I've written in previous devotionals that as Christians we need to put God first, others second and ourselves third. Well . . . this sounds nice when you say it . . . but living it practically is a bit harder. Let's explore the verse a little deeper and see what conclusions we can come to about this intriguing way to live our lives.

First, we see the likely outcome of generosity is prosperity. The word prosperity does imply financial reward; however, the broader definition includes a successful, flourishing or thriving existence, way beyond financial good fortune. It's this broader meaning that I want to look at more deeply. I believe God is showing us that something far greater than good fortune awaits those of us that pursue opportunities to pour out generosity toward others. Let's look at the second part of this precious verse, 'he who refreshes others will himself be refreshed'.

What's the application for you and me? Be a giver! That's right, be a giver. Not financially, although there are times when that might be appropriate, but think of the many other ways you can be a giver. Sometimes the simplest acts of generosity can be the most meaningful. I recall a very simple act of kindness when I gave up a table and chairs right next to the pool at a hotel. I offered it to two elderly women that would benefit from it being right next to the stairs into the pool. You would have thought I gave them a million dollars. They expressed immense gratitude for this simple act of kindness. It refreshed these two ladies but it also refreshed me! There are many benefits to living an 'others focused' life. I've had innumerable 'divine opportunities' to tell others about Jesus following a simple act of kindness. In fact, the older I get, the more aware I become of how God seems to orchestrate these opportunities. I just need to be sensitive enough to God's spirit to see the opportunity in front of me. Be generous in all ways! Be a giver. Not because of what you might get in return, but because of the wonderful opportunities that can come from giving. Remember . . . God first, others second and ourselves third!

Think about these things – keep studying the Bible – and have a blessed day!

Proverbs 11 NOTES

Proverbs 11 NOTES

Proverbs 12

*O*ne theme that runs through many chapters of Proverbs concerns foolishness. The Bible describes a fool as someone who believes there is no God. It is a sad thought . . . someone dying to a Christ-less eternity. That's why we need to be prepared to tell someone about the hope we have in Christ. I believe God brings people into our lives because He knows we are the perfect person to tell them about Jesus. I also believe that God wants to equip us through the active study of His Word, to be able to give a clear explanation of salvation. If you aren't prepared for this, then make today the day you decide to get prepared through prayer and Bible study so you are ready to share when the opportunity presents itself.

Today's devotional thought from Proverbs 12:1.

1 Whoever loves discipline loves knowledge,
but he who hates correction is stupid.

Well, Solomon doesn't beat around the bush on this one. You either grasp the benefits of discipline and correction or you're stupid! Don't blame me for this blunt statement, I'm just the messenger! It really does show the character of an individual if they can receive correction, counsel and reproof with a grateful heart. Willing acceptance of discipline shows a heart open to all that God has for someone. I'm not saying that it's always easy. In fact the easiest things in life are often not the best things in life. In Hebrews 12, we have this awesome reminder that God disciplines us for our own good:

11 No discipline seems pleasant at the time, but painful. Later on, however, it produces a harvest of righteousness and peace for those who have been trained by it.

So we see from God's own words; He disciplines us for our own good. Initially we may not like it very much. If you have received correction from someone that truly has your best interests in mind, then I believe the reason for the correction will become obvious to you in time. If you're thinking; *"What if the person correcting me isn't hearing from God?"* Well you don't have to worry about that either, because God will eventually discipline that person as well!

So what's the application for you and me? I think we should be very open to receiving correction. Hating correction only shows our own ungodly pride and immaturity. And the longer we ignore correction, the harder it becomes to receive it from others. We need to remain humble in our walk before God and man. The only thing I can offer is what the Bible teaches us through verses like Proverbs 12:1 and Hebrews 12:11 and my own life experience. I really am amazed at how much I have to learn and how much correction is still needed in my life. Brothers and sisters, we're all likely to do stupid things in life if we live long enough. Let's not be so thick-headed that we can't see when God sends someone or something our way that will have a long-lasting and course-correcting impact on our lives.

Think about these things – keep studying the Bible – and have a blessed day!

Today's devotional thought from Proverbs 12:2.

2 A good man obtains favor from the LORD,
but the LORD condemns a crafty man.

What an encouraging verse! We can obtain favor from the Creator of all things! How cool is that! What an amazing thing it is to know that we can have such an intimate relationship with God. Now this verse does say that it's a good man (or woman) that can obtain favor from the LORD. But doesn't the Bible say that none of us are righteous, no not one? Well that's true up and until the point of accepting Jesus as our Savior! When we accept Jesus, an amazing supernatural occurrence takes place. One moment, God looks upon us and sees only our sinfulness, and the moment after we repent of our sins, God sees us as white as snow. Why? Because Jesus wipes away our sin. Can I get an AMEN? So what's the application for me and you? We need to live like we've been rescued! The enemy of our soul (Satan) wants us to do at least two things after we become Christians. First, he wants us to doubt what we've done and second, he wants us to settle into a ho-hum, now I'm saved existence, whereby we don't really ruffle anyone's feathers about Jesus, but just live a peaceful life and not rob or murder anyone, right? Wrong! God has an amazing and wonderful plan for your life and the more you get to know Him, the more you'll understand that wonderful plan and purpose He has for you. Listen to what is stated in Colossians 1:10-14:

10 *And we pray this in order that you may live a life worthy of the Lord and may please him in every way: bearing fruit in every good work, growing in the knowledge of God, 11being strengthened with all power according to his glorious might so that you may have great endurance and patience, and joyfully 12giving thanks to the Father, who has qualified you to share in the inheritance of the saints in the kingdom of light. 13For he has rescued us from the dominion of darkness and brought us into the kingdom of the Son he loves, 14in whom we have redemption, the forgiveness of sins.*

Brothers and sisters, God has an awesome plan for your life and mine. We need to let Him speak to us through His word the Bible and we need to speak to Him through prayer. He has rescued us from the dominion of darkness and we should be living with this victorious mindset!

Think about these things – keep studying the Bible – and have a blessed day!

Today's devotional thought from Proverbs 12:4.

4 *A wife of noble character is her husband's crown,*
    but a disgraceful wife is like decay in his bones.

I've been happily married for over 40 years and the first part of this verse puts a smile on my face every time I read it! The mention of a crown makes me laugh for two reasons. The first reason is that the reference to a crown reminds me that I'm happier than a king on his throne because of the wife God has blessed me with. The second reason the mention of a crown makes me laugh is because most of us married men realize that our wives would have taken our crowns for their jewelry collection years ago! Sorry, I couldn't resist the tongue-in-cheek reference to jewelry, especially for those listeners that know my wife and her love of bling!

A man blessed with a good wife has much for which to be thankful. I rely very much on my wife, for advice and counsel and for feedback on day-to-day decisions and so much more. My wife is also my best friend and I love being with her whenever possible, except when she's heading off to the mall!

On a more serious note, I'm reminded of the many marriages that we've known during our 40 years together that haven't been as fortunate. As stated here in the second part of Proverbs 12:4, a disgraceful wife can make life miserable and can cause much harm when it comes to life and work. If your marriage isn't what it should be, I assure you that it can get better, but it takes a commitment from both husband and wife to live a life yielded to Jesus Christ; that is the key. God can work with a couple that is willing to listen and learn, but it takes both parties to humbly admit they need help. I assure you that it's well worth whatever it takes to get your marriage back on track. Believe me, the alternative is even harder. There's nothing easy about a broken family. God intended couples to marry for life because He knows how hard it is on everyone when marriages fall apart.

For the listeners that are not yet married but want to be, I offer this practical advice. Don't be in a hurry! Allow time for the infatuation period to wear off. Men and women don't think things through when they have just met someone. The wisest thing you can do the day you say; "let's get married" is to delay that decision for at least six months (or longer!) And never get married without going through pre-marital counseling. Someone needs to tell you that it's not always going to be easy. He's not always going to look like the cover of GQ, and she's not always going to look like Miss America! Marriage is one of the most important decisions you will ever make. Don't rush into something so critically important.

I can look back on virtually all aspects of my life and point to many decisions that I've rushed into that I've regretted. Yet I've never regretted waiting. There have been countless times that I've intentionally waited on decisions and that short delay has proven to be a blessing every time. I can hear the moans and groans already from all those young couples that want to get married and don't want to wait. I'm one more voice cautioning you to take your time. Trust me, you can wait. If your love is real, it will only grow more while waiting. And if it doesn't, then that's a red flag! In this waiting period, you may see things you never would have seen if you rushed into marriage. If he or she is the one, the wait will be worth it!

Think about these things – keep studying the Bible – and have a blessed day!

Today's devotional thought from Proverbs 12:15–16.

15 *The way of a fool seems right to him,*
   but a wise man listens to advice.

16 *A fool shows his annoyance at once,*
   but a prudent man overlooks an insult.

Here's a contrast in terms we haven't looked at together in any specific way, though I have certainly covered the topic of a fool. You might recall that the biblical use of the word fool would describe someone that believes there is no God. It's interesting to note that Verse 15 gives a subtle hint that the fool in this story does what seems right to him but makes no apparent effort to inquire of others. We get this sense from the second part of the verse, in its contrast to a wise man. Apparently the wise man took the time to get a 'second opinion' about whatever matter was at hand. We're admonished in many places in the Book of Proverbs to seek advice from others. Proverbs 19:20 states:

Listen to advice and accept instruction…and in the end you will be wise.

Proverbs 20:18 states: *Make plans by seeking advice.*

So the lesson for you and me is to seek counsel from others before making important decisions. Of course the first place we should go to seek counsel is to our Heavenly Father, who delights when we bring all our prayers and petitions before Him. Verse 16 gives us another glimpse at a fool and the better way of a prudent person. The fool is always quick to show annoyance when he or she is insulted or in some other way slighted or ignored. This is a result of thinking too highly of oneself. Many go through life, even Christians, thinking that God is fortunate to have them on His side. Many join a church with the attitude that the church should be rolling out the red carpet because this individual has chosen to bestow his or her many talents on this particular church! The awful taste of 'self' is so prevalent in this type of thinking.

It pains me to admit that there was a time when I thought God was fortunate to have *me* on His side. Fortunately, God graciously and patiently showed me in no uncertain terms that He was the Potter and I was the clay. It was only when I became a broken and humbled vessel, did I begin to see that only then would and could God use me for His plans and purposes. I am so grateful to my patient, gracious, forgiving Heavenly Father, that in spite of my foolishness, He gives me opportunities to serve Him. There is a great little paperback book called *The Calvary Road by Roy Hession*. I recommend this book for anyone wanting a good read on brokenness and humility. I've been walking with Jesus for about 40 years now, and I'm more aware than ever before just how much I need a daily dependence on Him. How about you?

Think about these things – keep studying the Bible – and have a blessed day!

Today's devotional thought from Proverbs 12:18.

18 *Reckless words pierce like a sword,*
    but the tongue of the wise brings healing.

There are a number of recurring topics that are written about in Proverbs but few are repeated as often as verses to do with the tongue. Today's devotional is about our words. All too often the references to our tongue are presented in the negative. Here in Verse 18 we see both a negative and a positive in one verse. First, the negative. Have you ever been spoken to in a way that quite literally felt like you were stabbed? I have! It's emotionally painful and it lasts long after the words have been spoken. I've counseled some folks over the years that tell me they can recall, sometimes decades later, the painful words spoken to them by a friend or family member. Negative words can cut like a knife! But here's the good news! Words can also be soothing and healing. Words can restore, reconcile and remedy hurtful circumstances.

What's the application for you and me? I think we can all grow in this area. I think it might be easier to eliminate hurtful words but more beneficial to learn how to add healing words. I think people hear far too much of the negative. We collectively err on the side of saying nothing when everything is going like it's supposed to but we shout out problems or criticisms from the rooftops. I believe you and I have a great opportunity being presented to us. I believe we should make it our goal to say at least one kind or encouraging word to someone every day. I think if we really took the time to work at this we could find ourselves looking for divine opportunities to bring a soothing word to someone every day. I'm not suggesting anything false or contrived, just a sincere comment offered to someone we speak to each day, on the phone or in person. I think we would all be amazed at how God could use this simple gesture to open doors for sharing our faith that we never would have imagined! The Apostle Paul in his letter to the Philippians penned these words describing the joy in his heart for the church in Philippi:

It is right for me to feel this way about all of you, since I have you in my heart; for whether I am in chains or defending and confirming the gospel, all of you share in God's grace with me. God can testify how I long for all of you with the affection of Christ Jesus.

If you got a letter like that do you think you'd just read it once and file it away or would you read it a number of times, very slowly, to let every word sink in and warm your heart? Let's all try to be a Paul in someone's life this week!

Think about these things – keep studying the Bible – and have a blessed day!

Today's devotional thought is from Proverbs 12:22.

22 *The LORD detests lying lips,*
but he delights in people who are trustworthy.

Today's topic is truth-telling. I recall a time a number of years ago when I had to tell my staff that I told a lie in a meeting the day before. I'll spare you the details but suffice it to say that I rationalized that a 'little' stretch of the truth wouldn't hurt anyone, which is a very common way we justify our lies. In this instance I found myself thinking about this 'stretch of the truth' the next morning . . . and I could almost hear God audibly telling me "you lied yesterday!" It was like a loving father giving his son a gentle smack on the side of the head saying "You knucklehead . . . why did you do that?"

Well . . . a few minutes later I opened my Bible to Proverbs 12 and started reading. When I got to Verse 22, I ran right smack into these words: 'The Lord detests lying lips, but he delights in men who are trustworthy'. Wow . . . did that get my attention. For some reason, it became clearer to me than at any other time in my 30 years as a Christian (at the time that this event happened) that I don't want to lie! Not just because God detests it but more importantly because He delights in when I speak truthfully.

About a third of the chapters in Proverbs deal with lying. A topic that appears in so many chapters must be important. That's why I love the Book of Proverbs as much as I do. I love the way Solomon communicates simple life principles that will make our lives better when we apply these principles to our lives.

122

Back to the story. A little later that same morning, I was listening to a Bible teacher on the radio. He asked a question that had a profound affect on me. He asked: "Is Jesus just a really important part of your life or is He the center of your life?" This was now two attention-getting moments in the same day! So . . . I confessed the sin of lying . . . and I renewed a commitment to allow Jesus to be my Leader and Lord. I found myself repeating the words of David in Psalm 139:23-24:

23 *Search me, O God, and know my heart;*
    test me and know my anxious thoughts.

24 *See if there is any offensive way in me,*
    and lead me in the way everlasting.

In conclusion...I'm reminded once again of the wonderful plan and purpose God has for each of our lives. He can do so much more with my life when it is yielded to Him. How about you? Is God giving you a gentle smack on the side of the head today? Anything you need to confess? We're all just a prayer of repentance away from a more solid walk with God.

Think about these things – keep studying the Bible – and have a blessed day!

Proverbs 12 NOTES

Proverbs 12 NOTES

Proverbs 13

*P*roverbs 13 is one of those chapters that has a meaningful principle in each of the 25 distinct thoughts being communicated. The best way to read a chapter like this is SLOWLY! Take your time, chew on the meaning of each separate thought. Read a verse at a time and then ponder it. Don't forget to journal your thoughts about what you're reading.

Today's devotional thought from Proverbs 13:3.

3 He who guards his lips guards his life,
   but he who speaks rashly will come to ruin.

This is one of many verses in Proverbs that deals directly with what comes out of our mouths! For most of us this is a *'work in progress'* but I'm learning more and more why God gives so much instruction on guarding our mouths. The book of James devotes half of Chapter 3 to the idea of *'taming the tongue'*. Why is it that we have so much trouble keeping our mouths shut? Growing up, if I heard my mother once, I heard her say a thousand times, (and you know what I'm about to say) *"God gave you two ears and one mouth so He must want you to listen twice as much as you speak!"* Well that humorous statement has more theology in it than we realize.

James 1:19 reminds us to . . . *"be slow to speak but quick to listen."*

Brothers and sisters, what we say really does matter. We need to learn to choose words carefully. A misspoken word can cause much unnecessary heartache. I need to remind myself, nearly daily, to listen more than I speak. It's taken a long time for me to learn that my opinion is *not* the only one worth hearing.

Our words can help or harm others! I have sat in on many counseling sessions where someone will mention a comment made months or years earlier that still has a crippling affect on them. Sadly, we often say hurtful things to those we love the most. I know I've had to confess to God on numerous occasions words spoken to my children when they were young, words that caused them deep pain and heartache. Having said that, each new day is a new opportunity to find godly ways to communicate to others.

Just as words can tear down a person, words can also be an unbelievable source of comfort and encouragement. Words like; *"What a terrific effort!"* - *"I appreciate you!"* - *"Thanks!"* Or words like; *"I'm sorry"* - *"I shouldn't have said that"* - *"Please forgive me!"* I think it's also worth mentioning that it's not just what comes out of our mouths. Avoid even *thinking* negatively!

Matthew 12:34 states that: *For the mouth speaks what the heart is full of.*

So this brings us back to that place where the ground is level for all of us . . . it brings us back to Jesus! We all need Jesus! We need to seek Him in prayer. We need to confess our poor use of the tongue. We need Jesus to speak to our hearts so that what we say matches what we feel. If you find yourself routinely saying the wrong things, hurtful and insensitive things then I urge you to run to Jesus. Confess your utter dependence on Him to purify your heart and He will. You have His word on it!

Think about these things – keep studying the Bible – and have a blessed day!

Today's devotional thought from Proverbs 13:4.

4 The sluggard craves and gets nothing,
  but the desires of the diligent are fully satisfied.

Here's an interesting proverb that shows us that our actions have consequences. Notice that the sluggard or lazy person in this verse craves the same things that the diligent person craves. The difference is that the lazy person won't do what the diligent person is willing to do. A lazy person wants everything handed to them. They don't want to work for things or apply themselves. I know people that are always quick to complain, usually about others, that they're smarter or richer or have more friends.

Never stopping to realize that they're smarter because they studied more in school and they're richer because they were diligent about saving a percentage of their income and not living beyond their means and they have more friends because they decided to live an 'others' focused life, always thinking of the other person rather than themselves. If the lazy person put the same energy they waste on complaining about their misery into more positive purposes, they too would be satisfied.

Note the subtle difference between the two types of people. The sluggard craves but the diligent desires. There's a difference. To crave something is to have an intense desire or urgent need for something. The word suggests the idea of begging yet not necessarily deserving. To desire something has a subtle difference. It's defined as a wish, a longing or even a request or petition. I see craving as wanting something no matter what, deserved or undeserved. I see a desire as something hoped for but only if it's God's will for them. One is selfish and one is selfless! The spiritual application is clear. The lazy person is 'self' centered. The diligent person is 'others' centered. One is always thinking they've been gypped in life and deserves more. The other finds pleasure in serving God and others. Laziness and self-centeredness are things we're all susceptible to. But the longer I live and the more I learn about God's plan for my life, the more I realize I'm happiest when I'm not thinking about me! Laziness and selfish thinking are the main ingredients in a recipe for disaster. Diligence and others-centered living will keep your eyes focused on the things of God, which is a far better place to be focusing our attention than on ourselves.

Think about these things – keep studying the Bible – and have a blessed day!

Today's devotional thought from Proverbs 13:6.

6 *Righteousness guards the man of integrity,*
but wickedness overthrows the sinner.

Let's start by stating the obvious, sin is destructive!

James 1:14-15 states:

14 *but each one is tempted when, by his own evil desire, he is dragged away and enticed.* 15*Then, after desire has conceived, it gives birth to sin; and sin, when it is full-grown, gives birth to death.*

Sin traps us and defeats us and ruins us for Kingdom work. But the Bible states here that righteousness guards the man of integrity. Our choice to pursue righteousness is rewarded, especially during the difficult trials of life.

Looking again in the book of James 1:12 we read:

12 *Blessed is the man who perseveres under trial, because when he has stood the test, he will receive the crown of life that God has promised to those who love him.*

What a precious promise from God. Brothers and sisters, in this life we're going to have many trials. It's how we handle these trials that matter. My first piece of advice is to not try to handle these trials on your own.

1 Peter 5:7 tells us:

7 *Cast all your anxiety on him because he cares for you.*

I make the mistake all too often of trying to get through trials in my own strength. How foolish that can be when I have these precious promises from God's word, assuring me that He is ready, willing and able to handle whatever life throws my way. Philippians 4:13 states; *"I can do all things . . . through Christ who strengthens me."*

Note the part about through Christ. It's what you and I can do in and through Him. Can I get an Amen to that? The man or woman of integrity will never really know all that God guards us from but we know from this verse that He guards us nonetheless. How cool is that? If we're living for God and if we're seeking Him daily, if we're studying, praying, fellowshipping and growing in Him, then we can rest in knowing that He has His Heavenly angels watching over us. He'll never leave us and He'll never forsake us! If we've repented of our sins, if we've accepted the free gift of salvation then we are His . . . forever!

Think about these things – keep studying the Bible – and have a blessed day!

Today's devotional thought from Proverbs 13:11.

11 *Dishonest money dwindles away,*
    but he who gathers money little by little makes it grow.

I think the principle being applied here is an interesting one. The thought is that money, power, prestige or anything we seek after that is not done from a right heart, will never be blessed. It doesn't mean that dishonest people will not be able to accumulate wealth, it speaks more to the heart of a person. I've always felt that if someone will do or say anything to get wealth or prestige then someone will do or say anything to maintain it and this could result in a life full of lies and deception. I'm convinced that in the end, people that live for many years in a life of deception will pay an enormous price for their ill-gotten gain. A life lived this way often leads to heartache, problems and pressure that causes marriages or relationships to suffer as a result. On the other hand and on a far more positive note, the person that achieves whatever level of wealth, large or small, if done with God and the Kingdom in mind, can rest in the fact that God will honor a life lived in obedience to Him. I believe this individual will receive from God and through people, many personal blessings that would never come to the dishonest man.

The principle here of small amounts of money over long periods of time is an investment principle that should still be practiced today. There is a strong need for individuals and families to begin a habit of routinely saving at least 10% of their earnings. My personal goal has always been to give at least 10% away, save at least 10% and live on 80%. If you were to follow this simple advice, you would wake up one day, 20 or so years from now and find that your small, but regular investments for the future have grown quite nicely. At the same time you would have grown a big heart for giving, and you will have learned how to live well within your means, rather than well beyond your means which is still one of the biggest pressure points in people's lives. There is a propensity, especially in America, to want more toys than we can afford. Of course we don't call them toys but since when have things like cable TV and gym memberships and breakfast lunch and dinner out every week become a necessity? So what's the application for you and me? Brothers and sisters, it's all God's anyway. The looser we hold onto things and the less we accumulate will actually provide us more time to live our lives 'others' focused. Think of how much more we could do for the Kingdom if husbands and wives didn't have to work demanding jobs that leave no time to invest in their homes and families, and in the lives of others. Friends, money has its place but it is not the answer to every problem. In fact it can just as easily be the cause of your problems! Why spend all our lives chasing after things that will all burn in the end anyway?

Think about these things – keep studying the Bible – and have a blessed day!

Today's devotional thought from Proverbs 13:14.

14 *The teaching of the wise is a fountain of life,*
   turning a man from the snares of death.

Here's a question to start the day. Do you ever stop to think about the eternal impact of sharing your faith with someone that has never trusted in Jesus Christ alone for their salvation?

I recently heard a very moving story about Pastor John Harper who was a passenger on the Titanic. It was reported by many survivors that Pastor Harper was seen assisting people onto lifeboats, and he was calling for women and children and those not yet believers in Christ! Wow! He understood so well that if not a believer then they were not prepared for eternity. Right up until the moment he sank below the sea it was reported that he was going from passenger to passenger asking them if they were saved and praying with them in the freezing water knowing that in minutes they would all be dead. The headlines used in reporting the tragedy around the world stated in stark terms; "711 SAVED, 1513 LOST!"

Are your friends, co-workers and relatives SAVED or LOST? If they died today, would they be SAVED or LOST? The answer to this question has eternal consequences. Friends, if we know the Lord, then we possess the fountain of life. We have Jesus! And He alone can turn a man from the snares of death. Are we living with that level of eternal purpose?

I heard a Pastor who recently asked this question: "If every Christian on the planet had a level of commitment equal to mine or yours, would the future of our faith be secure or in peril? That's a powerful question worth pondering. It's often been said that God has no grandchildren, only children! This means the current generation must win the next generation to Christ or they will be lost! Do you understand that? Do you believe it? Jesus said in His own words in John 14:6:

"I am the way and the truth and the life. No one comes to the Father except through me."

Brothers and sisters, the world needs to know the one and only 'Fountain of Life' and that is Jesus. Will you tell someone about Him today? If not you, then who?

Think about these things – keep studying the Bible – and have a blessed day!

Today's devotional thought from Proverbs 13:18.

*18 He who ignores discipline comes to poverty and shame,
      but whoever heeds correction is honored.*

I don't know about you, but this verse is a wonderful teacher to me each passing month. It's why I enjoy reading a proverb every day, week and month. It seems the more I learn . . . the less I know! What I mean is . . . there is more to learn than one lifespan can absorb. When you factor in the need to hear the same godly truths over and over again, we will reach the end of our lives wondering why we wasted so much time with trivial matters, wishing instead we would have spent more time sitting at the feet of Jesus.

I confess that I have all too often ignored discipline only to regret it later. I want more and more to heed correction as soon as the opportunity presents itself. I'm tired of lazy and undisciplined living. I want and need to spend more time at the feet of Jesus and more time in God's Word, and more time with others studying God's word. For many years my church back east had a mid-week Bible study. I attended faithfully for over 12 years. It was every Wednesday night for all those years, yet every week, I would find myself tempted to make alternate plans on Wednesday nights. On Wednesday afternoons I would find myself thinking about a dozen different reasons why I should skip church that night. "I'm so tired." "I have so much paperwork to do!" "I need to pay bills." "I have a headache!" I could go on and on. I would end up making it to church, sometimes kicking and screaming! But as soon as I would step foot in the church door, the battle would be over and I was glad I went. This is just one example where discipline has proven to be a great friend.

I have learned that I need to pre-determine that there will be certain absolutes in my life that must be non-negotiable, otherwise it could lead to poverty and shame. If I'm faced with a situation or circumstance in life, and I'm not prepared for it, I'm vulnerable to wrong choices. However, if I've predetermined certain absolutes . . . then the chance of falling in these areas lessens. At the end of the day, it's still a daily dying to self. But the more you do this the easier it gets. Is there an area of your life that needs correction? Take it to the (**the Jesus???**) Jesus right now! He is ready, willing and able to forgive you and guide you to right living.

Think about these things – keep studying the Bible – and have a blessed day!

Proverbs 13 NOTES

Proverbs 13 NOTES

Proverbs 14

*P*roverbs 14 offers distinct thoughts on topics that include wisdom, foolishness, wealth, poverty and more. As you read this chapter in your Bible, take your time. Read each verse as a separate thought. Pray! Ask God to speak to you through His Word. Then read one or more of the devotionals I've written from this chapter and see if any resonate with you. Don't forget to add your own thoughts about this chapter on the blank pages that follow.

Today's devotional thought from Proverbs 14:3.

3 *A fool's talk brings a rod to his back*
   but the lips of the wise protect them.

It's interesting to note that there are over three dozen direct references in Proverbs to the tongue or references to our words and what we say. The tongue, or our words, are often referred to in the negative, especially in the Book of Proverbs. The person described in Proverbs 14:3 is a proud individual that will end up getting what's coming to him because of his boastful talk. This individual thinks far too highly of himself and he usually ends up making a fool of himself. This type of person always ends up with his words bringing him down. He or she usually lacks wisdom and they try to compensate by being proud and boastful. Their opinion is the one that matters most. They lack tactfulness and often say the wrong things at the wrong time. They don't learn very well because this person talks far more than they listen.

Proverbs 16:18 reminds us that: *"pride goes before destruction, a haughty spirit before a fall."*

This person needs a broken and contrite heart. This person needs desperately to confess their proud and arrogant ways and ask God to mold them and make them into the person He wants them to be. I encourage you, if you know this type of person, pray for them because unchecked and unyielded to the loving and tender correction of our heavenly father, this person is going to end up lonely and miserable and we shouldn't want that for anyone. More importantly, at one point in our lives this most likely described me and you! I know as a young Christian, I was very rough around the edges. There had to be many a godly saint praying to God on my behalf because I spent my early years as a new believer thinking far too highly of myself. If you think this devotional might be describing you, then thank God you have eyes to see and ears to hear. If you think it describes you, and you want to be a kinder and gentler *'you'*, then ask God for His help, and He will provide it.

A pastor friend of mine often states; *"As a Christian, I'm not everything I want to be, but thank God I'm not what I used to be either."* I say amen to this! We are all a *'work in progress'*. Let me close with a comment on the last part of Proverbs 14:3:

It states: *"but the lips of the wise protect them."*

This is the precious promise to those that are yielding their lives to Jesus. This verse suggests that the wise person will choose carefully what they say and who they say it to. The wise person thinks first and talks second! This is a very smart way to go through life. We need to learn to be *'slow to speak'*. I can still remember my mother always telling us kids that: *"God gave you ONE mouth and TWO ears and that is because He wants you to listen more than you talk!"* I think Mom had it right on this one.

Think about these things – keep studying the Bible – and have a blessed day!

Today's devotional thought from Proverbs 14:7.

7 Stay away from a foolish man,
for you will not find knowledge on his lips.

Here's a great reminder for me and you. Who we invest our time with is a critical decision. Others will either draw you closer to God or move you away from Him. The thought being expressed here is a very strong one. Staying away infers the idea of going out of your way to avoid contact with this individual. I think of the expression: *"With friends like that, who needs enemies."* We've all uttered these words but do we ever sit down and really think about our associations? How much time are we spending with individuals that negatively impact our walk with God? I'm not suggesting for a minute that we eliminate contact with those that don't believe the way we do. On the contrary, I'm a strong advocate for spending time with those that don't know the LORD. I think we err when we isolate ourselves from non-believers. I've always preferred the word 'insulation' rather than 'isolation'. The world needs us to interact with them, specifically so they can see Jesus in us! We are the ones that need to be doing the influencing, not the other way around.

I have heard countless stories that go something like this: Mary was doing so well in her walk with God until she met Jim, or Bill or Brian or someone that began to be the dominant personality in the relationship and Mary didn't have the spiritual maturity to break away.

The definition of a fool is one who believes there is no God. You would be wise to avoid significant association with one such as this. Brothers and sisters, if we are sensitive to God's Spirit, He will guide us to people that can be a source of strength and encouragement to us. He will guide us to those He wants us to tell about Jesus. I just heard a great testimony of how God guided a couple from New Jersey to go to Mexico so they could meet another couple from New Jersey who needed to hear about Jesus. That story ended with the angels in heaven rejoicing over a sinner who repented and is now in the family of God. The application for me and you is to avoid foolish people with foolish talk on their lips. There are many people out there whose goal in life is to get others to believe the foolish things they believe. Make sure you're not the one being played the fool!

Think about these things – keep studying the Bible – and have a blessed day!

Today's devotional thought from Proverbs 14:12.

12 *There is a way that seems right to a man,*
but in the end it leads to death.

When I read a verse like this, I look back on close to 40 years of walking with the Lord and I see so many poor choices that I never should have made. It's so easy to deceive ourselves into thinking we know what's best for our lives. We say things in our heart like, *"It's okay God, I have this situation under control. I'll take it from here."* We never actually say these words, but our actions show them to be true.

With the benefit of hindsight, here are some 'red flags' that existed at times of my poorest choices. If you find any of these fit your life right now, it may indicate that you are setting yourself up for a fall:

- Isolation! When you see yourself separating from other people of faith. This one is subtle, because you can still go to church every week and still be isolated, because you're never expressing your heart to anyone. Get plugged into a Bible study or some other small group to avoid this trap of the enemy.

- Lack of time alone with God and His word. Once again, you need to develop a morning routine of time alone reading and praying. The Bible is God's primary communication tool with His children.

- Spending the majority of your time with people that don't know the Lord. They aren't bad people, just not people that are going to strengthen you in your walk with God. Too many of these associations will lead you further down the wrong path. Here's where an accountability partner or spiritual mentor is needed. Find someone that you can trust and confide in, someone that can pray with you and offer spiritual guidance. I recommend someone that has walked with the Lord for longer than you.

- Lastly, remember that this is a spiritual battle! We need to put on the armor and be prepared! Ephesians 6:10-17 should be read weekly and eventually memorized:

  10 Finally, be strong in the Lord and in his mighty power. 11 Put on the full armor of God, so that you can take your stand against the devil's schemes. 12 For our struggle is not against flesh and blood, but against the rulers, against the authorities, against the powers of this dark world and against the spiritual forces of evil in the heavenly realms. 13 Therefore put on the full armor of God, so that when the day of evil comes, you may be able to stand your ground, and after you have done everything, to stand. 14 Stand firm then, with the belt of truth buckled around your waist, with the breastplate of righteousness in place, 15 and with your feet fitted with the readiness that comes from the gospel of peace. 16 In addition to all this, take up the shield of faith, with which you can extinguish all the flaming arrows of the evil one. 17 Take the helmet of salvation and the sword of the Spirit, which is the word of God.

Brothers and sisters, we can't be lazy and careless about our walk with God. People all around us are dying to a Christless eternity and we need to be ready to give testimony of the hope we have in our Lord and Savior, Jesus. The time is short and the consequences are eternal!

Think about these things – keep studying the Bible – and have a blessed day!

Today's devotional thought from Proverbs 14:13.

13 *Even in laughter the heart may ache,*
  and joy may end in grief.

This verse seems to be a great reminder that all isn't what it seems to be with those we come in contact with, even those very close to us. We often use humor or we even 'put on a happy face' in the midst of chaos or confusion or turmoil in our lives. It may be a safety mechanism to avoid becoming overwhelmed. All too often it's more of a mask or a way to hide our true feelings. That's why I think it's important to look for ways to get past the typical surface conversations we often find ourselves in and be willing to ask deeper questions, and mean it. So many people are desperate for the peace that comes from knowing God, and you may be the only one at that moment to tell them about Him.

So what about the second part of this verse, the idea of joy ending in grief? Well to me this further explains that what we see is not always what is really going on in someone's life. Any joy one might seem to be experiencing may actually be a mask used to hide the grief in their life.

I got a wonderful call recently from a dear friend. We both have prodigal children *(as of this writing)* so we pray together regularly and lift them up to the Lord. We had talked just two days prior and he told me it seemed that his son was so very far from God. Then his son called him and said "Dad . . . I've been such a knucklehead! I just spoke with a pastor near where I live and I've decided to get right with God!" Well, my friend and I, along with the angels in Heaven, began rejoicing over this sinner who repented.

The other wonderful part of this was the son's words to his dad that he knew that no matter how rebellious he had become, his father still loved him. And our Heavenly Father still loves us and is in fact waiting for each of us to cry out to Him. True joy can only come through Jesus Christ! Everything else is a mere substitute, a copy of joy, and a poor copy at that. It comes in the form of money or job approval or alcohol or even humor, even though your life is really empty and miserable. I'll close today with the reading of Psalm 126. It's short and speaks so well to today's topic:

1 When the LORD brought back the captives to [a] Zion,
*   we were like men who dreamed. [b]*

2 Our mouths were filled with laughter,
*   our tongues with songs of joy.*
*   Then it was said among the nations, "*
*   The LORD has done great things for them."*

3 The LORD has done great things for us,
*   and we are filled with joy.*

4 Restore our fortunes, [c] O LORD,
*   like streams in the Negev.*

5 Those who sow in tears
*   will reap with songs of joy.*

6 He who goes out weeping,
*   carrying seed to sow,*
*   will return with songs of joy,*
*   carrying sheaves with him.*

Make today the day you commit or recommit your heart to Jesus!

Think about these things – keep studying the Bible – and have a blessed day!

Today's devotional thought from Proverbs 14:15, 18.

15 A simple man believes anything,
*   but a prudent man gives thought to his steps.*

18 The simple inherit folly,
*   but the prudent are crowned with knowledge.*

Let's look at these verses together since the key words of both are identical in most translations. Let's talk first about the words, SIMPLE and PRUDENT. These aren't words we use in everyday conversation . . . so let me give you two more words for each that will broaden your understanding of the meaning behind these words. When you hear the word SIMPLE . . . think of one who is IGNORANT or NAÏVE. When reading the word PRUDENT . . . think of DISCERNING or WISE.

We read in Verse 15 that the simple person (the ignorant or naïve person) believes anything and in Verse 18, we learn they inherit folly. When you hear FOLLY, think FOOLISHNESS! Now we're getting somewhere! How is a fool described in the Bible? A fool is someone who thinks there is no God. Tying these thoughts together, we see that this person is one that has not yet heard the life-changing and wonderful hope that comes from knowing God! We see that the prudent person is thoughtful and knowledgeable. The obvious difference here is that the prudent person knows God and the simple person doesn't.

I used to read these verses with a bit of a 'holier than thou attitude' . . . sort of like ha, ha . . . you're stupid. Well . . . God has smacked me on the side of the head for that poor thought. I need to have patience and compassion for the person that is ignorant about the things of God. I played golf with a young man that I'd known for a couple of years but hadn't talked with him about God. When I brought the conversation around to spiritual matters, it became apparent that I was speaking with someone that had absolutely zero understanding of the things of God. He was Jewish by birth but made it perfectly clear to me that there was zero religious thought or instruction in his home growing up. This 28 year old man had apparently never had a spiritual conversation with someone in his entire life. I had to do some fast praying! I proceeded to gently encourage him to open his heart and mind to God. We continued to have a friendly conversation that I hope will be a good start to future opportunities to talk with him. What's my point? I need to remind myself that there was a time not long ago when I was this young man. I am still grateful to the two dear friends that cared enough to take the time to talk with me about God.

The longer I live, the more apparent it becomes that many people have a total lack of understanding of God. I also have come to believe that most people are very open to listen to you explain why you believe in God. The next time you meet someone that knows nothing of God, quickly remind yourself that you were the same way at one time, and then lovingly tell them about your friend Jesus!

Think about these things – keep studying the Bible – and have a blessed day!

Proverbs 14 NOTES

Proverbs 14 NOTES

Proverbs 15

$\mathcal{I}$ have written six devotionals from this chapter. There are more that can be written from these 33 timeless verses. If you've been reading from **Page 1**, then you are nearly halfway though. Perhaps it's time for you to write your own devotional from your life? Why not take several minutes to read Proverbs 15, and then pick a verse(s) and start writing what you think about those verses as it pertains to your life. One day soon I hope you will begin to encourage your sphere of influence to start reading a chapter of Proverbs a day! **(This sentence doesn't make sense.)**

***Today's devotional thought from Proverbs** 15:1.*

1 A gentle answer turns away wrath,
  but a harsh word stirs up anger.

I don't know whether to laugh or cry when I read this verse. I laugh at my own stupidity in this area and I smile when I think I made it through 40 years of marriage and still have a wife who loves me even though too many times I have spoken harsh and ungodly words to her. Why do we seem to have less patience with those we love the most? I don't know another person on this planet more deserving of a gentle answer than my wife, yet all too often I take liberties with her that I would never take with others. I cringe when she responds to a harsh and unnecessary word from me with a statement like**:** "Would you ever respond that way to your boss, or our pastor, or a neighbor or your golf buddies?" Well you get the idea! And I really do want to cry on those occasions when

I miss divine opportunities to speak a gentle word but instead choose an angry response. God, please forgive me for such foolishness! Think about this . . . nothing can stir up storm clouds of anger and frustration faster than a harsh word.

Do you recall the story in 1 Samuel 25 when David asks Nabal if he and his men can be given some food and provisions? Keep in mind that David had risked his life and the life of his men by watching over Nabal's property and animals. You'll recall that Nabal responds by saying "jump in a lake" *(my paraphrase!).* David will have none of that! Nabal's harsh words stir up anger like you have never seen in David. He sets out to totally annihilate Nabal and all he owns. But the rest of the story shows us that Abigail; Nabal's wife, hears of her husband's foolish response to David's very reasonable request and she meets up with David and although the complete story is too long to tell now, we find that Abigail gives one of the most thoughtful and gentle answers possible and David's anger subsides in an instant! Take the time later to read this wonderful story in 1 Samuel 25. I can't help but imagine that as David grew older he would gather his children around him and tell these stories of his early life. Of course, Solomon, the writer of Proverbs was his son, and he would have very likely been thinking of this very story when he penned Proverbs 15:1.

It's cool to read God's word and think about the circumstances that prompted the divine inspiration to write. We learn from this story just how effectively a gentle answer can defuse a volatile situation. What Solomon offers us here is an absolute nugget of blessed teaching about the benefits of gentle words over harsh words. All we need to do is heed this practical counsel.

Think about these things – keep studying the Bible – and have a blessed day!

Today's devotional thought from Proverbs 15:3.

3 *The eyes of the LORD are everywhere,*
   keeping watch on the wicked and the good.

I am so grateful for the reminder that this verse brings to me each time I read it. The eye of God is always upon His creation and this brings me great comfort. We see from this verse that God sees it all and He watches all. I want to focus on the good and leave the wicked in the hands of God. We should never want to see God 'zap' the wicked, or anyone for that matter. Let's not forget that it could have easily been you or me getting zapped back in the days before getting our spiritual act together.

People living outside of God's plan for their lives are only doing what comes naturally to them. Our desire should be to pray for them and see them come to faith. For the Christian, this verse should bring great comfort, because God loves you with an everlasting love and He wants what's best for you and for me. We err when we view this verse in the negative, thinking that He will see us in our sin and then punish us for it. This is not the heart of God. We should be grateful that He loves us so much that if He sees us going in a wrong direction, He brings people and events into our lives to show us where we have gone astray. He gives us ample opportunities to repent. Isn't this comforting to you? It should be. God does see it all and we fool only ourselves to think otherwise.

I've lived long enough as a Christian to have seen numerous occasions where God has intervened at just the right moment to prevent me from doing something very foolish and I thank Him for that. We really should live our daily lives with the understanding that God sees it all. This is for your good and mine! If this verse worries you because you have something in your life that isn't God-honoring, then I suggest you confess it or pray you get caught! You'll look back in hindsight and see either confession or getting caught as having been the best thing that could have happened to you.

I'm so grateful to know that I serve a God who loved me before I was even born. Read these beautiful words found in Psalm 139:13-16:

13 *For you created my inmost being;*
    you knit me together in my mother's womb.
14 *I praise you because I am fearfully and wonderfully made;*
    your works are wonderful,
    I know that full well.
15 *My frame was not hidden from you*
    when I was made in the secret place,
    when I was woven together in the depths of the earth.
16 *Your eyes saw my unformed body;*
    all the days ordained for me were written in your book
    before one of them came to be.

I'm grateful that He watches over me. I'm grateful that He corrects me. I'm grateful that He will never leave me or forsake me. How about you? Take comfort in God's tremendous love for you that He cares enough to watch over you. He's not looking to catch you in some sin so He can punish you. No, He is looking to rescue you and me from our own foolish choices. He loves us that much!

Think about these things – keep studying the Bible – and have a blessed day!

Today's devotional thought from Proverbs 15:13.

13 *A happy heart makes the face cheerful,*
but heartache crushes the spirit.

I have a note in my Bible next to the first part of this verse. It reads: "This is my bride!" I've been with her many times and in many places when someone will comment that they think she's beautiful. I happen to agree! But more importantly is her standard response which goes something like this: *"Thank you so much but anything beautiful is because of Jesus living in me."* I love the way she turns the compliment into an opportunity to tell someone that she's a follower of Jesus.

But the bigger point here is this idea of a happy heart showing on our faces. Our joy in the Lord should be transparent, on our faces and in our words and actions. I often find myself in situations where I've just done some small act of kindness like helping someone struggling to load a car full of groceries. I try to make it a point to hand them a Bible tract or simply say *"God bless you and have a great day."* I try to leave someone with the connection between a kindness and a connection to Christ.

This also means that I have to be careful to not leave the opposite impression. When the car repair isn't completed on time am I just as determined to show kindness? The second part of this verse states: *"but heartache crushes the spirit."* If we indulge in some form of sorrow or bitterness, and if we allow some form of discouragement to affect our countenance then we are going to miss the opportunities that God sends our way to share the hope that is within us.

What's the application for you and me? It's to make a point to wear our faith on our sleeves and to wear it joyfully! This means we need to keep a short account of things that cause us heartache or sorrow. We need to find joy in the midst of whatever we are going through. Nehemiah 8:10 reminds us that *"the joy of the Lord is our strength!"* I believe God uses every single word that we utter, so use them wisely. So brothers and sisters, let's all commit anew to making sure our outward appearance matches our inward hope and the joy that comes from having Jesus in our hearts!

Think about these things – keep studying the Bible – and have a blessed day!

Today's devotional thought from Proverbs 15:23.

23 *A man finds joy in giving an apt reply—*
and how good is a timely word!

Let's talk today about finding time for others. The older I get, the more I realize the opportunities I have to be an example to those around me. For the most part it simply requires being a godly example. Showing kindness to others, treating my wife with graciousness and respect, and never being in a hurry. For me, the last one is often the hardest. Men by nature are mission or goal oriented. When we go somewhere it's always about the destination and never about the journey. That's why we often get into trouble if we're married, because our wives are all about the journey. But getting back to Verse 23, we see that it's not just what we say, but when we say it. I often wonder about the timing of some conversations I have, especially when a younger man asks me questions about business or marriage. I can almost sense in the midst of the question that God has orchestrated the encounter. When I am properly prepared and prayed up, I realize the significance of these opportunities to offer a timely word. What I don't want to do is find myself too busy or insensitive to these divine appointments. It's very easy to miss these if one is not looking for them.

The flip side of this is not making others a priority and not taking time for them. Having been a Christian for over 40 years, I have to be sure that what I soak in from God is equal to what I pour out to others. We all have a certain sphere of influence that we need to recognize and take advantage of. Have you ever stopped to think about the fact that God has placed you where you are for a reason? There really are no accidents with God. I have witnessed too many amazing coincidences to not see God's hand in so many of life's interactions with others. It's a good thing to think about the next time you find yourself frustrated about where you live or where you work. God might have you where you are for a very specific purpose. Think about the book of Esther and the amazing story of how she was raised up to become Queen just so she could be in a place to save the remnant of Israel from destruction. So the next time you are asked for advice or counsel or perhaps just when offering an unsolicited comment, consider the importance of a well thought word. What we say and when we say it can have far more eternal implications than we realize.

Think about these things – keep studying the Bible – and have a blessed day!

Today's devotional thought from Proverbs 15:29.

29 *The LORD is far from the wicked*
   but he hears the prayer of the righteous.

This verse gives us insight into God as both the merciful father and the righteous judge. The first part of this verse states that God is far from the wicked. Solomon is speaking here of the person that has set themselves at a distance from God. When you hear someone say: *"I don't feel God's presence"* you need to ask yourself . . . who moved? We know it wasn't God based on the second part of the verse wherein He assures us that He hears the prayers of the righteous. If you are truly calling out to God for any reason and with a sincere heart then be assured that He is listening. He's not only listening, He's waiting for you to speak to Him. We get a great picture of this in the story of the prodigal son found in Luke 15. Here we see that the father was constantly watching and waiting for his son's return. We know this because the father catches a glimpse of his son when he was still far off. What a beautiful picture! A loving father . . . never giving up hope that his son will return some day! The father in this parable is God and you and I are the son and God never turns away. And He never turns a deaf ear to our sincere prayers.

We get another awesome picture of how God judges our hearts. In Matthew 25 we have the parable of the sheep and the goats. Here we see the righteous being welcomed by God and being praised for things they didn't even know they did. What a great picture of how God judges the heart and that our relationship with Him is not based on works, because if it was, we would see in this parable a checklist of things we did for God that earned His approval. But we don't see that because our relationship with Him has nothing to do with what we can do for Him but what He has already done for us.

Here's the good news! If you find yourself far from God, you are only a prayer of repentance away from knowing He is close. It's not a magical prayer. God knows your heart. If you sincerely cry out to Him and confess you are a sinner that is repenting, He will forgive your sins and cleanse you from all unrighteousness. It's the single most important thing you can do!

Think about these things – keep studying the Bible – and have a blessed day!

Today's devotional thought from Proverbs 15:30.

30 *A cheerful look brings joy to the heart,*
  and good news gives health to the bones.

Brothers and sisters, I need this reminder each month. I have seen the benefits of a cheerful look and a joyful demeanor. I believe joy can be seen in our faces and I believe a lack of joy can be seen as well. Our very countenance is something that can draw someone to Jesus or drive them away! My pastor has stated many times that: "Christians are often the number one reason why people are attracted to Christ, and they are often the number one reason people are not attracted to Christ!" I think the point here is that we need to live our lives with the joy of the Lord and we need to show it on our faces and in our words.

I've known more than a few Christians that seem to drag themselves through life kicking and screaming all the way. Fans of Winnie the Pooh will recall the character Eeyore. He's the sad and depressed donkey that had a "woe is me" attitude about every aspect of life. Well there is no place for Eeyore's in the Christian life. That's not to say that there won't be times when we're sad or hurting over circumstances in life. This is normal and expected while on this side of heaven. Joy, however, is something we can have in the midst of tragedy. Very recently an internationally known Pastor experienced the tragic loss of an adult son. In the midst of his agony and just days after the news of his son's death, he gave a very moving fifteen minute talk that was aired all over the world. In it he spoke in an amazing way about his joy in the midst of such extreme sorrow. I'm still amazed at how he was able to express such hope during this agonizing trial. It reminds me of how foolish I can be when I mope around when it's drizzling outside. Or I get furious because of a few minutes of traffic.

But let me get back to Verse 30. A cheerful look can bring internal and external joy to the heart. The verse goes on to tell us that good news brings health to the bones. I have read many medical accounts of Christians with serious health problems that pull through near death illnesses and the doctors have no choice but to attribute their recovery to their faith. Think about this, the good news of Jesus has eternal and earthly benefits. Nehemiah 8:10 reminds us that the joy of the Lord is our strength! I've been out many times with my wife when someone will walk up to her and say something like *"you are so lovely"* or *"you have such a great countenance"*. She is always quick to respond that it's Jesus living in her, and I love the way she turns the compliment toward God. You and I should look for ways to identify ourselves as Christians whenever possible. Clearly, this needs to be handled in a casual way when the time seems right. I don't want people to think of me only as a nice guy, but as a nice guy *and* a Christian. I want people to see Jesus in me. How about you? I've heard it expressed this way; *"If being a Christian was a crime, would there be enough evidence against you for a conviction?"*

Think about these things – keep studying the Bible – and have a blessed day!

Proverbs 15 NOTES

Proverbs 15 NOTES

Proverbs 16

*H*ere's another chapter with 33 verses. One could conceivably write a lesson learned from each and every verse. Here are eight devotionals that you can read and ponder. Then pray and ask God what He wants you to learn from this chapter. Happy reading!

Today's devotional thought from Proverbs 16:1.

1 To man belong the plans of the heart,
*   but from the LORD comes the reply of the tongue.*

What a great reminder for me and you! Man has free will and freedom of thought. We can plan and prepare and chart our course the way we see fit. But there are limitations to what we can control. Our plans are finite, but God's are infinite! We can plan all we want but we have no control over tomorrow. You and I can't even be sure of our next breath let alone take any credit for it. It's this very fact that allows the humble and broken believer to lay all he has before the Lord and ask Him to use it for His honor and glory. Anything in us that is wise and good comes from God anyway!

Philippians 2:13 states: *"for it is God who works in you to will and to act according to his good purpose."*

God has complete control over His creation and this applies equally to the believer and the atheist. Not believing in God, no matter how sincere, just makes you sincerely wrong! No matter how hard we work or how diligently we plan, if God has a cross-purpose for our lives then He will have His way! For the believer that is fervently seeking God's best, this thought comes with an awesome promise! Look at what Jeremiah 29:11-13 states:

11 For I know the plans I have for you," declares the LORD, "plans to prosper you and not to harm you, plans to give you hope and a future. 12 Then you will call upon me and come and pray to me, and I will listen to you. 13 You will seek me and find me when you seek me with all your heart.

What a precious promise we see stated here! So what's the application for me and you? God has a wonderful plan and purpose for our lives, brothers and sisters. We need to be about our Father's business, seeking daily to know and understand the plan and purpose for our lives here on earth. There are people in your sphere of influence that need to know the Lord. There are opportunities to accomplish great things and to make a difference in this world! Spend time with God today in prayer! And humbly ask Him for the wisdom and ability to do above and beyond anything we could ever hope to do in our own strength. He's just waiting for you to ask!

Think about these things – keep studying the Bible – and have a blessed day!

Today's devotional thought from Proverbs 16:3.

*3 Commit to the LORD whatever you do,
    and your plans will succeed.*

I love this verse! It's a constant reminder to me to be a man of faith and to seek God in my day-to-day plans. Do you ever contemplate something important, perhaps a change in career or something a little less grand like whether to buy a new car or drive the old one another year? Now be honest, have you ever planned something like this without prayer or consideration for what God might want you to do? If you're anything like me you would have to answer in the affirmative! I've done this all too often. When I ran my own business I would routinely find myself deep into a new project only to realize sometimes days later that I never even prayed about it. What's that tell me? It tells me that I'm not looking at all aspects of my life through the prism of God's plan and purpose for my life. He loves me with an everlasting love! He loves my family. He loves my work. He loves everything about me! He has my best interests in His mind. So why would I ever want to make plans without seeking Him first? Are we planning first and seeking approval later? If so, we're doing things backwards! If I really want a project to succeed I had better be sure God is in it. More importantly, if I commit my ideas to the Lord first, I'm allowing Him to either confirm, deny or change my plan entirely. Shouldn't we want to be doing whatever we're doing with God in the equation anyway?

For me, this verse serves as a great reminder that I want to make sure all I'm doing is being committed to the Lord. And more importantly, that I'm willing to change my plans if I sense that God wants me going in a different direction. I really think we avoid going down wrong paths when we seek the Lord and then exercise the patience to wait upon Him rather than just hurrying into decisions. The plans of our heart, great and small must be committed to the grace of God and in submission to His will. Whatever pleases God should be what pleases us!

Think about these things – keep studying the Bible – and have a blessed day!

Today's devotional thought from Proverbs 16:9.

9 *In his heart a man plans his course,*
    but the LORD determines his steps.

Here's a very interesting proverb and one worth contemplating. God didn't create us as robots. He created us with free will and with an ability to choose our own course. Many of us choose to spend years directing our own lives and often with devastating consequences. The ideal scenario for the believer in Jesus is that we will choose to bend our self-will and self-directed tendencies to our Maker's direction for our lives. Brothers and sisters, His ways are far better than our ways. Our selfish natures will often choose poorly, unless we have made a conscious decision to allow God to be in the driver's seat.

A friend of mine recently wrote a book called: *"Jesus Take the Wheel."* The subtitle is *"Seven keys to a transformed life with God."* The author takes the reader on a two month journey that helps you understand God's plan and purpose for your life.

You and I will spend the greater part of our lives striving with our Maker - unless we choose to yield the driver's seat to Him! I could go on and on about my 40 years as a Christian, and talk about the wasted years spent pursuing what I thought was right for my life, believing I knew best and at times even telling God what He should do with my life! James 4:13-17 really captures the foolishness of the self-directed life. Listen to what James has to say:

[13]Now listen, you who say, "Today or tomorrow we will go to this or that city, spend a year there, carry on business and make money." [14]Why, you do not even know what will happen tomorrow. What is your life? You are a mist that appears for a little while and then vanishes. [15]Instead, you ought to say, "If it is the Lord's will, we will live and do this or that." [16]As it is, you boast and brag. All such boasting is evil. [17]Anyone, then, who knows the good he ought to do and doesn't do it, sins.

We boast about tomorrow as if we have some ability to control it. I happen to be one of those that read the obituaries most days. It always catches my attention when I see that someone has died in their 20s, 30s or 40s. I'm sure these poor souls thought they would live much longer. It's a reminder to me that I have no control over my life or my years. I want whatever time I have to be on the path He chooses for me and not on a self-directed path.

Friends, let me close with this final thought on the matter. I've never known a Christian that has ever regretted a more yielded life to Christ. Yet I've known all too many that have greatly regretted their years of striving with Him. Today's devotional is one of hope and happiness that is found in a life yielded wholly and completely to God.

Think about these things – keep studying the Bible – and have a blessed day!

Today's devotional thought from Proverbs 16:16.

16 *How much better to get wisdom than gold,*
    to choose understanding rather than silver!

Solomon seems to focus a lot of attention on several recurring themes throughout the book of Proverbs. The top five include the topics of wisdom and riches. It's interesting to contrast these two. And let's not forget that Solomon, when God asked him for whatever he desired, he asked for wisdom! Now think about that. God offers him whatever he wants . . . and he chooses wisdom. What would I have asked for? What would you have asked for?

Who of us hasn't imagined finding that little gold lamp and out pops a genie that could grant us three wishes? Or who hasn't imagined at least once, winning the lottery? I'll be the first to admit that I've imagined winning the lottery. *(And of course my imaginary story always includes giving away large portions of my winnings to God's work).* But how many of us have ever imagined getting a double portion of wisdom? We don't sit around thinking how a double portion of wisdom would solve all our problems, but we do imagine how a double portion of money would! I've said it many times before that if money solved all our problems then we wouldn't read daily or weekly headlines about the super wealthy or famous and their stories of drug abuse, divorce and suicide. The reality is that wisdom is better than gold and knowledge is better than silver. God and people are far more worthy of our time than things.

I remember hearing author and well-known speaker, Dr. James Dobson, telling a humorous story of buying a swing set for his children when they were very young. He went on and on about how this thing in his yard was now consuming all his time and money keeping it oiled and repaired. A swing set certainly isn't a bad thing, nor are cars, boats and houses. But we have to be wise in discerning if these things are what God wants for us or are they things we want for ourselves.

If we want to get real honest with each other we'd have to conclude that less time and less money spent on ourselves would open doors to spend more time and more money on others. And I have to believe if we look back on a life of personal sacrifice and a more modest lifestyle we'll find that we're actually far richer from an emotional and spiritual perspective than earthly riches could ever provide. So how about you? Why not decide today to take the advice of the wisest man of his time and choose wisdom and understanding over gold **and** silver. Choose God and choose people! That's a solid investment!

Think about these things – keep studying the Bible – and have a blessed day!

Today's devotional thought from Proverbs 16:17.

17 *The highway of the upright avoids evil;*
   he who guards his way guards his life.

This verse describes well the road that you and I need to travel. This highway or *path* should be a clearly marked and well-worn one. It's a road marked by truth, victory and strength. A road well-travelled by those that have gone before us. It might be helpful to picture the Bible as the entrance ramp to the highway. God's word is the road map that will take us to all we can see and experience on this road called life. Now, picture all those that have gone before us, those that have left their life lessons available for us to glean from. These are the rest stops along the road. I encourage you to make it a habit of reading books by Christian authors.

They have names like Charles Spurgeon, C. S. Lewis, Andrew Murray, E.M. Bounds, Alan Redpath or Oswald Chambers, to name a few. There is much to learn from those that have gone before us, those that have completed their travel down life's highway on earth.

We're fortunate to have the writings of godly authors that can guide us and guard us as we travel through this life. Those mentioned above and so many other godly men and women have spent decades at the feet of Jesus and have studied His word and have left us their accounts with God. What a precious gift we have in our modern age, to have such ready access to so many tools to help us in our walk with God. Are you and I committed to walking upright and avoiding evil?

1 John 1:7 states:

7 *But if we walk in the light, as he is in the light, we have fellowship with one another, and the blood of Jesus, his Son, purifies us from all sin.*

Charles Spurgeon states that *"to walk in the light is the opposite of walking in darkness, the willingness to know and be known."* This means we're willing to know the whole truth about ourselves. We're open to receive God's conviction and correction. When He shows us our sin, we deal with it. We don't toy with it, even for a moment. Everything that God's light shows us to be sin, we need to confess!

Here's what another great writer, Roy Hession has to say about 1 John 1:7:

"By the power of the precious blood we can be made more stainless than the driven snow; and thus continually abiding in the light and cleansed by the blood, we have fellowship with God."

Another great contemporary writer that I enjoy is Mark Cahill. In one of his very popular books, One Heartbeat Away, he comments on the problem with trying to sit on the fence when it comes to a godly walk. He states: *"Satan owns the Fence! You either choose to love Jesus Christ, or you choose to reject Him, one or the other."*

So my friends, why not make the choice today to go for it. Choose today to become a fully devoted follower of Christ! Remember, 95% devotion is still 5% short!

Think about these things – keep studying the Bible – and have a blessed day!

Today's devotional thought from Proverbs 16:18.

18 *Pride goes before destruction,*
a haughty spirit before a fall.

Today I'm going to talk about the problem of pride. I confess that at different times during my 40 years of walking with Jesus, that you would have thought I had an advanced degree in this subject! I still struggle with pride, and if you're honest with yourself, you do too! I think it's a universal struggle inherited from Adam and Eve.

The problem with pride is that a prideful person is usually the last one to know! The nature of pride is to think you're not prideful! This is extremely dangerous because a prideful person thinks themselves impervious to temptation and sin. When you begin to think you're too good to fall, I suggest you tie a pillow to your back because you're going down soon! Sadly, another problem with pride is that it often follows a person's season of truly great effectiveness. They often forget God's hand on them when they begin to experience success in life, business growth, co-workers recognizing their gifts and being commended for them or something similar. It may be that you see great growth in a Sunday school class you teach, or you're a pastor experiencing exponential numerical growth in the flock God has entrusted to you. You begin to take credit for things that God accomplished through you.

The more we begin to rely on our natural abilities, the less reliance we have on God's will for our lives. This is a dangerous place for any believer in Christ. Brothers and sisters, we can't take credit for what God alone has done through us! Any abilities we have are from Him! There's no easier way to be disqualified for effective ministry then to begin to think that it's all about you! So what's the application for us today? Our confidence needs to be found in Christ, not in self. Oh, how we need to remind ourselves that apart from Christ we can do nothing. Proud men and women are frequently most proud just before they're brought down by their own pride. The only real question remaining is whether we humbly repent or are permanently ruined by it.

Think about these things – keep studying the Bible – and have a blessed day!

Today's devotional thought from Proverbs 16:29.

29 *A violent man entices his neighbor*
  and leads him down a path that is not good.

I recall my daughter's first semester in college a number of years ago. All through High School, she had gone on missionary trips, sang in church, attended youth group. She did all the normal things a young Christian woman would do. Even with a strong foundation, she reported back that her very first week at college was a complete culture shock. And it was a Christian College! The number of students that were enticing her to sin was nearly overwhelming to her. It was a real eye-opener for her to realize that not everyone that calls themselves a Christian really wants to live for Christ.

So what's the application for you and me today? Christian or non-Christian, there are those in this world that truly want nothing more than to see us fall. I've mentioned in previous devotionals that misery truly does love company. Some individuals actually **take** get comfort in dragging others down to their level. The question we have to ask ourselves in regard to every friendship is this: who's doing the leading and who's doing the influencing? Are your relationships building you up or tearing you down? Another point that can't be mentioned enough is that Satan is always looking for ways to bring us down.

The devil wears camouflage. He never looks the way we would expect him to look. And remember this, the day you give your heart to Jesus is the day the devil becomes your enemy and begins looking for ways to make you fall. Let me remind you of just a few of the names given to Satan in the Bible. He is known as the angel of light (2 Corinthians 11:14), the father of lies (John 8:44), the power of darkness (Colossians 1:13) and the prince of this world (John 14:30). He doesn't try to turn you into an axe murderer because he's far more subtle than that. His simple goal is to cause you to be an ineffective Christian. He often uses well-meaning people and circumstances to bring you down.

There are paths we are tempted to take that seem okay at first glance, but nevertheless are traps of the enemy. So how do we get through these traps? Let me use an analogy I've heard a number of times. When new employees are hired at banks, they are never trained using counterfeit bills. They are trained using authentic bills so that they become so familiar with the authentic bills, that the counterfeit becomes easy to spot. I think we can take this advice into our Christian walk. The more we know the true God, the easier it is to spot the counterfeit Satan. 2 Corinthians 11:14 states: *"Satan himself masquerades as an angel of light."* But here's the good news! If you're a Christian then you'll want to understand 1 John 4:4 which states: (and I'm paraphrasing slightly); *". . . that because you are God's child you can resist the temptations of the enemy because the one who is in you, meaning God, is greater than the one who is in the world"* meaning Satan. So take heart in Jesus' own words in John 16:33 that *"I have overcome the world."*

Think about these things – keep studying the Bible – and have a blessed day!

Today's devotional thought from Proverbs 16:32.

32 *Better a patient man than a warrior,*
 a man who controls his temper than one who takes a city.

Whenever I hear the word 'patience' I always think of the humorous state-ment: *"Lord I need patience and I need it NOW!"* Patience is not some-thing that comes easily to most of us, especially in our fast-paced modern society. But let's start with the reality that patience is needed. Patience is a virtue! The writers of many of the Epistles mention patience extensively and I'll mention a suggested reading in a minute. I recently attended a men's retreat and the theme of the weekend was the life of Samson. We learned many things about Samson and in particular, we learned that he was a man that lacked patience and couldn't control his temper. Both of these topics are mentioned here in Proverbs 16:32. So what can we learn from the life of Samson? You can read the entire account in Judges 13-16, but the first thing we learn in Judges 14 is that Samson was impa-tient with his parents and with his future. He races into a marriage that is clearly outside the will of God. We see his temper problems at the end of Judges 14. Here's a man that for 20 years displays a pattern of impa-tience and anger and the resultant poor judgment and consequences of a life lived this way.

So what's the application for you and me? Are we like Samson? Are we patient with our children or our spouse or with our friends and co-workers? Are we even tempered or are we prone to fly off the handle? I encourage you to take time today to read the Book of James. It's a short letter with only five chapters, but interestingly enough the topics of both anger and patience from today's proverb are discussed throughout the Book of James.

It only takes about 15 minutes to read but you'll come away with many new truths to apply to your life, especially in relation to patience and anger. Brothers and sisters the world is watching us closely. As the pressures of life or financial and job pressures increase, people are looking for answers to life's problems. We have the answer! It's a life yielded to Jesus Christ! If you're reading this and you've trusted in Christ then ask Him for wisdom to become more patient and to have a controlled temper. If you've never trusted in Christ why not do so right now? Salvation is a gift from God and all you need to do is accept this free gift! Cry out to Jesus right now and confess you're a sinner in need of salvation. Ask Him to forgive you and to come into your life and to fill you with His Holy Spirit. He promises you He will come in if you simply invite Him. He is the ultimate promise keeper!

Think about these things – keep studying the Bible – and have a blessed day!

Proverbs 16 NOTES

Proverbs 16 NOTES

Proverbs 17

$\mathcal{T}$his chapter deals a lot with matters pertaining to those closest to us, our family members, and how we speak to them. I've had to confess to the Lord on numerus occasions about how poorly I have spoken to my wife and children. It's unfortunate how we sometimes speak to those we love the most. We often use harsh words we would never use when speaking to others. Lord, help me (and you) to heed the advice found in this chapter, and to choose our words wisely!

Today's devotional thought from Proverbs 17:1.

1 Better a dry crust with peace and quiet
  than a house full of feasting, with strife.

Several thoughts come to mind when reading this verse. First is the reference to peace and quiet. I think this is more important than we realize. Most of us spend a great deal of our lives outside the home and in work environments that are not what you would call godly settings. This requires that the time we spend at home be as stress-free as possible. Our homes need to be places that we look forward to coming back to each day. This necessitates a commitment from all family members that the time at home is going to be a place where the family gathers to be replenished and re-energized. A stress-free zone whenever possible. I recently made my own adjustment that has reduced stress in my own home. I was always in the habit of coming home and sitting right down to read the paper. What I didn't stop to think about was that my wife looks forward to me coming home and asking me about my day and telling me about hers. She didn't want to deprive me of the paper because she knows of my desire to stay abreast of news and current events. I decided I didn't want my paper to compete for attention with my wife so I made a simple adjustment. On weekdays when our time is more limited I take the paper to work and read it when I get a chance or not at all. The point is, I needed to recognize that the newspaper was creating a source of stress that was very easy to eliminate with a very simple adjustment to my routine. Now I come home and I'm able to focus my attention on my bride! This has turned into a highlight of our day!

The second point to this verse makes it very clear that without peace and harmony in the home everything else becomes nothing more than distractions and adds to the stress. You can have the nicest home on the block, the biggest outdoor grill, a home theater with surround sound, the best manicured lawn in town, a refrigerator full of food, and it will all be meaningless if your home isn't a place filled with love and a place where you can come to be filled and renewed, physically, emotionally and spiritually. What's the application for me and you? I suggest you spend some time this week as a family and sit down and discuss ways to make your home a more peaceful and quiet place for everyone. You may find a few simple changes can make a world of difference.

Think about these things – keep studying the Bible – and have a blessed day!

Today's devotional thought from Proverbs 17:3.

3 *The crucible for silver and the furnace for gold,*
   but the LORD tests the heart.

Here's a great proverb and a great reminder for the believer in Christ! What is the purpose of a crucible you might ask? A crucible is a container that is made to withstand tremendously high temperatures. Temperatures hot enough to turn metals like silver and gold into liquids. The reason this is necessary is so that impurities can be burned off of the fine metals. The impurities will float to the top of the crucible and are then able to be scooped away leaving the pure metal. One interesting fact is that the way to know if all the junk has been removed is if the liquid metal looks like a mirror. When you can see your reflection in the metal you know it's pure.

I find this analogy in Proverbs 17:3 fascinating! You see, left to ourselves our hearts get filled with junk. Jeremiah 17:9 states:

9 *The heart is deceitful above all things*
   and beyond cure.
   Who can understand it?

This is a difficult but important reality to understand. This scriptural picture of man's true nature is in direct opposition to the secular world view that says that man is basically good and with education and understanding of people, animals and the environment we can learn to live in harmony with all mankind. The Bible states otherwise and in many places. In fact the very first reference to the heart in Genesis 6:5 states:

[5] *The LORD saw how great man's wickedness on the earth had become, and that every inclination of the thoughts of his heart was only evil all the time.*

So you might be asking, where does that leave you and me? Is godly living a hopeless endeavor? Not in the slightest! On the contrary, for those of us that come to the end of ourselves and yield our hearts to God by accepting the gift of forgiveness and eternal life found through faith in Jesus Christ, we are accepting the fact that we need Christ to purify us and cleanse us from all unrighteousness. Once He has melted our hearts and cleaned away the junk we begin to reflect Jesus in our lives. People stop seeing us and start seeing Christ in us. When we let go of the self-directed life and give our hearts to Him, dying daily to ourselves, God is able to refine us and makes us purer until that glorious day when we see Him face-to-face! Are you reflecting Jesus in your countenance today?

Think about these things – keep studying the Bible – and have a blessed day!

Today's devotional thought from Proverbs 17:9.

9 *He who covers over an offense promotes love,*
   but whoever repeats the matter separates close friends.

Here's a timely word from the Book of Proverbs and one we all need to hear again and again. If there's ever been a glaring problem in relationships and especially in the church it would have to be in this area of gossip. I know the word gossip isn't used here in Proverbs 17:9 but Solomon speaks extensively about the tongue throughout this chapter and throughout many of the Proverbs. This particular warning has to do with *'retelling'* stories that have no value beyond hurting the person you're speaking about. The really hurtful comments are those that start off with: *"Did you hear what so-and-so said about you?"* This is your chance to say no! End it right then and there! Don't give the person the satisfaction. We need to learn that these things are better left unsaid. We never get it right anyway. There are always facts and details that get lost in the translation and usually causes unnecessary pain and heartache. It would be so much better if we were just willing to give others the benefit of the doubt. We often say or do things that if we would have had even one more minute to think about we would choose to bite our tongue.

There is a ripple effect to what we say so choose wisely what you repeat. Here's a thought that might quiet your tongue. What conversations could other people be having about you right now? Who among us doesn't have a blind spot? Wouldn't we hope and pray that someone would pray for us rather than talk about us? I'm reminded of Matthew 7:3:

3 Why do you look at the speck of sawdust in your brother's eye and pay no attention to the plank in your own eye?

It's so easy to see shortcomings in others but not in ourselves. Don't we all deserve the benefit of the doubt? Romans 12:18 seems a fitting verse for our topic today:

18 If it is possible, as far as it depends on you, live at peace with everyone.

Why not stop right now and pray for that person that has recently offended you. Start praying for them every day and watch and see what God does.

Think about these things – keep studying the Bible – and have a blessed day!

Today's devotional thought from Proverbs 17:14.

14 Starting a quarrel is like breaching a dam;
so drop the matter before a dispute breaks out.

Well friends, I've been married for 40 years so I confess I've done my share of dam breaching! Many of us will remember an old movie classic called "Force 10 from Navarrone.(it's **Navarone**)" You may recall the dramatic scene right after the soldiers try to blow up the dam that will eventually knock down the bridge that will stop the invading army and win the battle. Remember the next thing that happens? The charges are set and the explosion occurs. There's some rumbles . . . but nothing major. But wait! In a few minutes, there is just the very slightest little crack in the foundation. And slow but sure the little crack grows and grows until the dam is finally breached and millions of gallons of water come crashing down wiping out everything in its path.

So what's the analogy for me and you? I think this proverb is telling us that a quarrel has the same affect! One thoughtless word, one complaint that is not shared in love, will lead to another and another until eventually you are trying to stop a torrent of harsh words that can never be recalled!

So what does Solomon recommend we do? Drop the matter before a dispute breaks out! And this requires us to hold our tongues! Why is holding our tongues such a difficult thing for so many of us? The answer is, we're selfish! We think that whenever we're feeling hurt or angry about something that it needs to be verbalized.

Here's where we err. The promise of God's Word, not our feelings, needs to be our authority. The Christian needs to live by faith in the trustworthiness of God and His Word. Feelings are deceiving. God's word teaches us in many passages that we are to guard our tongue. James 1: 26 states very clearly about our obligation to keep a tight rein on our tongues. The words we speak can either build up or tear down.

How do we apply this to our lives? Let's start with keeping our mouths shut! Contrary to popular belief we don't have to have the last word on a subject. And there are many times when we shouldn't have the first word on a subject either. God help me in this area of my life. Let's take this wise advice and apply it to our lives today. I'm confident of this, we'll all be better off being careful with our words. There will be many arguments that never happen because we die to ourselves and live for Christ!

Think about these things – keep studying the Bible – and have a blessed day!

Today's devotional thought from Proverbs 17:17.

17 *A friend loves at all times,*
and a brother is born for adversity.

Today's verse speaks so beautifully about friendships. My personal observations are that the busier our lives get, the less opportunity to develop friendships. Having said that, I can't think of anything more precious than a good friend! Deep friendships rarely just happen. Friendships are nurtured. Friendships have to be worked at and developed over time and circumstances, and as this verse indicates, so that when difficulties arise in a friend's life you're there for them.

You might have a friend that goes through a health crisis and you're the only friend that person has. In the words spoken in the Book of Esther, you are there for such a time as this. You might have a friend that makes a mistake that lands themselves in prison and you're the only friend that person has. You're there for such a time as this.

This type of friend is not a fair weather friend. The friendship described in today's verse is a friend through thick and thin. I can't help but think of a deep friendship we see in the Old Testament, a friendship born for adversity as this verse describes, and that was the friendship between David and Jonathan. This was an unlikely friendship to say the least, King Saul was Jonathan's father and Saul spent 15 years trying to kill David. Jonathan's friendship with David came at great personal risk, yet he still loved David as a brother. You can read about this beautiful friendship in 1 Samuel 20.

Here's the application for me and you. There are only two things that will last for eternity and that's God's word and people. We should make others a priority in our lives. We should value friendships the way we value our time with the Lord. You see we'll only be able to experience true friendship with others if we spend time pouring our lives into them. It won't happen on its own, the same way a deep love for God won't happen unless we spend time with Him every day. Friendships do take time, no question about that. Friendships are hard, risky and **time**-consuming. But the older I get the more I have come to realize that it's all worth it. The time you and I spend pouring our lives into others is time well spent.

Think about these things – keep studying the Bible – and have a blessed day!

Today's devotional thought from Proverbs 17:24.

24 *A discerning man keeps wisdom in view,*
    but a fool's eyes wander to the ends of the earth.

Here's a verse filled with great advice and the principle is an easy one to capture. The idea of keeping wisdom in view suggests a man or woman that has their eyes fixed on the things of God. It's often been said that you'll never hit your target if you don't know what you're aiming at! For the follower of Christ, if we know what our mission and purpose is we're more likely to accomplish it and less likely to get distracted by the many things this world offers, things that are not part of God's plan for our lives. Picture here a horse getting ready for a race. The horse has blinders on. These are small leather pads that block the horse's vision to the left and right. They block things that could distract the horse during the race.

We need to go through the Christian life with spiritual blinders on. Another analogy we often use when driving a car is to be aware of blind spots in our rear view mirror. A blind spot is that area that we can't see in the mirror or out of our peripheral vision. We refer to it as a blind spot, meaning what we can't see could be dangerous.

So what's the application for you and me? If we are discerning properly, we will keep God's blueprint for our lives in full view. Proverbs Chapter 8 teaches us that Jesus is wisdom, so by keeping Jesus in full view of our eyes, we'll make wise decisions with what we see and what we do with our lives. We learn here also that the fool's eyes are not fixed. The fool's eyes are constantly wandering around, always looking to see if something over there is more interesting or appealing.

The fool allows his or her imagination to run their lives. They make silent observations: if my spouse was only taller or shorter or smarter. Maybe I need a new spouse? Or, if only my boss understood me better. Maybe I need a new job? If only my church appreciated me more, maybe I need a new church. Or maybe, if you and I would simply focus our eyes squarely on Jesus and let Him be our source of wisdom and discernment for our lives, then maybe these other things wouldn't seem to matter anymore.

Think about these things – keep studying the Bible – and have a blessed day!

Proverbs 17 NOTES

Proverbs 17 NOTES

Proverbs 18

By now you will have noticed that one topic that repeats itself throughout the Book of Proverbs is the use of words. Proverbs 18 is no different. All too often God has to rebuke us for the harsh words we use. I pray I will one day have greater victory over how I speak and the words I use, especially with those closest to me.

Today's devotional thought from Proverbs 18:2 and 4.

2 *A fool finds no pleasure in understanding*
   but delights in airing his own opinions.

4 *The words of a man's mouth are deep waters,*
   but the fountain of wisdom is a bubbling brook.

I want to look at these verses as good contrasts to one another. In Verse 2 we see an individual that talks much, but says little. Always talking but never listening! This individual quite literally loves to hear himself talk! That's a problem! It states here that he loves to air his own opinions. Do you get the sense that no other opinion would be welcome anyway? I'm quick to think of people I have known over the years that are like this but before I jump to others, I need to ask myself if I listen to others. Do I bother to take the time to really hear other people's opinions or do only my opinions matter? Do I blurt out my opinion on something as if that should somehow be the end of the discussion? Do I think too highly of myself, or too little of others to think they can't have something meaningful to contribute to a discussion. I pray that you and I would find little resemblance to this individual.

But let's contrast Verse 2 with Verse 4. This dear saint has a heart that seeks after God. This person, when they do speak, shows a well-thought position that literally flows forth just like water flows from a bubbling brook. This individual is slow to speak. Most likely because he or she is in prayer while others are voicing their opinions, taking that extra minute to ask God for wisdom. And this person will only add a comment if they deem it beneficial to the discussion. How different from the person that can't wait to prove how smart they are and that always has to be sure their opinion is heard the loudest. Lord, I want to be slow to speak, or not to speak at all - unless it's God guiding my mouth. I've wasted too many years being the one that had to be heard. Thank you God, for showing me that Your ways are so much higher than my ways. Your thoughts so much better than my thoughts. So what's the application for me and you? If you're like me, you've put your foot in your mouth on a few too many occasions. Hopefully, we are all growing in this area. I know that God hears our prayers so join me in asking Him to give us quiet and gentle mouths and hearts!

Think about these things – keep studying the Bible – and have a blessed day!

Today's devotional thought from Proverbs 18:4.

4 The words of a man's mouth are deep waters,
*   but the fountain of wisdom is a bubbling brook.*

What a tender way this expresses how our words can have an impact on other people's lives! The person that could fit this description would have spent many years studying God's Word, and also spends much time in prayer and communion with God. This is the only way that we can get to a place where the very words we speak could be described in such poetic terms. Wouldn't it be nice to walk away from a conversation with someone, and describe their comment or instruction to you as that of a fountain of wisdom! What would it take in my life and yours to have someone describe our advice or counsel as a fountain of wisdom? I think this can only happen when we learn how to die to ourselves and to our flawed and worldly wisdom and earnestly ask for wisdom and knowledge from God. It's what Solomon asked for…and received!

Read his petition here in 2 Chronicles 1:9-10:

⁹ Now, Lᴏʀᴅ God, let your promise to my father David be confirmed, for you have made me king over a people who are as numerous as the dust of the earth. ¹⁰ Give me wisdom and knowledge, that I may lead this people, for who is able to govern this great people of yours?

I believe our main problem is our tendency to apply human solutions to spiritual problems. We don't measure our circumstances next to God's word. All too often we apply our own wisdom to a situation never seeking godly wisdom from others or far more importantly taking the matter before our Heavenly Father.

My biggest problem in living the Christian life - is me! What's my mistake? I try to live the Christian life. The mere fact that I even try shows that it's all about me! As long as I'm in control, God can do little with me! It's only when I reach that place when I yield my life fully and completely to Him that God can use me fully and completely. Listen to what Jesus tells us in John 15:5:

⁵ I am the vine, you are the branches. If a man remains in me and I in him, he will bear much fruit; apart from me you can do nothing.

If you snap off a branch from the main vine it will die in a matter of hours! We all know this and understand this but isn't this what we're doing when we apply human solutions to spiritual problems? Aren't we thus separating ourselves from the main vine? If you and I want to be truly used by God in any significant way we'll need to gain victory over the needs of self!

Self-seeking, self-indulgence, self-pity, self-defense, self-consciousness . . . it's all about SELF!

We're the problem but God is the solution. Would you join me today in bowing our stiff necks to God in humility and ask Him to have full rein over our lives? Only then can we hope to impact this world for Christ's sake! May we so fully yield our lives to our creator that He can begin to use us to impact this world in ways we never thought possible. Amen!

Think about these things – keep studying the Bible – and have a blessed day!

Today's devotional thought from Proverbs 18:8.

8 *The words of a gossip are like choice morsels;*
they go down to a man's inmost parts.

This is another of the many times that Solomon addresses the topic of gossip in the book of Proverbs. Paul also talks about it to the church in Corinth, in a list of sinful things that are affecting their fellowship. I've always used a pretty simple system of bible study. If something is mentioned multiple times in scripture it's probably something I should pay close attention to. I've seen the effects of gossip up close and personal and it's never good. The true gossip has in their heart an intentional desire to hurt someone. They will always present a morsel of true information in the worst possible light. They will always add a juicy detail that is often untrue, but is closely connected enough to the actual circumstance to fit. It's usually someone's own perspective on a real situation.

There is something about gossip that appeals to us. Maybe it's the feeling of having insider information or sometimes the person being gossiped about is someone that we might not like and the tasty morsel gives us more proof that we were right all along!

Well friends, gossip is always wrong. At its core it is always intended to bring doubt and hurt about the person being gossiped about. Here's some great advice that I've been given about how to handle gossip when you hear it. The first thing you can immediately do no matter how tempting is not to listen to it! Wouldn't it be better to stop someone right in their tracks and suggest you pray rather than speak? Here's another great idea I got from a pastor friend. Ask the person that is about to tell some juicy tale if you can quote them on what they are about to say! This will usually end the conversation right then and there.

If you're reading this and are thinking that you're guilty because you've gossiped, well so have I! But I have grown much in this area and so can you. So what's the application? Gossips are usually easy to spot because they tend to be consistent in their sin. I would avoid conversations with them. If you are really bold you can admonish them in a loving way that what they are doing is wrong. Finally, begin praying and ask God to give you sensitive ears to be able to discern gossip as soon as it starts and then choose not to listen. It gets easier and easier to not listen to gossip. I'm learning how, and so can you.

Think about these things – keep studying the Bible – and have a blessed day!

Today's devotional thought from Proverbs 18:10.

10 *The name of the LORD is a strong tower;*
    the righteous run to it and are safe.

What a powerful reminder for the believer in Christ! Our heavenly Father is a strong tower! We can cling to Him when the storms of life are buffeting us. We can rest in Him when we are weary and life's burdens weigh us down. We can receive shelter from Him when enemies of the faith try to attack us. We can be lifted up by Him when we have fallen into temptation. He is limitless where we are limited. He is always there when everyone else abandons us. We can run to Him when evil thoughts are haunting us. We are safe and secure in His embrace. His arms are always extended in our direction! Take a moment and consider all this.

Here's the bad news: friends, family, co-workers, children, parents, spouses, pastors and priests will all fail us! Here's the good news: God never will!

Joshua 1:5 in stating an attribute of God . . . says: *"I will never leave you or forsake you!"*

Rest in the fact that you can never end up in a place where God can't find you and rescue you. These words *"I will never leave you or forsake you"* are words that contain within them a covenant between God and man. The only requirement on our part is to accept the free gift of salvation that God has provided for us through Jesus Christ. God loves us so much that He had to provide a way for us to be able to have fellowship with Him. That's how precious you are in His sight.

If you're reading this devotional then you fall into one of two categories because there are no others. You are either safe and secure in His arms because you've accepted Jesus as your Lord and Savior or you are still lost in your sins and relying on your own strength, ability and good works. You're either trusting in some grand scale in Heaven that will one day weigh your good deeds against your bad, hoping to come out on top or you believe you are nothing but dust and when you die it's all over. Friend, if that's you, no matter how sincere you believe in this path, you are sincerely wrong. But don't take my word for it. Something as important as where you'll spend eternity is worthy of your research.

Search the Bible. Find a church that teaches verse-by-verse from the scriptures, or ask around about a Bible study. You do a lot of research before you buy a new TV! Don't you think searching for the truth about eternity is worth the effort?

Think about these things – keep studying the Bible – and have a blessed day!

Today's devotional thought from Proverbs 18:17.

17 *The first to present his case seems right,*
till another comes forward and questions him.

I've always been fascinated with a good courtroom drama. I'm dating myself when I say that one of my favorite programs growing up was Perry Mason. I always enjoyed how a strong case would be made to show how the defendant was guilty as charged and the evidence presented was seemingly an open and shut case. Then, the other side would present their case. All of a sudden you would see the circumstances from a completely different perspective. I was always fascinated by how different the same scenario looked when presented from the other side.

So what's the application for me and you? First, I think we should avoid being too hasty in forming opinions when someone comes to us for counsel or advice. Not that we should enter every conversation with a suspicious attitude but more importantly with an attitude of humility, recognizing that we have a limited understanding of whatever points or facts are being presented. These principles apply equally whether for circumstances at church, business or life in general. There are always multiple ways to see every situation. There will always be reasons for positions to be presented with a specific goal or intent in mind.

A wise individual will always weigh carefully the words or comments spoken and will prayerfully consider a response but always with the thought of hearing from all parties involved. It's too easy to side with the first person to present their case, especially if it's an individual that we know and respect. There's nothing wrong with someone speaking up in defense of a particular position. The challenge for all of us is to be willing to hear an alternate viewpoint. And the real sign of maturity is when the wise counsel of others tips the scale in their favor of a position and we are willing to go in another direction. We would be wise to heed the counsel of James 1:19 and *"be quick to listen and slow to speak."*

Learn to listen with discerning ears in all circumstances. Then choose carefully how you respond. You will most likely have a lot less words to regret and you'll have learned how to develop discernment that will prove helpful for the rest of your life.

Think about these things – keep studying the Bible – and have a blessed day!

Today's devotional thought from Proverbs 18:24.

24 *A man of many companions may come to ruin,*
but there is a friend who sticks closer than a brother.

This verse deals primarily with the topic of friendships. Friendships matter greatly! Who we develop relationships with will have great impact on our lives, both now and into the future. The first part of this verse addresses the problems associated with too many acquaintances and no deep friendships.

Social acquaintances have their place but the reality is, you can spend weeks and even months going here, there and everywhere with social friends and never have a meaningful discussion about important matters of life. Deep friendships, the kind mentioned in this verse are friendships that are often closer than a brother or sister. These are friendships that require effort. This type of friendship needs to be developed and nurtured. Sadly, our fast-paced lifestyles have made it more and more difficult to devote proper attention to meaningful relationships.

Women are better at this than men, but all of us could do a better job than we currently do. Here's the application. You and I need these friendships for our future well-being. And we need to be a friend to others for their future well-being. The irony here is that the person with many companions is actually hurting his or her chances of developing deeper relationships and our excuse is that we're too busy for friendships! Ironic isn't it? What can we learn from Jesus and His example? He had the opportunity for many companions. Just add up the number of people he healed, spoke to or fed. There would have been literally thousands of men and women that would have loved to be His friend. Except for a very few exceptions, His time was spent almost exclusively with 12 men. He devoted Himself to growing deeper with a small number rather than surface relationships with many. Let me restate my opening point. Who you spend time with matters greatly. We need friendships that allow for conversations to go deeper than how was your week. Why not pray and ask God to guide you in this area. Start spending more time with fewer people and see what God will do. And while we're on the topic of friendships, I can't imagine a friendship more worthy of our time than a deep friendship with Jesus! This eternally significant friendship is available to all of us!

James 2:23, speaking of Abraham states:

23 And the scripture was fulfilled that says, "Abraham believed God, and it was credited to him as righteousness, and he was called God's friend."

Revelation 3:20 expresses a great commitment to an everlasting friendship: *"behold, I stand at the door and knock. If anyone (you or me) hears my voice and opens the door, I will come in and eat with him and him with me."*

Do your best to develop a closer friendship with fewer godly individuals that will draw you even closer to God, but make sure God remains your best friend! How's that for some 'friendly' advice!

Think about these things – keep studying the Bible – and have a blessed day!

Proverbs 18 NOTES

Proverbs 18 NOTES

Proverbs 19

       roverbs 19 contains 29 verses. All are rather distinct and stand on their own. Earlier in my book, I offered the suggestion to write a 'T' in your Bible next to verses that deal with the tongue. Starting in this chapter, consider writing an 'R' next to the verses that deal with our 'relationships'. There are quite a few if you take the time to find them! The challenge in reading Proverbs is to not rush through a chapter. You have to read each verse as a stand-alone thought. This requires time to ponder the words and to consider what God wants to teach you today. It's best to read this book with a pen in hand. This way you can just keep a finger in the blank pages at the end of the chapter, and write your thoughts as they come to mind. You can take extra time by going back to your notes and expanding on your thoughts. If you take the time to do this, I think you will find it to be a joyful effort!

Today's devotional thought from Proverbs 19:3.

3 *A man's own folly ruins his life,*
    yet his heart rages against the LORD.

This topic touches on something that started at Creation and haunts us to this very day. In Genesis 3:1 we read these words of Adam: *"The woman you put here with me—she gave me some fruit from the tree, and I ate it."* Adam blamed God! A man's own folly ruins his life yet his heart rages against God! Friends, I have seen this repeat itself so many times in life. Someone makes a mistake and gets drunk. Then they get into a car accident, get their driver's license revoked, insurance surcharges get tacked on, community service and many more headaches, all because they chose to drink and drive. Then when finances get tight and they can't see their friends because they can't drive because they lost their license, they murmur and complain to God about their miserable life. All the time forgetting that none of these circumstances would exist if they didn't get drunk!

This devotional really isn't about drunkenness, although if the application hits home for you, then take it as something from God. The application for me and for you is much broader than drinking. It's about our choices and how those choices affect our future and how our choices affect our relationship with our heavenly Father. I have a clipping on my refrigerator that I read from time to time and it goes like this: "Men don't decide their future. They decide their habits and their habits decide their future." This is always a helpful reminder to me that most of the difficult places I've found myself in were a direct result of choices I made! But pointing negative things out to others, especially those close to us, must be done in love and not with an, *I told you so* attitude. I've made this mistake all too often with my own two children. God has had to show me that instead of pointing the finger, I should be pointing the way to better decision making. The way to wiser choices. The way of the Lord! These precious opportunities won't last forever. One day you'll wake up and find your children are in their 30s and you'll see that you missed too many opportunities to exchange correction for guidance, finger pointing instead of problem solving and lecturing instead of loving. So what about you? Are you mad at God when you should be mad at yourself? Are you correcting others instead of counseling and encouraging others? Why not start today to pray more, plan more, read more and grow more. That's how your life can take on new meaning and purpose.

Think about these things – keep studying the Bible – and have a blessed day!

Today's devotional thought from Proverbs 19:6.

6 *Many curry favor with a ruler,*
and everyone is the friend of a man who gives gifts.

Human nature being what it is, coupled with our modern day culture and the emphasis Hollywood and Wall Street places on fame and wealth, we often find ourselves in awe of these people. I understand why we do this and I've done it myself. But I've also lived long enough to have seen many that we hold in high esteem fall into disgrace as a result of drugs, alcohol, promiscuity or financial impropriety. Even on a smaller scale, we can find ourselves drawn to people with local prominence or wealth.

What's the application for you and me? There may be times when individuals come into our lives that are in a position to give gifts. There's nothing wrong with this as long as we see this as a blessing from God and we don't start to see these individuals as more deserving of our time or attention. Here are a few practical examples. A friend works for a company that has box seats at the pro stadium in your city, and on occasion you get invited to a game. You might have another friend that is a member of a private golf club or some similar membership. The important thing in these situations is to be grateful for the friendship for as long as God has it for you. More importantly, be sure the friendship isn't one-sided. You don't want to find yourself using a friendship just for what you can get out of it.

Every person God brings into your life becomes an opportunity to tell them about Jesus or strengthen them in their walk if they already know Him. Friendships are important but they can easily become a distraction. I often mention to people struggling with their relationships, to consider who they are spending great amounts of time with. Spend time with people who will be crying at your funeral. And remember that nothing is more important than your friendship with Jesus. Friends will inevitably let you down but Jesus will never leave you or forsake you. You have His word on it!

Think about these things – keep studying the Bible – and I have a blessed day!

Today's devotional thought from Proverbs 19:11.

11 *A man's wisdom gives him patience;*
it is to his glory to overlook an offense.

A great lesson can be gleaned from this verse. It's not surprising that the words wisdom and patience should be found in the same sentence. The idea being expressed here is multi-faceted. There are so many good attributes tied together to show us what makes us better men and women of God. We learn here that the ability to overlook an offense is the mark of a wise and patient person. I want to be that person! I want to be the one that gives the benefit of the doubt. I want to exercise self-control. How about you?

We learn here that wisdom, knowledge and patience are all areas we can grow in as Christians, and that these attributes will serve us well in all aspects of life. The ability to overlook an offense as mentioned here is something you and I should work at and develop.

There are so many things that happen in the course of a day that could cause us to overreact or react too quickly. By waiting a day or sometimes even just a few hours to respond to something can change the whole outcome.

What's the application? First, observe that wisdom and patience go hand-in-hand. Applying this verse to our daily lives will result in greater self-control, less anger, more ability to forgive others and less thoughts about getting even! If you're thinking;

"But Brian, you don't understand, So-and-so said this-and-that and I need to set the record straight."

No you don't! Why not let God handle it? Why not let Him be your defender? If we need defending, He can do a better job than you can. Proverbs 26:2 states:

"Like a fluttering sparrow or a darting swallow, an undeserved curse does not come to rest."

You can spend the rest of your life trying to defend yourself or set the record straight. Unless it's a legal matter or something with substantial repercussions, I say let it go. If you are walking with integrity, the people in your life that matter will consider the source of a negative comment.

Here's the bottom line; time is too short to waste it on anger, impatience and others transgressions. Psalm 39 offers us a great reminder of the shortness of life and the need to keep our eyes on what will matter for eternity.

In Psalm 39: 4-7 we read these words:

4 "Show me, O LORD, my life's end and the number of my days;
   let me know how fleeting is my life.

5 You have made my days a mere handbreadth;
   the span of my years is as nothing before you. Each man's life is but a breath.

6 Man is a mere phantom as he goes to and fro:
   He bustles about, but only in vain; he heaps up wealth,
   not knowing who will get it.

7 *"But now, Lord, what do I look for? My hope is in you."*

What really matters are the things that bring us and others to Jesus!

Think about these things – keep studying the Bible – and have a blessed day!

Today's devotional thought from Proverbs 19:17.

17 *He who is kind to the poor lends to the LORD,*
*   and he will reward him for what he has done.*

Jesus reminds us that the poor will always be among us. He states this clearly in three of the four Gospel accounts. We need to consider the poor among us for at least two reasons. First, we need to have hearts of compassion for those around us that are needy. There are many references to the poor in the Bible and our need to give to those less fortunate. But 1 Corinthians 13:3 reminds us that it's not enough to just give to the poor, but to have love and compassion for the poor.

A tender heart for those less fortunate keeps us humble. I can still remember my first few years of marriage and how very little we had in the way of finances and possessions. I try to remember those lean years so that I never forget the little blessings we received from friends There were many times we would be invited to someone's home after church for a great meal because they knew we had very little back home.

The second reason for remembering the poor is so we can be active participants in meeting the needs of the poor whenever possible.

James 2:15-16 states it this way:

15Suppose a brother or sister is without clothes and daily food. 16If one of you says to him, "Go, I wish you well; keep warm and well fed," but does nothing about his physical needs, what good is it?

This verse is a great reminder to put our money where our mouth is. The second part of this verse is a gentle reminder that God knows our hearts. Our motives need to be right so we never want to give with the thought of getting. When we start thinking that way, we've missed the purpose completely. Once again I'm reminded of the way God works in our hearts. The person that benefits most by giving to the poor, is the giver! That's right! The recipient is blessed as well, but I think God has designed it so that the giver receives a far greater blessing.

I was part of a church back east that had a food and clothing ministry. They distributed to needy families every week of the year, but at Thanksgiving and Christmas the fellowship pulled out all the stops and blessed hundreds of families. They received complete Thanksgiving dinners and for Christmas, the church would find out the ages of all the needy boys and girls…and distribute new toys and clothing and gifts to each child. My wife and I have been blessed to participate in this distribution and we gave a few dollars to the cause but we received far more than what we gave. We've seen the faces of the mothers that are given an entire holiday meal when they didn't think they would have one. I've seen the faces of children that were given an unexpected Christmas gift and that's been priceless! Whatever we do for the least of those around us we do for God!

Think about these things – keep studying the Bible – and have a blessed day!

Today's devotional thought from Proverbs 19:27.

27 *Stop listening to instruction, my son,*
   and you will stray from the words of knowledge.

This is a good cautionary verse, especially for readers that have been walking with the Lord for several decades. I look back on my 40 years as a Christian and I can recall different times in those years when I really felt like I had a good handle on my relationship with God. Yet as a whole, I'm more aware now than any other time in my life how little I really know. There will never be a point where any of us will know it all while living life this side of Heaven. More importantly we have a very clear warning here. As soon as we stop listening to godly instruction we become vulnerable to teachings that are not biblical. The only way we'll ever be able to turn a deaf ear to false teachings is if we can identify truthful teachings! I've mentioned this analogy in past devotionals, but it bears repeating; when a new employee is hired at a bank they are never shown or asked to handle counterfeit money. They only handle genuine bills so that they become so accustomed to the genuine that the false becomes easy to spot!

The application should be obvious, we need to be absorbed in true godly teaching so we can spot false teaching easily, before it has a chance to influence us down a wrong path. God has a wonderful plan for our lives. He has given us a wonderful instruction manual that provides answers to all of our questions and equips us to share what we learn with those in our sphere of influence. And we can share with confidence!

The Bible contains 66 books written by 40 authors over a period of 1500 years and in three different languages. Thousands of years later, it's still guiding and instructing us and showing us God's plan and purpose for our lives. We're living in a time of unprecedented expansion of knowledge. I read recently that all the combined knowledge of the world is doubling every 18 months. Think about that! We're doing things in science and technology today that only a decade ago seemed impossible. With each passing year and with every new discovery there has never been a single reputable fact that has ever disputed a single word in the Bible. In fact the Bible becomes harder and harder to dispute with each passing year! Why? Because the author of the Bible is also the creator of all these scientific and technological discoveries! He is the great "I AM". It should be obvious to anyone with an open mind that the Bible is divinely inspired. Consider this: every single year there are books on science, mathematics, philosophy, child-rearing, health and so on that have to get revised or tossed because they are no longer considered accurate. Yet the same Bible text that was read and studied thousands of years ago is still read and studied today and without contradiction. It seems evident to me that it's the divinely inspired word of God. Shouldn't that be reason enough to make reading and studying the Bible an important part of your daily life?

Think about these things – keep studying the Bible – and have a blessed day!

Proverbs 19 NOTES

Proverbs 19 NOTES

Proverbs 20

$\mathcal{T}$here are 30 verses in this chapter. There are two verses that always catch my attention the most. The first is Verse 9. It's a great reminder that sin is universal, and we can't save ourselves. That's why God sent us Jesus! The second is Verse 29, simply because I have a full head of gray hair! Throughout my life, it is often those older than me that have been the most helpful in guiding me. Now at 60 years old, I admire youth, but I honor those older than me. I hope you enjoy my devotionals from Chapter 20.

***Today's devotional thought from Proverbs* 20:1.**

1 *Wine is a mocker and beer a brawler;*
   whoever is led astray by them is not wise.

As a Christian for 40 plus years, I've heard every viewpoint there is about alcohol. There are as many opinions on consuming alcohol as there are brands of the same! So I will make no attempt at convincing you one way or the other. That's something for each individual to determine in their own homes as to whether it's right or wrong for them. But here are a few points we can all agree on. Alcohol is a mind-altering drug. There have been many studies done, and no one disputes that alcohol alters our brains. It affects our reasoning. It stunts personal development. And abusing it will inevitably have negative consequences. Instead of wasting time on endless discussions about whether Christians can or should consume alcohol, why not take this verse for what it states; if you allow yourself to be led astray by alcohol then you are not wise! This is the clear and simple message of this verse. Alcohol has caused more deaths, car accidents, unplanned pregnancies, lost virginity, arguments, fights and divorces than any other single thing that anyone can point to. This is the reality of what alcohol causes. Another reality is that alcohol costs a lot of money and just like ice cream or manicures or anything else that you could argue for or against, at some point, brings into question whether this is a good use of the finances God has blessed you with. So what's the application for you and me? The question shouldn't be 'can I or can't I consume alcohol'? In my opinion that question has already been answered. 1 Corinthians 6:12 states:

"Everything is permissible for me"—but not everything is beneficial.

"Everything is permissible for me"—but I will not be mastered by anything.

This verse has to do with anything related to the body so it's not about can I or can't I, but a question of should I? Do I want to bring something into my life, marriage or family that has such a high risk of a negative outcome? One person can have a glass of wine on a special occasion and not have another glass for months! Others have just one single alcoholic beverage or smoke one cigarette and then spend decades trying to break an addiction. Which one are you?

Think about these things – keep studying the Bible – and have a blessed day!

Today's devotional thought from Proverbs 20:3.

3 *It is to a man's honor to avoid strife,*
      but every fool is quick to quarrel.

So many wonderful life principles are captured in this simple yet compelling verse. Any fool can start a fight, but it takes great wisdom and maturity to avoid one. One thing I've learned in life is that you have to find a way to get along with all types of people. It's far too easy to jump into a quarrel, and all too often people allow a simple disagreement to escalate to a full blown altercation. Note the word honor used in this verse. The honorable man or woman will withdraw from an argument, they will drop a controversial discussion, and they'll overlook an offense. They will learn how to get along with even the most difficult of people. The foolish man or woman talks first and thinks second. Their goal in life is to always have the final word no matter what. They make the mistake of verbalizing everything they think.

Here's a suggestion for those of you that are in the habit of reading a chapter of Proverbs every day. I've done this and I've found it helpful. Whenever I read Proverbs and come across any verses that have anything to do with the tongue, I write the letter 'T' next to the verse. It's very enlightening to see how many verses are devoted to our foolish tendency to speak before we think! Let me state just a few of them here;

Proverbs 10:19: When words are many, sin is not absent.

Proverbs 15:1: A gentle answer turns away wrath, but a harsh word stirs up anger.

Proverbs 18:7: A fool's mouth is his undoing, and his lips are a snare to his soul.

Proverbs 21:23: He who guards his mouth and his tongue keeps himself from calamity.

These are just a few of the dozens of verses in the Book of Proverbs that can prove helpful to you in this area. So what's the application for me and you? The next time you find yourself in a discussion that seems to be quickly turning into an argument, make a concerted effort to avoid strife. Challenge yourself! Word a quick prayer to God and set your heart on calming the situation. You'll be amazed at the outcome!

Think about these things – keep studying the Bible – and have a blessed day!

Today's devotional thought from Proverbs 20:9.

9 *Who can say, "I have kept my heart pure;*
I am clean and without sin"?

Brothers and sisters, sin is universal! The sooner a person realizes this, the sooner they can turn to the only one who can cleanse their sin and make them righteous before a holy God and that's the Savior, Jesus Christ. I remember quite clearly the weeks just before giving my heart to Jesus. I was living in New Jersey and someone from California that I had never met shared the salvation message with me. It was the very first time anyone took the time to tell me that God loved me and had a wonderful plan for my life!

It was less than 30 days later that I accepted Jesus as my personal Savior, but my initial response was: *"thanks but no thanks."* I remember thinking that I must be okay with God because I never killed anyone and because I lived a good life and cared about others. I was doing the two things that most everyone gets wrong.

First, I was measuring myself horizontally, meaning I was comparing myself with others and it was always *others* who were far worse than me. By measuring ourselves this way, we can always point to the murderer or the thief or the drug addict because next to them, we will always look better. There's just one problem with this way of measuring ourselves. We need to be measuring our life next to a holy and sinless God, and a holy and sinless Savior! When we measure vertically, we will quickly conclude that we fall far short!

My second mistake was very similar. I was trusting in a God who would grade me on a curve. I had this picture of heaven that many people have, that there will be a giant scale at the entrance to the pearly gates and God will weigh my good deeds against my bad. And because I never killed anyone, the scale would magically tilt in my favor.

This might sound good to you, and you may be very sincere in believing this, but you would be sincerely wrong. Because that's not what the Bible says! Romans 3:23 states: *"For all have sinned and fall short of the glory of God."*

I heard a great analogy that might be a helpful word picture. If you were to fill a glass with water and then added a single drop of cyanide to the glass, would you drink it? The answer of course is no. Why? Because the one drop has now defiled the whole glass. See the point? The cyanide represents sin, and it only takes one sin, or even one ungodly thought to condemn us before a Holy God. One single drop defiles the whole vessel! Sin is universal and we can't save ourselves! So what can we do?

Romans 6:23 gives us the blessed answer:

[23] *For the wages of sin is death,* **but** *the gift of God is eternal life in Christ Jesus our Lord.*

What is a wage? It's something we earn or payment for what we've done. The Bible makes it clear in Romans 3 and elsewhere that none are righteous, no not one, for we all have sinned and fall short of the glory of God.

But here in Romans 6 we are also told that the gift of God is eternal life in Jesus Christ. You see, friends, a gift is the complete opposite of a wage.

197

A gift is something we can't earn. All we can do with a gift is choose to accept it or reject it.

Jesus sacrificed His sinless life for you and for me! It's through Jesus that we can have access to God. Jesus washes away our sin. We can't ever say we're clean and without sin but we can say we've been cleansed from our sin if we've accepted Jesus as our Lord and Savior! If you've never asked Jesus to come into your life, if you've never confessed your sin to Him and asked for His forgiveness, why not do so right now? If you believe in your heart that Jesus is Lord, the Bible says you will be saved!

Think about these things – keep studying the Bible – and have a blessed day!

Today's devotional thought from Proverbs 20:12.

12 *Ears that hear and eyes that see—*
the LORD has made them both.

Here's a precious reminder from God. I thank Him that He gave me ears so that I could hear His voice and eyes so that I could see His beauty and the beauty of His creation. This verse reminds me of one of the first times I shared my faith as a Christian. It was at least 40 or more years ago. I was a brand new Christian and only a few months in the Lord. I was a newlywed as well, which plays into the story so read on. I was out to lunch with four coworkers, all salesmen with the same company I worked for at the time. I was the newest and youngest man at the table. I mention this to give you a picture of the intimidation factor that was about to be presented to me. One of the men at the table was a man named Charlie and he was just a few weeks away from his wedding day. So out of the blue and with just a touch of sarcasm, Charlie says to me: *"So Brian, now that you're married and an expert on marriage, what is the secret to marital happiness?"* Keep in mind that at this moment, I had been married for less than a month!

I paused just long enough to say a silent prayer for God's help and I answered him this way; *"Charlie, as best I can tell, it's by you and your future wife yielding your hearts to Jesus Christ. As each of you grow closer to Jesus, you will then grow closer to each other."*

There was an awkward moment of silence and then Charlie replied with the words, *"Please pass me the ketchup!"*

I'll never forget that moment as long as I live. Nothing more was said that day. The topic of conversation was quickly changed to something else and it was never brought up again. I left that company a short time later and had no further contact with Charlie. Fast forward about seven years. I am now the founder of my own company in a totally different industry. I'm sitting at my desk and I can hear from the front office a distinct voice that I hadn't heard for over seven years. It was the voice of Charlie asking if this was where Brian Rechten worked. I immediately came out of my office and greeted him warmly and invited him in. After exchanging a few pleasantries he got more serious and began to tell me, with tears in his eyes, about some struggles he had been having in his marriage. He and his wife were not able to conceive, and this and other factors had put a significant strain on their marriage. He loved his wife and didn't want to lose her. So one day, when he was alone and quiet he recalled the advice I had given him seven years earlier in that diner in Bayonne, New Jersey. Charlie cried out to God that day and gave his heart to Jesus! By the time he tracked me down it was about nine months later and he and his wife were now both Christians and they were in the process of adopting a little baby girl.

Well the application is obvious. God gave Charlie ears to hear and eyes to see. God uses all things however small or seemingly insignificant to draw people to Himself. Take every opportunity to tell others of the hope that is within you because you never know what will come of it.

Think about these things – keep studying the Bible – and have a blessed day!

Today's devotional thought from Proverbs 20:29.

29 *The glory of young men is their strength,*
  gray hair the splendor of the old.

Having a full head of gray hair, I figured I needed to speak on this verse. I call it gray hair but my wife calls it "distinguished!" Young people define distinguished as . . . old! This verse has something to say for both the young and the old.

I like the fact that this verse points out that both the young and old have their advantages. It's far too easy for those of us with gray hair to pick on those younger as having a long way to go, but we throw the baby out with the bathwater when we do that, because we ignore the many benefits of youth. There's something to be said for strength and stamina. I spent a week in Mexico on a Mission's trip several years back. We built a home for a family in a little town called Vicente Guerrero. I confess, I was the oldest of the 11 men on the trip. In fact most of the men were half my age! By about the third day I recall it being such a blessing to have these younger and stronger men do a bit more of the heavy lifting. I turned out to be quite the supervisor! By week's end, several were referring to me as *'dad'*.

It turned out to be such an honor to work side-by-side with this wonderful group of younger men. You may recall the Apostle Paul reminding Timothy that he should not let his youth cause him to be bashful about his ministry.

In 1 Timothy 4:12-14 Paul states:

[12]Don't let anyone look down on you because you are young, but set an example for the believers in speech, in life, in love, in faith and in purity. [13]Until I come, devote yourself to the public reading of Scripture, to preaching and to teaching. [14]Do not neglect your gift, which was given you through a prophetic message when the body of elders laid their hands on you.

In the same way, those of us that have been around the block a few times have a lot to contribute, as well. Those of us that are older have the benefit of hindsight to grow from our mistakes. When we fall down, we can get up. The Bible is full of examples of older folks that made amazing contributions to the kingdom in their later years. Think of men like Noah and Abraham and Moses and Daniel, and all they accomplished late into their lives'.

I've been blessed to know young and old that have this in common: they love God with all their heart, soul, mind and strength. What a privilege it is for young and old alike, to serve God together side-by-side!

Think about these things – keep studying the Bible – and have a blessed day!

Proverbs 20 NOTES

Proverbs 20 NOTES

Proverbs 21

here is much to learn from these 31 verses. The following devotionals are thoughts from just five of these verses. There's plenty more to be written. Perhaps I'll publish a second book that will include devotionals on all the verses yet to be written. With each passing year, God reveals more of His plan and purpose for my life. I know the same is true for you. Keep reading, and keep journaling. God has a plan and purpose for your life too!

Today's devotional thought from Proverbs 21:1.

1 The king's heart is in the hand of the LORD;
   he directs it like a watercourse wherever he pleases.

I could sum this verse up in one sentence and that is this: God is completely in control! No matter what your personal circumstances or circumstances in your family, in your state, nation or world, God is in control. God never says: *"I never saw that coming"*

As this verse implies, even the King's heart is in God's hands. This is a great reminder for each of us when we find ourselves in difficult situations, like a new job or a new boss or unemployment or illness or any number of other things. These are things you can bring to God in prayer. His arm is not too short to deal with these matters. He actually wants you to come to Him in prayer. He can put people into our lives and he can move people out of our lives! He directs our lives and He is in control and this should bring us peace.

Several years ago I had a pretty amazing small world 'God thing' occur that was such a clear reminder to me that God orchestrates all things for his purposes. In my previous business role as the General Manager of an east coast Christian radio ministry, it was my job to be on the lookout for great Bible teachers to join our ministry line-up. I sent an email to a particular west coast pastor just before leaving for Maui with my wife to celebrate our 30th wedding anniversary. We left for Maui on a Friday, but just two days prior, this west coast pastor was at our home church in New Jersey on a Wednesday evening. My wife (Patti) attended that mid-week service and came home raving about his teaching and what a great night it was. She mentioned how inspired she was as a result of his teaching and proceeded to tell me his entire message! So I mentioned all this in my email asking this pastor to consider partnering with our radio ministry. The pastor's Wednesday night teaching was all about the importance of sharing our faith with those we meet. That Friday morning we had a short layover flight from New Jersey to Cleveland on our way to Maui.

Here's Part 1 of the amazing 'God thing' that occurred. We began a conversation with our seatmate that ended with us praying with him to receive Jesus as his personal Lord and Savior. It was an amazing 'open door' and he quickly recognized his need for salvation! Needless to say, we were pretty excited. I added all these details in my email to this pastor, since it was his inspiring teaching that prompted us to be more aware than ever for opportunities to tell others about Jesus. I added one final sentence in my email, mentioning that it was such a great way to start our anniversary trip to Maui!

The next morning we awoke to Part 2 of the 'God story'. I opened a reply email from this pastor stating: *"You're in Maui? So are we!"* What are the chances of Patti hearing a west coast pastor speaking in New Jersey two days before, and then we both end up in Maui, 10 minutes apart in the same week? We ended up having dinner together with our wives that same evening and we developed a friendship that never could have happened any other way. By the way, the pastor thought it far more than a mere coincidence, and that night at dinner he informed me that his radio program would be joining the ministry line-up and he's been on that radio station ever since!

So what's the application for me and you? Live each day expecting God do something unexpected. There are no accidents or coincidences in life that God doesn't know about. When you enter into a conversation with someone in a bank line, in the grocery store, at a restaurant, at a park or even at church, then it's safe to say that it's an opportunity to speak to them with confidence that God has allowed the encounter, and to make good use of the opportunity. I've had more unplanned spiritual conversations than I can count, I just needed to be faithful with the opportunity before me. Expect the unexpected and always remember that you're God's hands extended! Be bold! People need to hear that God loves them and has a wonderful plan for their lives!

Think about these things – keep studying the Bible – and have a blessed day!

Today's devotional thought from Proverbs 21:3.

3 *To do what is right and just i*
s more acceptable to the LORD than sacrifice.

This is an interesting topic to consider and one that is guaranteed to stir the pot. Humankind spends a great deal of time and energy pursuing man-made religious ceremonies. God tells us in His word that if our motives or the intended outcome is an attempt on our part to bring pleasing rituals to God we are to be pitied. Verse 3 tells us in a very simple way to do what is just and right and to do it as an outward expression of an internal decision to follow God and love Him completely. We routinely get this backwards. We do good works because we think this somehow earns us points with God. Some even think church attendance, prayer and communion are somehow done for God's benefit. These are things we should desire for our good, not to earn points with God!

In Amos 5:21 we read:

21 *"I hate, I despise your religious feasts;*
I cannot stand your assemblies.

We see here that God hates empty rituals. External actions without an inward desire are despised by God. These are strong words . . . and spoken by God through His prophet Amos! (They're not my words!) This makes me want to do a soulful attitude and heart-check pretty regularly. I want to pray the prayer of David in Psalm 139:23-24:

23 *Search me, O God, and know my heart;*
test me and know my anxious thoughts.

24 *See if there is any offensive way in me,*
and lead me in the way everlasting.

Isaiah 1:11-14 shows us in even clearer terms how much God disdains empty rituals with no sincere desire on our part to worship Him and know Him more:

11 *"The multitude of your sacrifices—*
   what are they to me?" says the LORD.
   "I have more than enough of burnt offerings,
   of rams and the fat of fattened animals;
   I have no pleasure
   in the blood of bulls and lambs and goats.
12 *When you come to appear before me,*
   who has asked this of you,
   this trampling of my courts?
13 *Stop bringing meaningless offerings!*
   Your incense is detestable to me.
   New Moons, Sabbaths and convocations—
   I cannot bear your worthless assemblies.
14 *Your New Moon feasts and your appointed festivals*
   I hate with all my being.
   They have become a burden to me;
   I am weary of bearing them.

What are the right and just things God accepts from us? First we must accept God's provision of salvation and eternal life by recognizing we are sinners in need of a Savior. We need to put our faith and trust in Jesus Christ alone for our salvation. What we do from there is a direct result of our gratefulness to our Savior for His sacrifice on our behalf.

We get the next step in our spiritual journey from Jesus' own words before His ascension and that is an admonition to go into the entire world and tell others about Him. We should tell others about Jesus because we have the privilege of showing someone how to spend eternity with Jesus and not be doomed to eternal damnation. We should not be telling people about Jesus for any selfish motives or some type of imaginary heavenly point system.

Spend a few minutes now to refocus your thoughts on all that God has done for you. Reevaluate your daily routine and make sure that you're doing what is just and right and that you're doing them for all the right reasons!

Think about these things – keep studying the Bible – and have a blessed day!

Today's devotional thought from Proverbs 21:5.

5 *The plans of the diligent lead to profit*
   as surely as haste leads to poverty.

These few simple words have more to say than we may realize at first. How I would have avoided so many wasted days and wasted dollars had I heeded the wisdom of this Proverb.

Fortunately, scripture is always speaking to us and it's never too late to learn a new principle, or to learn from our mistakes.

Let's face it, most of us are far too hasty in our decision-making. There are so many scriptures that deal with this topic, that we should quickly realize that this is an area of vulnerability for many of us. I think of Proverbs 15:22 that states:

"Plans fail for lack of counsel, but with many advisors they succeed."

If we followed this simple advice, how much trouble would we avoid? I've heard many wise financial counselors recommend that every purchase we make should have a 24 hour waiting period before we buy. Think about the wisdom of this simple suggestion. How many times do we make impulse purchases in the course of a day, week or month? Some of us spend more time deciding on a brand of laundry detergent than we do on a new car! The main thought of today's devotional is the idea of proper planning. The opposite of planning is to do things on impulse. And if we really get honest with ourselves, we would most likely admit to making far too many impulse purchases in our lives. Aren't there many decisions you've made, that given a chance to do it over, you would make a different decision? All too often though, we don't get a chance at a do-over so we're forced to live with the consequences of a hasty decision.

I've made many investments, small and large . . . that have turned out to be disastrous. I can look back and see that had I just spent an extra day praying, or asking the opinion of a friend, or someone more knowledgeable in that area of finance, I would have made an entirely different decision.

Maybe you're reading this right now and you're considering a significant purchase or investment, and you're realizing that you haven't even prayed about this matter. Perhaps you need to take a day to pray about it. Call a friend and get some additional advice. It might be a really great investment, or maybe it's not!

Let me get back to the topic of do-overs. One decision you'll never regret, is the decision to recommit your life and your plans to God. God is the God of endless do-overs, and He is ready, willing and able to give you a fresh start in whatever aspect of life you may be struggling with. Have you made bad investments? God will grant you a do-over! Let God have His way with you. He has a wonderful plan for your life if you will only let Him have control. Let me close with one of the most precious promises in scripture from the Old Testament book of Jeremiah 29:11-13:

11For I know the plans I have for you," declares the LORD, "plans to prosper you and not to harm you, plans to give you hope and a future. 12Then you will call on me and come and pray to me, and I will listen to you. 13 You will seek me and find me when you seek me with all your heart.

Think about these things – keep studying the Bible – and have a blessed day!

Today's devotional thought from Proverbs 21:20.

*20 In the house of the wise are stores of choice food and oil,
   but a foolish man devours all he has.*

Here's a very practical verse that deals with being good stewards of all that God provides us with. The main thought being expressed here has to do with the idea of living within our means. Sadly, America has become a nation of excess. We tend to live way beyond our means instead of well within them and this creates problems that are far greater than financial.

Perhaps you have heard the same survey that I've heard, that more marriages end in divorce due to finances than any other reason. I think it points to the heart of man. We never seem to be satisfied.

We tend to measure everything in our lives horizontally, meaning we compare ourselves to those around us. If they have more toys, than we want more toys, and the person with the most toys wins! Well I'm sorry to be the one to disappoint you but my experience in life and what I've seen first-hand in the lives of many friends and associates is, the one with the most toys usually loses, and sometimes they lose everything.

I know of destroyed marriages, drug addiction and even suicide that has been a direct result of having too much money. This verse captures well the true heart behind our wants and our needs.

The older I get and the more I look at the world around me, the more I realize how desperately we need to be about our Father's business. Time is short and if I'm too busy working harder and longer hours, I'll miss the divine opportunities God sends my way. Opportunities to invest my time and knowledge into the lives of others. What's the application for you and me? It's not about who has the most toys, but who has the most time.

Time is a far more precious commodity than silver, gold, houses or cars. Time to pour into those we come in contact with. Time to sit at God's feet in prayer and in His word. Time for spouses and children. Time for others. Now that's time well spent!

Think about these things – keep studying the Bible – and have a blessed day!

Today's devotional thought from Proverbs 21:24.

24 *The proud and arrogant man—"Mocker" is his name;*
he behaves with overweening pride.

What a great reminder we have in today's verse from Proverbs! That blessed reminder to not think too highly of ourselves. We've all known proud and arrogant people. We've all walked away from this type of person at a dinner party or at a business function wondering if they knew how obvious their disdain for others was. Some people simply think too highly of themselves. We need to exercise great wisdom when around this type of person, lest we enter into their condemning words for others.

I want to take a look at this verse from another perspective and it might hurt a bit as I've been guilty of this error in my own life. Here's what I'm talking about. Have you ever seen someone visit church that looks different than you? Perhaps they pull into the parking lot, get out of the car and take one last drag on a cigarette before stamping it out and coming into church. Your first thought is that they just littered the parking lot. Your second thought is that you don't want to end up sitting next to a person smelling of smoke. Or perhaps you see a woman walking into church and she's wearing something you deem inappropriate for church. Your first thought is that she should know better. Your second thought is that she's going to cause men to pay too much attention to her.

Now here's the part that might hurt. We're being proud and arrogant when we do this. Shouldn't our first thought be, "I'll bet he or she are visitors today. Perhaps they've never even been to a church before. Perhaps they have no idea that they are doing anything questionable, or anything that you have deemed wrong."

Churches are not country clubs for Christians but hospitals for sinners. Meaning people like me and you, and smokers and drinkers and people that curse and dress differently, men and women that are just living the only way they know how to live, which is just like we did before coming to faith in Christ. We should have our radar up for these very people. We should anticipate that they might be nervous or uncomfortable in church. We should be making a beeline to these individuals and welcoming them to church and asking if we can assist them, show them where the bathrooms are! Ask them if they want to sit with us and introduce them to our friends! And watch and see what God does in their lives. Wouldn't our churches be a warmer and safer place if people felt welcome there?

Think about these things – keep studying the Bible – and have a blessed day!

Proverbs 21 NOTES

Proverbs 21 NOTES

Proverbs 22

*P*roverbs 22 through 24 introduce us to 'Sayings of the wise' and 'Further sayings of the wise'. These separate and distinct thoughts can help us live a more godly life. These saying start at Verse 17 of Proverbs 22 and continue into chapter 24. Take your time when reading these three chapters. There is much to learn from the words written here. Take a moment to pray before you start reading, and ask God to open your heart and your mind to receive great wisdom from these three chapters.

Today's devotional thought from Proverbs 22:1.

1 A good name is more desirable than great riches;
  to be esteemed is better than silver or gold.

This verse offers us powerful teaching on so many levels. First, as I pondered this simple verse I was able to see that some of the men and women I respect the most in my life are not people of great wealth. And second is the awesome reminder that the more you and I are respected, the more we can influence others for Christ! Let's explore the first point about wealth. Someone can have great wealth and can also be a very well-liked and respected person. I'm just making the point that wealth is not what gains us respect. It's how we live our lives before God that dictates how well we're respected by men. To be well respected is something to be desired because of the opportunities it brings to influence others toward Christ. There's no reason to work for or strive for respect. It's something that should be a by-product of how we live our lives. How

I pray that others will see Christ in us. Not like an overcoat that we're wearing to look good to our fellow man but more importantly, to be well spoken of by others may actually cause someone to seek God, because of the testimony of our lives. Sadly, many are esteemed only because of their silver or gold. It's their wealth that gets them attention.

But Solomon reminds us that a good name is far more valuable than anything this world can provide you. Wealth can even bring everything but respect. Great wealth brings attention to the possessor. For the Christian, a good name brings glory to God! What's the application for me and you? Let Jesus be your model for life! In Luke 2:52 we learn that even at an early age Jesus increased in wisdom and stature and in favor with God and man. I want to be growing every day, in favor with God and man! Don't you? I want my life to count for eternity. Don't you? Silver and gold have their place but I don't know anyone that came to Christ because they were impressed with someone's wealth. Yet I know many people that have come to Christ through the quiet witness of a respectful spouse or a caring co-worker. How about you? Won't it be great if one day you stand before God and you find that you're surrounded by others in Heaven that are there because of the great testimony of a godly life lived for Him?

Think about these things – keep studying the Bible – and have a blessed day!

Today's devotional thought from Proverbs 22:3.

3 *A prudent man sees danger and takes refuge,*
but the simple keep going and suffer for it.

The Book of Proverbs offers several verses on this theme of a prudent person vs. a simple person, and the decision-making process for each of them. I've commented in the past that the only real way to be prepared for danger, especially the spiritual kind, is to be knowledgeable enough of God's word to be able to spot spiritual danger as soon as it is apparent. This requires being on your guard and making sure that you are wearing the armor of God outlined in Ephesians 6:10-17:

[10] Finally, be strong in the Lord and in his mighty power. [11] Put on the full armor of God, so that you can take your stand against the devil's schemes. [12] For our struggle is not against flesh and blood, but against the rulers, against the authorities, against the powers of this dark world and against the spiritual forces of evil in the heavenly realms. [13] Therefore put on the full armor of God, so that when the day of evil comes, you may be able to stand your ground, and after you have done

everything, to stand. [14] *Stand firm then, with the belt of truth buckled around your waist, with the breastplate of righteousness in place,* [15] *and with your feet fitted with the readiness that comes from the gospel of peace.* [16] *In addition to all this, take up the shield of faith, with which you can extinguish all the flaming arrows of the evil one.* [17] *Take the helmet of salvation and the sword of the Spirit, which is the word of God.*

The thought being expressed in the second part of today's verse regarding the simple person is that they see the same danger as the prudent man, except that they make a conscious decision to ignore the danger and they pay the price for their actions. When reading verses like this one, I like to recommend the classic book called Pilgrim's Progress by John Bunyan. It was written in the 1600's and it's as timely today as it was when originally penned. In this book the main character and his friends are routinely faced with danger. Their choices often dictate whether the danger lessens or increases. Several of the stories show very vividly how our choices affect the future. Christian, the main character in the story will decide to go in one direction and find safe passage and another character will choose the opposite direction and will meet their demise.

So what's the application for me and you? At the end of the day it always comes down to our faith and trust in God. Are we letting Him have complete control over our lives or are we determined to captain our own ship. I find myself choosing God's way more and more. I haven't always done this and sometimes I still find myself coaching God on how to handle certain situations. I foolishly think that I know more about what's best for my life than God does. I'm in awe over His patience and love in spite of my foolishness at times. So . . . when you and I find ourselves facing uncertainty we would be wise to seek God first! And more importantly, study His instruction book, the Bible before we're faced with a situation requiring wise choices. Put on the full armor of God each day! We'll never know the danger that we avoid because we were already prepared.

Think about these things – keep studying the Bible – and have a blessed day!

Today's devotional thought from Proverbs 22:6.

6 *Train a child in the way he should go,*
   and when he is old he will not turn from it.

Many parents cling to this verse as a guarantee when in fact this verse states a probability. My wife and I have prayed many times for our two children, and at the time of this publication, they are both what the church refers to as 'prodigals'. If you are so inclined, please word a prayer for our children. (Thanks!) This verse is both a problem and an opportunity.

The problem is simple, we can't claim godliness for our children. I wish we could! One doesn't become a Christian by being born into a Christian home. Christianity can't rub off on someone. Christianity can be observed, it can be explained, it can be viewed and it can be shared with others. The principles of Christianity can be taught, and we can tell others all about the object of our affection, which is our leader and Lord Jesus! There's a phrase you've likely heard and used yourselves that states that the ground is level at the cross. We all have to come to Jesus the same way, as sinners in desperate need of salvation.

Many parents, me included, have beaten themselves up over a prodigal. If only I had done this better or that better, or played more baseball or baked more cakes, read more books, prayed more! At the end of the day, our responsibility if we're a Christian is to seek the Lord, learn His plans and purposes and train our children accordingly. It is the child's choice at some point in their life to make Jesus their choice . . . or not! It's difficult to watch our children make poor choices, especially when we know that Jesus is the answer. But they have to want this for themselves.

Here's the opportunity! God knows! He never stops seeking our wayward children! He never stops seeking a more intimate relationship with any of us. My advice? Love your prodigals even when it's hard to do. Trust God. Cry out to Him to be the hound of heaven in the lives of your prodigals. The probability is still a good one, that one day everything you taught them will finally make sense and they too will turn their lives over to Jesus, making Him the center of their life.

For those who have children walking with the Lord, that have been spared a season of wandering in the wilderness, thank the Lord for that and pray for the prodigals of which you are aware. In the story of the prodigal son in Luke 15 we see a beautiful picture of God's tremendous love and patience. In this parable the father is God and the wayward son is me and you. The sinful living in the story represents all the sins you and I have ever committed. Here's the part of the story to cling to. Where do we see the father in this story? Waiting and watching! He is longing for the sons return, the same way God is longing for our prodigals to return! God is standing watch daily. He's not waiting to pound on our prodigals, but instead to clothe them in righteousness! What an awesome God we serve!

Let me close with this. If you've never cried out to Jesus. If you've never come to him as a sinner desperately in need of salvation, than why not cry out to him now. Confess you are a sinner in need of salvation. God's response? You were dead in your sin, but you will be alive again! You were lost but now you have been found.

What are you waiting for?

Think about these things – keep studying the Bible – and have a blessed day!

Today's devotional thought from Proverbs 22:10.

10 Drive out the mocker, and out goes strife;
quarrels and insults are ended.

I find it interesting that the word mocker, which means to ridicule, challenge or defy is used multiple times and almost exclusively in the Book or Proverbs and the Book of Psalms. There are quite a number of teachings or *'life lessons'* that can only be found in these two books of the Bible. Interestingly enough, the only other time mockers or the word mock is used in scripture is in the gospel accounts of what the soldiers did to Jesus before His crucifixion and then again in Isaiah 50, which is the prophetic passage that predicts that the mocking of Jesus would take place more than 500 years into the future. To mock or ridicule someone today is just as detestable as it was when the soldiers did it to Jesus.

It's not surprising to read here in Proverbs 22:10 that when you get rid of the mocker, then strife, quarrels and insults also go away. So what's the application for you and me? To mock or ridicule someone is going to cause great harm and will inevitably lead to larger and greater problems between individuals or groups.

One sad commentary on politics in America is the degree in which mocking and insults between candidates is so commonplace. There is no shortage of mocking and ridiculing that goes on. And just as this proverb suggests, quarrels, insults and strife end up pitting entire people-groups against each other.

I realize that the nature of political campaigns is going to cause this, but at the same time this verse is a great reminder that mocking someone is always wrong. If you look up mocker or mockery in a thesaurus you will find the word 'sarcasm' listed. Someone once said to me that sarcasm is

217

always wrong. I recall that I foolishly tried to defend the fact that sometimes it's okay to be sarcastic. Thank God I've gotten wiser with age! It's never okay to be sarcastic!

I've now come to the conclusion that there are certain traits or mannerisms that are always wrong and mocking, sarcasm and insults are among them. I can't for the life of me think of a scenario when mocking someone could be beneficial in a situation. I think the application is clear for us today. By eliminating mocking from your vocabulary, you can be fairly certain that there will be far less strife, fewer quarrels and fewer insults occurring in your life. As best I can tell, that's a good thing for everyone! If you're like me, and have used mocking or insults to try to control a conversation or show how clever you are, then take a moment now to ask God to forgive you, and ask Him to do 'heart surgery' on you so this kind of talk never leaves your lips. Honor God in this way and watch the good that begins to be evident in your relationships!

Think about these things – keep studying the Bible – and have a blessed day!

Today's devotional thought from Proverbs 22:13.

13 The sluggard says, "There is a lion outside!"
   or, "I will be murdered in the streets!"

Proverbs talks often about laziness. I've noted in the past that whenever scripture speaks multiple times on the same topic it's probably important enough to see how it applies to our lives today. We observe from this verse that it's the lazy sluggard that will use any excuse possible to avoid things he or she doesn't want to deal with. An example might be the person that can't keep a job, or has a job but never seems to advance up the ladder. They find too many excuses to stay home and miss work, hence they never get promoted.

This verse certainly applies to this type of lazy or underperforming worker but I think the application for us can and should be much greater. This verse can apply to many types of people and many circumstances. The man or woman that chooses to live with their significant other, often because they're simply too spiritually lazy to do the right and godly thing and get married, and instead turn their relationship into ungodly fornication. That's not my word but the Bibles! Or maybe it's the friend that won't risk a relationship to point out a character flaw that would actually be helpful for someone to know about.

The sluggard or lazy individual is the person that has an excuse for everything they do, or don't do! In this verse there is no lion outside. This is nothing more than a fabrication to avoid another action. It's no different than the person who refuses to call a family member to resolve a dispute because they rationalize that the family member won't appreciate the call. The truth is, one will never know without trying. Anything else is nothing more than a lazy attitude about things. This individual goes on to say that they can't go outside because they might be murdered in the streets. This is nothing more than spiritual and physical laziness. They no sooner believe there is a lion outside than to believe the moon is made of cheese.

So what's the application for you and me? Let's start with the fact that there is a lion outside, but only in a spiritual sense. One of his many names is Satan or the Devil.

1 Peter 5:8 states: *"Be alert and of sober mind. Your enemy the devil **prowls around** like a roaring lion looking for someone to devour."*

The devil would like nothing more than to murder you, physically or spiritually, making you ineffective for Kingdom work. The devil will do everything in his power to make you feel inferior, unloved and unwanted. This leaves you vulnerable to becoming a real life sluggard, someone that allows themselves to be defeated by the enemy and becomes too lazy to make a difference in their sphere of influence. Don't let this verse ever describe who you are. God has a wonderful plan for your life.

Matthew 6:33 states:

33 But seek first the kingdom of God and His righteousness, and all these things shall be added to you.

Don't be lazy about knowing God and his plans and purposes for your life!

Think about these things – keep studying the Bible – and have a blessed day!

Today's devotional thought from Proverbs 22:24-25.

*24 Do not make friends with a hot-tempered man,
do not associate with one easily angered,*

*25 or you may learn his ways
and get yourself ensnared.*

There are two thoughts being considered here. They are anger and our associations (who we spend our time with). There's obvious risk in having an angry person as a friend. The angry person has within them a character flaw that can come out at any time, usually when least expected. By nature, an angry person is, among other things, easily provoked, moody and one who can fly off the handle at any time. If you've made friends with this individual, it's inevitable that you are going to end up in the middle of one of their outbursts. The expression, "you're just asking for trouble" comes to mind. I'm not suggesting for a minute that you shouldn't pray for or even offer counsel to someone with an anger problem. But I am strongly urging caution in developing friendships with an angry person. Verse 25 cautions that it's easier than you think for this person's ways to rub off on you.

I remember when our daughter went off to college in North Carolina. We went down to see her in a play mid-way through her first semester. The first thing we noticed was how she had picked up a bit of a southern accent and she had picked up some phrases and mannerisms of her roommate as well. I remember thinking how easy it is to become more like those with whom we spend time with. It's a natural thing that occurs and I find no fault in it, unless of course it's a negative trait that is being rubbed off!

Who we associate with is important! I remember when my children were in their teen years and how my wife and I would caution them about their friendships. I would remind them that in all relationships, someone is doing the influencing. Anger in and of itself is a snare to all of us anyway. We're all prone to getting angry. We're impatient. We rarely give others the benefit of the doubt and if we're late and in traffic then every slow driver is our enemy. I could go on but I think you get the picture.

So what's the application for me and you? Let me ask, in your relationships, are you doing the influencing or are you the one being influenced? Do you spend time with one who is easily provoked? These verses are a good reminder to periodically review where and with whom we are investing our time.

Think about these things – keep studying the Bible – and have a blessed day!

Today's devotional thought from Proverbs 22:29.

29 *Do you see a man skilled in his work?*
He will serve before kings;
he will not serve before obscure men.

What would happen if you had a goal of being the best at what you do? This is a business and life principle more of us should take heed to. I always like reading the account of the building of the first temple by Solomon. There's a passage in 2 Chronicles 2 when the King of Tyre tells Solomon he's going to send a man by the name of Huram-Abi, a man of great skill, trained to work in gold, silver, bronze, iron, stone, wood and fine linen. He is skilled in all kinds of engraving and can execute any design given to him! Now that's a testimony of a man skilled at his work! So what would happen if you had a goal of being the best at what you do? First, you'd most likely never be out of work! Second, you'd most likely be paid at the higher end of the pay scale for what you do! And third, you'd set a standard for all others to follow.

And if you're a Christian, you'd be a powerful and living testimony of what it means to honor God in all your work. As Christians, we really should be the best employee or employer you can find. Too many times, I hear stories of Christian businesspeople that make an appointment at 9:00 am and show up at 9:30! Or say they'll finish a job by Tuesday and it eventually gets done . . . the following Tuesday! We can and should be better than this. We should be the best at what we do, and we should do it all with joy and integrity!

Brothers and sisters, we need to start each day with a good hearty meal, and I mean feeding on the Word of God. Just like the body needs physical nourishment, our souls need spiritual nourishment. We need to ask God to fill us afresh with His Holy Spirit. This will help us to 'stand out' from the crowd. Let me ask you this question? Do your neighbors, coworkers or customers know you're a Christian? Are you and I splashing Jesus everywhere we go? Do you see a person skilled in their work? I can think of no better testimony you can have! There's another Proverb; 24:30 that describes a businessperson that made no effort to be skilled at his work. He was a farmer and he allowed thorns to come up everywhere, and weeds to cover the ground. His business ended in poverty! All too often we blame our circumstances, or our boss, or coworkers, or the weather, or a bad economy for low pay or unemployment. Granted, these things can often be real factors but I still believe if we work hard and study hard, and developed our skills with our testimony in mind, we would have more job security and be a better Christian witness than the farmer that allows weeds to overtake his land.

Think about these things – keep studying the Bible – and have a blessed day!

Proverbs 22 NOTES

Proverbs 22 NOTES

Proverbs 23

*A*re you being blessed by reading through the Book of Proverbs? Are you spending time contemplating the wisdom written on these pages? Why not take a few minutes right now and consider rededicating your life to God! Renew your commitment to Him and watch what happens. Please be sure to journal your own thoughts as God reveals them to you. Happy reading!

Today's devotional thought from Proverbs 23:1-3.

1 *When you sit to dine with a ruler,*
   note well what is before you,

2 *and put a knife to your throat*
   if you are given to gluttony.

3 *Do not crave his delicacies,*
   for that food is deceptive.

The analogy before us in these verses centers on food. I often try to imagine what Solomon might have experienced just before writing this Proverb under the influence of the Holy Spirit. Perhaps he just completed a meal at the palace with some visiting dignitaries and noticed someone that ate or drank too much or just engaged in bad manners. The warning here has to do with luxury, excess and self-satisfaction. We see here someone that approaches life, not just the dinner table, with a focus on self. The life of the Christian should be 'others' centered, never self-centered. By nature we will always struggle with self-centeredness but we need to remind ourselves daily that for the Christian that has trusted in Christ, we have God's Spirit living within us. We have God's help available to us in all aspects of decision-making. We need only ask! We err when we insist on taking over the throne of our lives when in fact we should be welcoming God to have His rightful place in our lives. Yes, Philippians 4:13 states that: *we can do all things,* but it goes on to state; *through Christ who strengthens us.* Once again, we're reminded that it's not about us! From time-to-time I like to recommend a good book in addition to reading the Bible. If you've never read *The Calvary Road* by Roy Hession, I encourage you to get it. This small little paperback is one I've read four or five times, and I get something new from it each time I read it. Let me quote just one short passage just to give you a feel for this man's godly wisdom. Here goes:

"You see, the only life that pleases God and that can be victorious is His life – never our life, no matter how hard we try. But inasmuch as our self-centered life is the exact opposite of His, we can never be filled with His life unless we are prepared for God to bring our life constantly to death. And in that we must co-operate by our moral choices."

We learn here that how we react to external challenges and disappointments shows us if we are filled with Him or filled with ourselves! We need to restrain ourselves in regard to what we want and instead consider what God wants, for us. We quite literally need to guard ourselves against self-pleasing, be it in the form of food, riches, cars, houses or any other thing that competes for our time and talents, things that can be used more effectively for Kingdom work. At the end of our lives we will very likely regret the time we wasted on ourselves that could have been spent on others.

Think about these things – keep studying the Bible – and have a blessed day!

Today's devotional thought from Proverbs 23:4-5.

4 Do not wear yourself out to get rich;
*   have the wisdom to show restraint.*

5 Cast but a glance at riches, and they are gone,
*   for they will surely sprout wings*
*   and fly off to the sky like an eagle.*

I think people in general, and certainly Americans, spend far too much time thinking about money and finding ways to get more of it. People are literally wearing themselves out trying to get rich! Our desire for 'stuff' is very strong but attainment is often disappointing! Studies show a majority of Americans live way beyond their means. This is defined as spending more than one makes! This is accomplished through the excessive use of credit cards, equity loans or by refinancing their mortgages.

When there is a financial correction in the marketplace, which is normal, healthy and is a virtual guarantee every few years, the first people to get into trouble are those that are over-extended.

These verses also remind us that the future is uncertain. Who will care about their bank account when they find out a family member is diagnosed with cancer? What happens to the family that buys a plasma TV or a new barbeque set when they should have purchased health insurance?

To be sure, these verses are not saying that every creature comfort is wrong, but Verse 4 clearly states our need to exercise wisdom and to show restraint. There are very few people in this world that have everything they we want or need, and that's probably best.

1 Timothy 6, starting at Verse 3 and to the end of the letter, is loaded with practical counsel regarding riches, and provides a very healthy way to view money:

These are the things you are to teach and insist on. ³ If anyone teaches otherwise and does not agree to the sound instruction of our Lord Jesus Christ and to godly teaching, ⁴ they are conceited and understand nothing. They have an unhealthy interest in controversies and quarrels about words that result in envy, strife, malicious talk, evil suspicions ⁵ and constant friction between people of corrupt mind, who have been robbed of the truth and who think that godliness is a means to financial gain.

⁶ But godliness with contentment is great gain. ⁷ For we brought nothing into the world, and we can take nothing out of it. ⁸ But if we have food and clothing, we will be content with that. ⁹ Those who want to get rich fall into temptation and a trap and into many foolish and harmful desires that plunge people into ruin and destruction. ¹⁰ For the love of money is a root of all kinds of evil. Some people, eager for money, have wandered from the faith and pierced themselves with many griefs. ¹¹ But you, man of God, flee from all this, and pursue righteousness, godliness, faith, love, endurance and gentleness. ¹² Fight the good fight of the faith. Take hold of the eternal life to which you were called when you made your good confession in the presence of many witnesses. ¹³ In the sight of God, who gives life to everything, and of Christ Jesus, who while testifying before Pontius Pilate made the good confession, I charge you ¹⁴ to keep this command without spot or blame until the appearing of our Lord Jesus Christ, [15] which God will bring about in his own time—God, the blessed and only Ruler, the King of kings and Lord of lords, [16] who alone is immortal and who lives in unapproachable light, whom no one has seen or can see. To him be honor and might forever. Amen.

[17] *Command those who are rich in this present world not to be arrogant nor to put their hope in wealth, which is so uncertain, but to put their hope in God, who richly provides us with everything for our enjoyment. [18] Command them to do good, to be rich in good deeds, and to be generous and willing to share. [19] In this way they will lay up treasure for themselves as a firm foundation for the coming age, so that they may take hold of the life that is truly life.*

[20] *Timothy, guard what has been entrusted to your care. Turn away from godless chatter and the opposing ideas of what is falsely called knowledge, [21] which some have professed and in so doing have departed from the faith.*

Grace be with you all.

The best advice I ever received when I was just a young Christian was the principle of giving away 10% of my income, saving 10% and living on the remaining 80%. These percentages can be adjusted to fit your personal circumstances but the principal will keep you living on less than you earn and this will always have great long-term results. Pray about these matters and examine your spending habits. Are you spending far too much time chasing riches? If riches were the answer to all our problems, I don't think we would hear so many stories of the rich and famous going in and out of rehab clinics, divorcing or committing suicide!

Think about these things – keep studying the Bible – and have a blessed day!

Today's devotional thought from Proverbs 23:9.

9 *Do not speak to a fool,*
*   for he will scorn the wisdom of your words.*

Everyone is worthy of our time and attention. Everyone we come in contact with could be a divine appointment from God and an opportunity to tell someone about Him! Having said that, keep in mind that there will always be people that will scorn anything you have to say. Regardless of how meaningful, wise or well-intentioned your words, some people are pre-determined, due to their own foolishness, to be unwilling to receive any counsel you offer them. We learn from this verse that there are definitely times when we're actually better off not speaking, then to waste our time on foolish men or women that are predetermined to not hear whatever we have to say.

Some people can't sense good and godly counsel even if they tripped over it. Their lives leave a trail of poor choices and damaged relationships because they refuse sound counsel. You may recall from previous devotionals that the biblical definition of a fool is a person that believes there is no God! That's a sad thought for those of us that know God and know He is the answer to this world's problems. So what's the application for you and me? I think it's for us to realize that there are times when enough is enough. The advice Solomon gives us here is for our own good. All too often it's the people we know or love the most, those that we have counseled and advised over and over that scorn godly advice and leave a trail of poor choices and failures.

God is telling us through this verse that it's okay to stop trying to convince someone beyond their ability to see the good we are trying to pass on. There are people that God brings into our path all the time! For every fool there's a thirsty soul longing for the living water that is available through our Lord and Savior Jesus. Take time today to pray that God will bring someone into your path this very day that needs to hear about the hope that is within you. God is faithful to answer that prayer and provide you with a glorious opportunity to tell someone about our wonderful Savior.

Think about these things – keep studying the Bible – and have a blessed day!

Today's devotional thought from Proverbs 23:12.

12 *Apply your heart to instruction*
   and your ears to words of knowledge.

There are two mistakes a Christian is prone to make. The first is to underestimate the power of God in their life and the second is when that same person neglects to apply the Word of God to their daily life. This verse speaks to these two critical points.

Our hearts represent our life. Without a heart we can't live, so the word '*heart*' in this verse would represent the Christian's whole self. Their heart, soul, mind and strength. We are to apply everything in our lives to what the Bible has to say. The Bible is God's instruction book for how we are to live our lives. Everything you and I need to know about life can be found in the Bible. Do you need help in your marriage? The Bible speaks to this topic. Do you need help raising children? The Bible speaks to this topic, too. Do you need help running your business? Yes, the Bible has something to say about this, too! Need help with how to be a good employee or employer? Need financial wisdom? Need wiser decision-making? Yep! The Bible speaks to all these issues . . . and more! There isn't a single topic I could list here that I couldn't find a chapter and verse in the Bible to help me in that area of my life. That's why I encourage you to make the Bible your life book. Read it. Study it. Apply it!

The Bible really is our instruction manual for life, and much more! The author is also our Savior! And the Holy Spirit helps us interpret and apply all these principles to our daily lives. The Bible is quite literally alive in our hearts!

So what's the application for me and you? I'm reminded of the practical advice given to me over the years about the importance of learning and application. It's not enough to just know something intellectually. We err when we learn but never apply what we've learned. An example might be the person that is praying fervently for a job but never takes the step of filling out a job application. This verse reminds us that our heart and our minds need to be fully engaged in our walk with the Lord. What we hear and are taught needs to get filtered through our minds but then it needs to make that eighteen inch journey from our head to our heart! The heart applies the instruction when the instruction is applied to the heart! But it doesn't stop there. We need to put feet to our prayers. God doesn't want us to just pray. He wants us to pray and then take action on our prayer. This is what God is waiting for. For the person praying for a job; start with prayer, then put together an amazing resume. Then post your resume on job boards. Go on interviews. Get better and better at interviewing. Now, watch what God does because you have taken action steps to find a job! Apply this same principle to every aspect of your life. God is waiting patiently for you to seek Him with all your heart, soul, mind and strength!

Think about these things – keep studying the Bible – and have a blessed day!

Today's devotional thought from Proverbs 23:17-18.

17 *Do not let your heart envy sinners,*
but always be zealous for the fear of the LORD.

18 *There is surely a future hope for you,*
and your hope will not be cut off.

I have to confess that in years past I enjoyed watching a program on TV called *"Lifestyles of the Rich & Famous"*. I would look at the homes and the gardens and the cars and I would listen intently to how the people being featured would jet-set all over the world with paparazzi and their cameras flashing wherever they went. And I couldn't help imagining myself as the famous and wealthy person being featured. It's only natural to be curious about the rich and famous.

But it's never more than a few weeks before reading the paper or watching the news, that the headline that day is about another rich and famous person that is getting divorced, losing custody of their children, getting arrested for drunk driving or worse, dying due to a drug overdose or suicide. Tragic! What point am I trying make? We tend to envy others that seem to have every wonderful treasure this world can offer. The only question for me and you is whether or not we can have all these things and still be zealous for the Lord?

For some the answer may be yes! For most, these things would become stumbling blocks or distractions that would keep us from being fully devoted followers of Christ.

The word envy means:

A feeling of discontent or covetousness with regard to another's advantages, success or possessions.

The 10th Commandment tells us that we shouldn't covet, so we know it's wrong, but we also know we are prone to covet. The only advice I can offer is what I find in Verse 18, that my future and my hope can only be found in the Lord. The more I stay focused on God and others, the less likely I am to be thinking about me!

I like what the Apostle Peter tells us in 1 Peter 4:8-11:

[8] Above all, love each other deeply, because love covers over a multitude of sins. [9] Offer hospitality to one another without grumbling. [10] Each one should use whatever gift he has received to serve others, faithfully administering God's grace in its various forms. [11] If anyone speaks, he should do it as one speaking the very words of God. If anyone serves, he should do it with the strength God provides, so that in all things God may be praised through Jesus Christ. To him be the glory and the power for ever and ever. Amen.

I want to be fully devoted to God and I want to be others-minded! When we view life horizontally, comparing ourselves to others, we will always get in trouble. When we view life vertically, meaning we are looking to God for our sufficiency, we will be far more likely to keep our lives and our priorities in proper order!

Think about these things – keep studying the Bible – and have a blessed day!

Today's devotional thought from Proverbs 23:23.

23 *Buy the truth and do not sell it;*
get wisdom, discipline and understanding.

Here's a very compelling verse for us to ponder today. What is meant by this thought of *buying the truth*? It's an interesting choice of words.

Truth is the principle that our hearts must be guided by. Truth is what keeps back sin. The more we know and understand God's Word, the more equipped we become to protect ourselves from all the flaming arrows of the evil one described in Ephesians 6:6:

⁶ *In addition to all this, take up the shield of faith, with which you can extinguish all the flaming arrows of the evil one.*

Here's the thought being conveyed here. We can't buy it, yet we must be willing to part with anything and everything to get it! We must be willing to pay any price for what is available for free! So what is the price? We must be willing to put aside the things that keep us from gaining it. We must be willing to carve out time for gaining wisdom, discipline and understanding. We can't buy it, yet we must be willing to pay any price to get it. Listen to what Isaiah says in chapter 55:1-3:

1 *"Come, all you who are thirsty,*
come to the waters;
and you who have no money,
come, buy and eat!
Come, buy wine and milk
without money and without cost.

2 *Why spend money on what is not bread,*
and your labor on what does not satisfy?
Listen, listen to me, and eat what is good,
and your soul will delight in the richest of fare.

³ *Give ear and come to me;*
hear me that your soul may live.

We need to see God's Word as the only thing that can satisfy our hunger and thirst for right living. I think it's interesting that Solomon, the richest man that ever lived, would use an analogy of buying something that we can't actually buy, but once gained, we would not sell for any price! Brothers and sisters, we need to develop a discipline of studying God's word daily. When we understand something we read it helps us distinguish between truth and error. In a sense, we buy it. When we hear a spiritual application that helps us in our walk with Christ, we buy it! When we see an opportunity to tell someone about Jesus . . . we buy it!

Friend, God has a wonderful plan for your life. He loves you! He loves you so much that He sent His Son to die on the cross for your sins. 1 Corinthians 6:20 reminds us that:

20 you were bought at a price. Therefore honor God with your bodies.

So, our Proverb for today tells us to seek truth! Don't part with it for pleasures, fame, honor or riches in this world. Never let go and never give up!

Think about these things – keep studying the Bible – and have a blessed day!

Today's devotional thought from Proverbs 23:30-32.

30 Those who linger over wine,
who go to sample bowls of mixed wine.

31 Do not gaze at wine when it is red,
when it sparkles in the cup,
when it goes down smoothly!

32 In the end it bites like a snake
and poisons like a viper.

There are as many opinions on the topic of alcohol as there are brands of the same. Verses like those found here are so easy to misunderstand, or at least misunderstand the underlying meaning. Let me start by saying that I believe Solomon is simply speaking plain talk here. He's not saying that a glass of wine is wrong or sinful but he is saying that much trouble can come from indulging in routine consumption of too much wine, or any fermented beverage.

Here's the problem with an opinion on verses like these. For the person that believes wine should never touch the lips of a believer reads too much into these verses and the person that thinks there is nothing wrong with regularly consuming wine or alcohol reads too little into these verses.

We often miss the broader application of these verses, that of self-denial of things that can cause a brother to stumble or the idea of avoiding excesses in life, whatever they may be. Speaking personally, Ben & Jerry's ice cream can be far more sinful in my life than wine would ever be. My point is this, wine may or may not be a stumbling block for you, but there are other stumbling blocks in your life and mine that we would be wise to avoid.

These verses and others like them should be viewed as big red danger flags in our lives. Your excess may be work, sports, alcohol or whatever else it is that causes excess or over-indulgence, often to the detriment of something else more wholesome or worthwhile in your life.

So what's the application for you and me? I like what is stated in Philippians 4:8:

8 Finally, brothers, whatever is true, whatever is noble, whatever is right, whatever is pure, whatever is lovely, whatever is admirable—if anything is excellent or praiseworthy—think about such things.

Let's not get hung up on the do's and don'ts in our Christian life. Let's focus instead on what is pure, what is lovely, what is admirable, the things that we can be doing with and through our lives that can have an eternal impact on others!

Think about these things – keep studying the Bible – and have a blessed day!

Proverbs 23 NOTES

Proverbs 23 NOTES

Proverbs 24

I really love Proverbs 24. I've written seven devotionals from this very rich chapter that is loaded with practical thoughts that will help you live a godly life. Don't forget to write down your own thoughts on the blank pages at the end of this chapter.

Today's devotional thought from Proverbs 24:3-4.

3 By wisdom a house is built,
and through understanding it is established;

4 through knowledge its rooms are filled
with rare and beautiful treasures.

Here we see Solomon using a physical structure to express a spiritual principle. We know that a home is more than the brick and mortar that holds it together. And we know that the real treasures that occupy the rooms of our homes are not the lamps and chairs and wall hangings but the memories, the special events, the birthday parties and the precious time spent with those we love. But even more than this are the things that will last for eternity; the things done for God. You and I will only be fully used by God when we come to understand that most of what we pursue in this life is temporary and empty and really nothing more than a distraction. If you ponder this thought I think you'll agree that what will really make our memories great memories will be the ones we spent serving others.

I recently heard a pastor give a great teaching from the Bible on the word 'servant'. It seems Bible translators starting from around the 1600s all the way to modern times have done a poor job in translating this word. The actual meaning of 'servant' or 'bond servant' is slave. This causes us to dramatically reread what it means to be a 'servant' of Christ. Or when in Matthew 6:24 Jesus says: *"No one can serve two masters,"* - we begin to better understand this verse. Basically, it's saying we can't be a slave to two people. A slave is owned. A slave is totally subject to his master, therefore he or she can only be owned by one person.

So, back to the verse for today and the application for me and you. Are we building our house and collecting treasures for ourselves? Or are we dying to ourselves and living for Christ? Are we subjecting our wills for His 'perfect' will for our lives? I don't say these words lightly. I realize it's not easy to do this but I also realize that it's the ultimate answer to a fruitful life in Christ. The more we strive with our Maker over our own desires the more we miss out on God's better plan. Why not join me today and present ourselves as a living sacrifice to God, and see how He uses us? Listen to the words of the Apostle Paul in Romans 12:1-2:

[1] Therefore, I urge you, brothers, in view of God's mercy, to offer your bodies as living sacrifices, holy and pleasing to God—this is your spiritual act of worship. [2] Do not conform any longer to the pattern of this world, but be transformed by the renewing of your mind. Then you will be able to test and approve what God's will is—his good, pleasing and perfect will.

Now that sounds like a house built on a solid foundation!

Think about these things – keep studying the Bible – and have a blessed day!

Today's devotional thought from Proverbs 24:10.

*10 If you falter in times of trouble,
        how small is your strength!*

I'm writing this devotional at a time of great economic and political turmoil in our nation. I will be the first to confess that I've been spending far too much time watching the news and wondering and worrying about the future.

This verse was a startling reminder that I'm exercising a very weak faith when I allow myself to falter in times of trouble. I was challenged this week in my own heart to make sure that I don't allow these global distractions to overshadow the importance of keeping the main thing the main thing. For the Christian, that's living our lives as an example to others, and seeking opportunities to tell others about Jesus.

Think about the fact that it's during periods of great turmoil that people will be more open to look beyond themselves for help in these uncertain times. This is a season of opportunity to tell others of the hope that is within us. I don't want to sound like everyone else when I'm asked my thoughts on tough economic times. I believe this is when Christians are being watched more carefully by others. Are we miserable and complaining like everyone else or are we confident that God is in control and nothing catches Him off guard. Many people outside of faith in Christ are insecure, worried and in many cases are quite miserable. They are looking for hope, and the Christian should be the most hopeful people out there!

I need to put my eyes squarely back on God where they belong! The next time I'm asked to comment on the economic or political future I'm going to try to turn the conversation in a spiritual direction.

So what's your greatest need right now? Do you need someone to stand in the gap? Jesus is your Mediator! Are you hungry? He's the Bread of Life! Are you troubled? He's your Counselor! Are these dark times overwhelming you? He's the Light of the World! Are you in need of security and protection? He's the Good Shepherd! Do you need help? Jesus is your helper. If you've already trusted in Him for your salvation, then you're His! He will never leave you or forsake you. If you're not His, if you've never put your faith and trust in Jesus Christ alone for your salvation, then do it now.

Confess you're a sinner . . . and repent!

1 John 1:9 assures us:

[9] *If we confess our sins, he is faithful and just and will forgive us our sins and purify us from all unrighteousness.*

Think about these things – keep studying the Bible – and have a blessed day!

Today's devotional thought from Proverbs 24:13-14.

13 *Eat honey, my son, for it is good;*
   honey from the comb is sweet to your taste.

14 *Know also that wisdom is sweet to your soul;*
   if you find it, there is a future hope for you,
   and your hope will not be cut off.

I love the way Solomon uses the things around him as teaching tools. We know that from the time leading up to the nation of Israel entering the Promised Land that the country flowed with milk and honey. Honey was a common and inexpensive food. Solomon was likely watching his son eat some honey when God inspired him to write this proverb. Honey is sweet to the taste and therefore enjoyable.

Wisdom is like honey in that it is sweet to the soul and we should want to feed on it all the more. Honey is sweet, but wisdom, truth and godliness are even sweeter! Honey satisfies for the moment, but wisdom has a present *and* future value. Wisdom is spiritual nourishment that can last a lifetime!

We have much we can learn from the Book of Proverbs. Practical truths that serve as a light on our path in this dark world. I think it's worth noting that Solomon talks of a future hope for those that seek wisdom. You see, we'll never fully understand the great value of spending time each morning reading our Bibles, praying and seeking wisdom and knowledge. What new or better decisions might we make as a direct result of our study? What dangers and snares might we avoid as a direct result of our study? We may never know how often that time of study and humility before God has spared us from a temptation that would have ruined a weaker believer. We'll never fully understand how a seemingly insignificant conversation with a friend or coworker can ultimately lead them to a decision to accept Jesus as their Lord and Savior, simply because we shared a little bit of wisdom that we didn't even know we had because of faithful time spent learning and growing in Christ.

I think this is what Solomon means when he speaks of the future benefits of gaining wisdom. Have you ever walked away from a conversation and said to yourself *"where in the world did what I just said come from?"* I'm talking about times when you share a bit of godly counsel that you didn't even know you possessed! When you quote scripture you didn't even know you knew! This is why wisdom is sweet to your soul. I recently had a conversation with a man who had just started coming to church. A man very new in the Lord. We spoke for only a few minutes and off we went. Two weeks later I saw him again and he proceeded to tell me that our conversation had a profound impact on him and that he made several significant changes in his life. He wrote a letter to a friend to confess a wrong he had done and on and on he went about the value of our conversation. I could barely recall the conversation and I didn't think it was all that significant, yet it certainly was to him!

This just means that our time with the Lord each morning can have lasting value even if we don't realize it at the time. So the next time you feel like skipping devotions and prayer time, don't! Someone next week, next month or next year needs to hear what you're learning.

Think about these things – keep studying the Bible – and have a blessed day!

Today's devotional thought from Proverbs 24:16.

16 *for though a righteous man falls seven times, he rises again,*
  but the wicked are brought down by calamity.

I have always found great encouragement in this proverb. The righteous man stated here can be me and you! The righteous man or woman is the person that when they fall, quickly come back to God with a repentant heart, seeking His forgiveness. And God in turn, through His infinite mercy and grace, grants us forgiveness and restoration. It's this aspect of restoration that I want to speak about today.

We have an absolute assurance from God's word, the Bible. We serve a God of the second chance! And in this reference to falling seven times, we should read seven to mean infinite. God knows our hearts. He knows if we're sincere and He longs to see a fallen man restored.

The problem as I see it is more man's problem. Are we as willing to grant the same second chance to the man or woman who has sinned us? The church can be a difficult place for the repentant sinner. God forgets our sin as far as the east is from the west, but man seems to have a very long memory for another person's sin. I need to remind myself that "but by the grace of God go I", meaning that today it's the other guy that falls, but tomorrow it can be you or me!

It should be our desire to welcome a sincerely repentant sinner back into fellowship. Luke 15:10 reminds us that "the angels in Heaven rejoice over a sinner who repents." I've never read this to just mean when someone prays to receive Christ for the first time. I believe Heaven rejoices every time a believer falls, sincerely confesses, and seeks sincere forgiveness.

I realize some readers of this devotional may be believers in Christ that have walked away from the local church because of a particular sin, perhaps a very public one, that has them feeling they are no longer welcome. That may have actually happened to you but it doesn't make it right. The church is made up of fallen men and women and we are prone to handle things poorly. There are churches that would welcome you back.

So this verse is a good reminder to us that all are sinners *and* saints at different times as we walk through this period of life we call sanctification. I'm asking you to err on the side of grace with those around us. Tomorrow it might be you that is needing that very same grace!

Think about these things – keep studying the Bible – and have a blessed day!

Today's devotional thought from Proverbs 24:21-22.

21 *Fear the LORD and the king, my son,*
  and do not join with the rebellious,

22 *for those two will send sudden destruction upon them,*
  and who knows what calamities they can bring?

Devotion to God and loyalty to those that govern us really do go hand-in-hand. We can't have one without the other and still be honoring our faith commitment. Now this statement presupposes that government doesn't ask you to compromise your faith. At the end of the day we must obey God rather than men. Let's focus for a moment on fearing God.

If you're a Christian then think about what God has done for you! Listen to how it's stated in Micah 7:18-19:

18 *Who is a God like you,*
  who pardons sin and forgives the transgression
  of the remnant of his inheritance?
  You do not stay angry forever
  but delight to show mercy.

19 You will again have compassion on us;
    you will tread our sins underfoot
    and hurl all our iniquities into the depths of the sea.

Think about these points: God forgives us! He doesn't stay angry! He is merciful! He is compassionate! Through Jesus and His sacrificial death on the cross we have been given eternal life, if we've trusted in Him. If you're reading this and haven't cried out to Jesus for salvation, why not do so today? The second part of Verse 21 goes on to state that we should avoid associations with rebellious individuals. This means any individual or group that lives their lives contrary to the teachings of the Bible.

There's always room for voicing dissatisfaction with positions and policies of our leaders. We should stay active and aware of laws and positions that are in direct contradiction to godly principles and there is ample room for voicing our discontent. I think the application for me and you is to honor God and Honor our leaders. We should pray for them and ask God to guide our lives in such a way that we are a sweet fragrance to those we express differing views with. We should pray for our leaders and we should unhesitatingly voice our concerns if we see our leaders moving in a direction that is in opposition to our Christian worldview.

The two words that describe too many Christians when it comes to faith and politics are: ignorance and apathy, which can be defined as: *"I don't know and I don't care."* Ignorance and apathy should have no place in the life of a Christian. There's another verse in Micah that I'll end with, that captures this thought:

8 He has showed you, O man, what is good.
    And what does the LORD require of you?
    To act justly and to love mercy
    and to walk humbly with your God.

I recommend you and I make this our motto for life!

Think about these things – keep studying the Bible – and have a blessed day!

Today's devotional thought from Proverbs 24:27.

27 Finish your outdoor work
    and get your fields ready;
    after that, build your house.

Here's a practical bit of advice that we should all think about more than we do. The basic idea is that of proper planning. For those of us that like to shoot from the hip this verse has some challenges. Shooting from the hip is an expression that grew out of the days of the old west when men carried guns. Picture Clint Eastwood in one of those old westerns. When someone would shoot from the hip, they would draw their gun and shoot before ever lifting their arm all the way up, hence they got the shot off faster. The risk of course, was that accuracy could be lost in the haste of getting off a quick shot.

When we use the term these days it usually means dealing with things as they come up. There are times when shooting from the hip is necessary but I think this verse challenges us to be better at proper planning in all aspects of our lives.

The analogy used in Verse 27 is an agricultural one. The thought expressed is to make sure your fields are cultivated and your crops are planted before you build your house. Without food and the income from the harvest, a home is of no value.

The principle goes much further though. Here we see the importance of forethought in all of our decision making. It's too easy to shoot from the hip with regard to important circumstances in life. People often make significant purchases without any forethought. I know couples that have admitted to getting married and starting families with less thought than they used to plan a vacation.

Solomon offers us this little reminder to think before we act. Are you seeking God first, before going forward with major decisions? Or are you making decisions and then asking God to fix the mess you've made? Here's an even bigger question. Do your plans start with Kingdom purposes in mind? Problems start with a poor foundation. Our very decision-making process all too often puts God's plan and purpose for our lives as an afterthought. Matthew 6:19 offers us a great reminder to make sure we are laying up treasures in Heaven rather than on earth:

19 "Do not lay up for yourselves treasures on earth, where moth and rust destroy and where thieves break in and steal;

What a healthy reminder for me and you, the concept of making sure our plans have been bathed in prayer and wise counsel before we make a decision. I can almost guarantee you that you'll look back on your decisions and see God's guiding hand keeping you from a laundry list of poor decisions.

Think about these things – keep studying the Bible – and have a blessed day!

Today's devotional thought from Proverbs 24:30-34.

30 *I went past the field of the sluggard,*
   past the vineyard of the man who lacks judgment;

31 *thorns had come up everywhere,*
   the ground was covered with weeds,
   and the stone wall was in ruins.

32 *I applied my heart to what I observed*
   and learned a lesson from what I saw:

33 *A little sleep, a little slumber,*
   a little folding of the hands to rest-

34 *and poverty will come on you like a bandit*
   and scarcity like an armed man.

This topic is one that is fairly common in Proverbs and that's the subject of laziness or slothfulness. I always try to imagine myself sitting in a corner of Solomon's court listening in on some of the problems and situations that are brought before him to settle. His writings in Proverbs later in his life were clearly designed to help others avoid similar pitfalls he found so many falling into.

Based on today's verses, Solomon must have heard many sad stories that were a direct result of laziness or an unwillingness to learn from others and avoid disaster.

Verses 30-34 have great application for us today. Solomon uses an agricultural analogy; *a field that has been neglected, thorns everywhere, the ground covered with weeds and stone walls in ruins.* A more modern day analogy might be; *the restaurant parking lot needed to be repaved, the floor was filthy, the food was brought out on dirty dishes and the dessert case had duct tape covering a large crack in the glass!* This restaurant example is actually a true story. I knew the owner! He was always complaining about why business wasn't better than it was. I pointed out some of the problems I saw, but he made no effort to correct them.

The point I'm making here is that this proverb could easily describe many modern day business failures or someone's home that has been allowed to fall into disrepair, all as a result of laziness and poor judgment. I've seen many situations like the one I described and sadly the individuals involved never understood why things failed! So what's the application for us today? Do what Solomon did. He applied his heart to what he observed, he learned a lesson from what he saw! Life presents many opportunities for us to learn and grow, even from other people's mistakes and especially from our own.

And what is that lesson?

33 A little sleep, a little slumber,
*   a little folding of the hands to rest-*

34 and poverty will come on you like a bandit

This describes the dangers of a lazy attitude about our relationship with God. Do we choose a nap or TV over time alone with God? That's what the sluggard does! Do we find ourselves too busy with work or recreation to invest in church or Bible study? That's poor judgment! The advice is clear and it's here for us to read and learn and grow from, so we can see the problem before it happens.

This is where ears to hear and eyes to see comes into play. Are we teachable? Do we have spiritual receptivity? Or are we doomed to repeat the same failures over and over? I hope not! We need to apply what we learn from Proverbs, and then pass it on to others so they too can avoid these same pitfalls. That's what Solomon did by writing this!

Think about these things – keep studying the Bible – and have a blessed day!

Proverbs 24 NOTES

Proverbs 24 NOTES

Proverbs 25

*J*like chapter 25! Most of the 28 thoughts written in this chapter start with the words "Like" "Like apples of gold . . . Like an earring of Gold . . . Like a snow-cooled drink . . . Like clouds and wind!" These are just a few of the many thoughts that start this way. I'm confident you are really going to like this chapter!

Today's devotional thought from Proverbs 25:11.

11 Like apples of gold in settings of silver
*   is a ruling rightly given.*

I love this simple, yet profound verse! Wise, thoughtful and timely words. What we say and when we say it and how we say it is a lifelong study! Our words can help and heal or they can hurt and scar. I want to talk more about this in a moment, but I think it important to state that you and I desperately need our hearts yielded to God's Spirit when it comes to our words. I've learned too often the hard way, that what I say to people, especially those close to me, has a lasting impact. If you remember nothing else from today's devotional, please remember this. Don't ever go into an important discussion without prayer. Don't do it when rushed or tired, either. Words can't be taken back so choose them wisely.

But let me shift to the positive side of our words! This verse tells us that a word aptly spoken is like apples of gold in settings of silver. Now that sounds real nice to me! Our words can be such a source of encouragement to others. In Ecclesiastes 9 and 10 Solomon goes on to say that our words should be quiet, calming . . . and gracious! I've heard it said that a word of praise or encouragement has to be spoken 10 times to have the same weight as one criticism. The point is this. People may need to hear correction but they need to hear gracious words as well. I try to look for opportunities to speak a gracious word to people. Most of us don't hear them enough. I've had countless opportunities to share Jesus with strangers simply by starting the conversation with a gracious word.

My wife and I recently had a meal at a restaurant where we went out of our way to encourage an otherwise frazzled waitress. When we left our tip we also left a Bible tract that stated that she was someone special. She followed us outside and down the sidewalk to tell us that the tract meant the world to her and was more important to her that night then all of her tips. What am I trying to say? Err on the side of graciousness even in those conversations that require correction or discipline. A word aptly spoken sounds nice all by itself! I know we know this already but I need the reminder and I think it might be one of the reasons Solomon repeats himself on this topic because we have a tendency to forget these simple truths. That's why I regularly encourage those I meet to make a habit of reading a chapter of Proverbs every day! Routinely reading Proverbs has helped even a thick-headed individual like me in these areas of practical daily living. In closing, I want to remind you of a few words spoken by Jesus that at the end of our lives will mean more to us than any other words ever spoken. Here they are: *"Well done thou good and faithful servant!"* Matthew 25:21

Think about these things – keep studying the Bible – and have a blessed day!

Today's devotional thought from Proverbs 25:13.

13 *Like the coolness of snow at harvest time*
is a trustworthy messenger to those who send him;
he refreshes the spirit of his masters.

What a truly great proverb! And what a great message of encouragement we will find as we dig down just a little deeper into this verse. Like me, I'm sure you've experienced a cool rain after an extremely hot day or maybe you've stopped along the road and treated yourself to a refreshing Italian Ice on a hot summer day. If this thought puts a smile on your face, then you can get a sense of the smile we put on God's face when we boldly proclaim our faith in Him to those we meet along life's journey. Are you bringing the good news of Jesus Christ to those He puts in your path? This verse says that a trustworthy messenger refreshes the spirit of his master. The master is God and we are His messengers. There is no greater joy we can bring to our Heavenly Father than to tell others about Him!

Read the words of the Apostle Paul in 2 Corinthians 2:14-15:

[14] But thanks be to God, who always leads us in triumphal procession in Christ and through us spreads everywhere the fragrance of the knowledge of him. [15]For we are to God the aroma of Christ among those who are being saved and those who are perishing."

We learn from these verses that God orchestrates opportunities for us to tell others about Himself! We just need to be a faithful and pleasing aroma. I've stated in the past that I believe God arranges divine opportunities to tell others about Him all the time. The only problem is, we don't always pay attention to them. We rationalize that it's not the right time or the right place or the right person.

I want to encourage you to keep these opportunities front of mind. We err by not taking advantage of them. Friend, if He's our Master then we are His slaves. When He commissions us we had better be ready. There really is no greater joy than to see someone respond to God in prayer, accepting Jesus as their Lord and Savior!

A friend of mine is a well-known pastor from Atlanta by the name of Dr. Michael Youssef. He shares a humorous story in his book titled, *"You Want Me to Do What?"* There was a man who was under the conviction of the Holy Spirit. He felt God wanted him to witness to others about Jesus Christ. But he always seemed to have plenty of excuses for not doing it. Every time God gave him an opportunity to witness, he'd say, 'Lord, is this really the right time? Is this really the right person?' And he would procrastinate until the opportunity was lost. One day he boarded an empty bus. An EMPTY bus! He went past the driver and took the very last seat in the very last row of seats. At the next stop, one lone man boards the bus. He scans the empty rows of seats and proceeds to walk to the back of the bus and takes a seat next to the Christian man. Remember, there is not another soul on the bus! This new rider then turns to the Christian man and says: *"Please mister, my life is a mess. I'm desperate. I want to know Jesus. Can you please tell me how I can be saved?"* The Christian man looked out the window and prayed, *"Lord, is this really the right time?"* The Christian man was obviously insecure about sharing his faith. But the divine opportunity could not have been any clearer! If a similar scenario presents itself, I say go for it! You will be glad you did. If God commissions us, then I assure you, it's the right time!

Think about these things – keep studying the Bible – and have a blessed day!

Today's devotional thought from Proverbs 25:14.

14 *Like clouds and wind without rain*
   is a man who boasts of gifts he does not give.

If you're a farmer, the worst thing that could happen to you is to not have enough water for your crops. Think of how disappointing it would be to look up into the sky and see the signs of rain: clouds, darkness and wind, (only to see not a drop of rainfall!) This verse shows us how empty words are the same as empty clouds! I'll give a few examples to help you see the point I'm trying to make here.

This is something that I've been guilty of doing myself and I think it's a blind spot for many of us, this idea of saying things that we really have no intention of doing. What am I talking about? Simple things, like:

I'll call you later!

We want to have you over!

Let's get together for dinner soon!

We really need to get together!

I'll get back to you tomorrow!

Ouch! I probably hit a nerve with some of you on this one! Well, I've already confessed to doing this myself but studying this verse has caused me to consider the impact of these empty promises in a new light. In the time period that this proverb was written, the lack of rain to a farmer could mean a death sentence. Their crops were their livelihood. To see all the signs of rain and then not get a drop is heartbreaking.

This puts into perspective the disappointment and heartache we can cause when we say we're going to do something and then we never do it! What's the application for me and you? I think we just need to be careful about things we say, promises we make, gifts or assistance we offer and then make no effort to actually accomplish what we said we would do! Something as simple as saying we're going to call someone later raises an expectation that, when left unmet, causes disappointment. Be a person of integrity. It would be better not to promise a return phone call, but you make it anyway. It would be better to never mention you want to have someone over to your home for dinner until you actually call them and invite them. This way you don't build up an expectation only to forget you even said it. We often say things with very good intentions and then forget we said them. The problem is that all too often the other person doesn't forget and every time they see you, they're wondering if this is the day you're going to confirm the date! We can't possibly know if we're the first person or the 21st person to make a promise and then fail to keep it. If this person has experienced this disappointment multiple times, you can really do damage to their self-esteem. Is there someone coming to your mind right now? Someone you promised something to? If so, why don't you give them call?

Think about these things – keep studying the Bible – and have a blessed day!

Today's devotional thought from Proverbs 25:20.

20 *Like one who takes away a garment on a cold day,*
or like vinegar poured on soda,
is one who sings songs to a heavy heart.

This verse in Proverbs deals specifically with the subject of knowing what to say and knowing when to say it! This isn't always easy. It's one of those things that we tend to get better at with age and maturity. As its stated here, the last thing you want to do to someone on a very cold day is take away their coat. This gives us such a great visual of just how inappropriate this would be.

Have you ever gone somewhere and weren't prepared for a change in weather. Think how uncomfortable you were when you were freezing cold and couldn't do anything about it. This same feeling is conveyed when you say the wrong thing at the wrong time. What are some situations we can find ourselves in that cause us to run the risk of saying the wrong thing? How about at a funeral or sitting at a sickbed or being the first to talk to someone right after they lose their job.

Our motives are usually good but sometimes we still manage to say the wrong thing. I always view verses like this as opportunities to ponder the thought being expressed before I have to apply it. It's always best to pray before speaking, anyway, especially in difficult situations.

Verse 11 of this chapter reminds us that there are great blessings that can come from choosing our words wisely. Personally I think people are worth the risk! I've been reminded regularly by many sermons I've heard over the years, that there are only two things that will last for eternity and that's God and people! So what's the application for me and you? God and people are where we should be investing our time. God first, others second and ourselves third! That's a recipe for success, not just in our choice of words but in how we live our lives.

Think about these things – keep studying the Bible – and have a blessed day!

Today's devotional thought from Proverbs 25:27.

27 *It is not good to eat too much honey,*
nor is it honorable to seek one's own honor.

I've never read a truer proverb! Notice the very clever point being made here. First let's consider honey, which is one of the sweetest foods known to man. Eat just a small amount and your stomach is well pleased. Honey was a staple commodity found throughout Israel, so it's not surprising that Solomon uses it as an analogy more than once in the Book of Proverbs. You see, honey is great to eat and very satisfying to the taste. But if you eat too much of it and you can feel sick to your stomach!

Going out of your way to seek the praise of men will have the same effect, only it will be everyone else who will get sick. Sick and tired of hearing about you! If eating too much honey is unhealthy, drawing too much attention to ourselves and our accomplishments is unhealthy too.

We can't accomplish anything good in and of ourselves anyway because every gift, talent and ability we possess is from God. He should get the glory! Not you and not me! Just two chapters later in Proverbs 27:2 we read these words of wisdom:

2 *Let another praise you, and not your own mouth;*
someone else, and not your own lips.

What's the application for me and you? We must not be greedy for too much honey nor too much praise or attention to ourselves. I'm not talking about a positive comment someone makes about a job well done. If someone chooses to encourage you for one reason or another, receive it and be glad. I'm addressing the issue of seeking after the praise of men. Making yourself popular or craving compliments. If we do well then God sees it and that should be enough. In fact you hurt yourself and all the good you do, especially when it comes to Kingdom work because God sees the heart and judges the motives.

These things aren't always easy especially when you feel like no one is noticing. Well friend, that's probably a good thing. I love hearing stories about unsung heroes or even witnessing them. I was on a mission's trip to Mexico several years back. The plumbing was a major issue at the mission facility we were staying at, so the requirement was to leave all the toilet tissue in a trash can and not in the toilet. This is certainly not something Americans are accustomed to doing, but we followed the rules. One of the other men I was on the trip with took it upon himself to empty the trash cans every morning and every evening. He never told anyone he was doing it and he didn't wait to see if someone else would. He never mentioned to a single person that he was doing it. I just happened to notice him a few days into the trip. He was happily and quietly singing songs to the Lord while cleaning up all the bathroom stalls. How cool is that? This is the kind of attitude we should have about all we do for friends, neighbors, co-workers and employers! Remember this, at the end of the day we are doing it all for God!

Think about these things – keep studying the Bible – and have a blessed day!

Proverbs 25 NOTES

Proverbs 25 NOTES

Proverbs 26

In the 28 verses found in Proverbs 26, Solomon takes direct aim at fools, and foolish actions. When you consider that the Biblical definition of a fool is someone that believes there is no God, you begin to see the mess that people can make of their lives when they lack a Biblical foundation. Join me in praying for those we know and love that are not Christian's. Pray that today would be their day of Salvation! I hope you enjoy reading the seven devotionals I've written from this chapter.

Today's devotional thought from Proverbs 26:2.

2 *Like a fluttering sparrow or a darting swallow,*
   an undeserved curse does not come to rest.

I love this verse and here's why. Because of human nature! That's right, because human nature is what it is and our first thought when we hear someone say something about us that is untrue or inaccurate, is to defend ourselves! We feel a need to 'set the record straight'. We worry about our reputation and sometimes we feel a need to get even. This verse suggests to us that whatever unkind or inaccurate words are spoken about us, they need not be defended. Basically this verse tells us that if we're living a godly life, that negative comments will go in one ear and out the other! The people that would listen and believe these comments aren't going to be swayed by your attempts to clarify or explain anyway!

So what's the application for you and me? Don't worry about unkind and undeserved things that are said about you. What should you do? Love

God with all your heart, soul, mind and strength. Serve others whole-heartedly and let God be your defender.

Having said that, this verse doesn't mean that you get a free ride if what-ever you are being accused of is true. If you're being ungodly in word or deed it's still wrong for people to speak to others without first speaking to you but you should also be reminded that *"your sin will find you out".* Numbers 32:23. So, keep a short account before God and remember that you are only a prayer of repentance away from being right with Him.

One final thought. There is often a little kernel of truth even in under-served comments. What am I getting at? If you do hear that a negative comment has been said about you, take it to the Lord in prayer. You should remain open to praying about what was said and be willing to ask God if there is even a shred of truth to the comment. Sometimes, although undeserved and unfair, a comment can reveal a character flaw that might be very small and minor but something you may want to work on. Beyond that, trust God to be your defender. Let the curse simply fly away just like the sparrow mentioned in this verse. If the words of gossip or innuendo are underserved then let God return the comment back onto the head of the person who uttered it. He can handle it much better than you and I can anyway!

Think about these things – keep studying the Bible – and have a blessed day!

Today's devotional thought from Proverbs 26:12.

12 *Do you see a man wise in his own eyes?*
   There is more hope for a fool than for him.

Solomon wasn't just a wise man, he was also a wise teacher. We can glean from this verse that the hardest person to teach is the one who thinks he has nothing to learn. This person thinks far too much of them-selves. They're conceited and full of what they think is important and this becomes a barrier in their ability to hear and learn from others. They're too busy expressing themselves to hear from someone else that's offering them wise council. If you're familiar with the list of woes and judgements found in Isaiah 5, the fifth woe states: *"Woe to those who are wise in their own eyes and clever in their own sight."*

Well friends, one thing that I can say about writing a daily devotional in Proverbs is that I still see too much of 'me' in me! Here's the application.

When we read God's word we need to read it with open hearts and minds. We need to get into the habit of praying before reading and asking God to reveal our true inner selves. I can read a verse like today's three different ways.

First: I can read it with other people in mind. Those foolish people!

Second: I can read it thinking I'm usually open to receiving wisdom from others.

Third: I can read it with a prayerful and sincere desire to grow in this area of my life. Then I'm able to focus on the times that I still get it wrong! If you're still tracking with me, all I'm saying is that there is still room for improvement for each of us. I want all that god has for me, so I try to stay open to learning from others.

1 Corinthians 3:18 states:

[18] Do not deceive yourselves. If any one of you thinks he is wise by the standards of this age, he should become a "fool" so that he may become wise.

Our hope comes in the form of humility before God. We need to be willing to see our own foolishness and in humility ask God to mature us in areas where we have room for improvement. It's worth it brothers and sisters because the more times we get it right, the more opportunities we have to glorify God and be a better example to those around us.

Think about these things – keep studying the Bible – and have a blessed day!

Today's devotional thought from Proverbs 26:20.

20 *Without wood a fire goes out;*
    without gossip a quarrel dies down.

Solomon devotes many of his wise Proverbs to the topic of gossips. Gossiping certainly is a weakness for many and it often has dire consequences. This verse really captures the essence of how to properly deal with gossip. If you add wood to a fire it causes it to blaze longer and hotter and in the same way, if you pull a piece of wood out of a fire and leave it by itself, it goes out in no time. This same principle applies to gossip. If you keep it going by spreading it further, it blazes longer and hotter! The best thing any of us can do with gossip is to let it die.

My pastor back east would often suggest that when you hear what sounds like gossip just ask the person talking if it would be okay for you to quote them on what they are saying. That will quiet them down in a heartbeat! There are many negative consequences to our sinful nature and gossip is certainly one of them. What we say, what we listen to and what piques our curiosity has been affected by the fall of man in the Garden of Eden.

Our tongues and our nature, good and bad, is captured well in the book of James. Look at what is stated in James 3:6-8:

⁶ The tongue also is a fire, a world of evil among the parts of the body. It corrupts the whole person, sets the whole course of his life on fire, and is itself set on fire by hell. ⁷ All kinds of animals, birds, reptiles and creatures of the sea are being tamed and have been tamed by man, ⁸ but no man can tame the tongue. It is a restless evil, full of deadly poison.

Let's shift gears because I want to focus on the only way I know of to overcome the temptation to share gossip or even to listen to gossip and that's to fill our hearts and minds with something else. It's not surprising to me that James ends chapter 3 with a discussion about wisdom. He offers wise counsel about filling ourselves with spiritual fruit that will bless us and others. Listen to his wise and anointed words in James 3:17-18:

¹⁷ But the wisdom that comes from heaven is first of all pure; then peace-loving, considerate, submissive, full of mercy and good fruit, impartial and sincere. ¹⁸Peacemakers who sow in peace raise a harvest of righteousness.

So the application for me and you is to fill our hearts with godly thoughts and godly purposes. You see, friends, what we're filled with the most is what will pour out of us. If our hearts are pure, considerate, submissive and merciful than this is what will come from our overflow. Isn't this better than participating in gossip?

Think about these things – keep studying the Bible – and have a blessed day!

Today's devotional thought from Proverbs 26:22.

²² The words of a gossip are like choice morsels;
  they go down to a man's inmost parts.

Given the many times Solomon repeats his warnings about gossiping, we can be sure that this is a sin that many struggle with. There are so many parties that can be hurt by the whisperings of gossip and we'd be wise to steer clear of this temptation.

This verse captures well the thought that for some people, gossip is as tasty as the sweetest gourmet dessert you can eat. For some, gossip has the same effect as a drug addict when he gets high. He or she gets so excited about what they hear that they can't wait to get more! The words, *"this is confidential"* only makes it that much more of a desire to hear it and pass it on. A gossip will almost always embellish a story to make it even juicier! This is a damaging sin that has no place in the life of a Christian. We see in the Bible that an entire church can be damaged by gossip. Paul's concern for the church at Corinth included a number of problems, but one that made it onto his list of things he feared for the church was, in fact, gossip.

The latter part of 2 Corinthians 12:20 states:

20 I fear that there may be quarreling, jealousy, outbursts of anger, factions, slander, gossip, arrogance and disorder.

Gossip was a problem in the church 2000 years ago, and it remains a problem in the church today. It may sound harsh, but the best thing that could happen to the gossip is stated in Proverbs 26:27:

27 If a man digs a pit, he will fall into it;
if a man rolls a stone, it will roll back on him.

Gossip will and should come back and bite you. In fact, it's the best thing that can happen to you because it may make you see the great damage that can be caused by the tongue. I've suggested in previous devotionals that when someone comes to you with a tasty morsel of gossip, simply ask them if you can quote them on what they're about to tell you! That will likely put an end to it right then and there. So the only remaining question for me and you is: are we gossips? Does Proverbs 26:22 describe you or me? Take this to God in prayer, confess as needed and make a decision to stop this sin in its tracks. We're either the giver or receiver of gossip, and it can stop with us! And it should!

Think about these things – keep studying the Bible – and have a blessed day!

Today's devotional thought from Proverbs 26:24-26.

24 *A malicious man disguises himself with his lips,*
   but in his heart he harbors deceit.

25 *Though his speech is charming, do not believe him,*
   for seven abominations fill his heart.

26 *His malice may be concealed by deception,*
   but his wickedness will be exposed in the assembly.

These verses offer a fair warning that there are those all around us that seem like the nicest people on the planet but in reality are people with evil intent. Note the clever way this individual can cloak themselves with charming speech. The American Indian saying; *"he speaks with forked tongue"* comes to mind. The meaning of a forked tongue is the idea that a person says one thing but their intent is the complete opposite of what they say. Christians need to be wise in this area because the person with the big and caring heart is often the target of this type of deception.

For you and me these verses also offer us a reminder to check our hearts and to be sure we don't speak deceptively. It's another great reminder that we need to be continually baring our souls before God, every day, and to be asking Him to reveal any wicked way in us. We need to keep a very short account of sin and ungodly thoughts.

These verses remind me of the Genesis account of Joseph and his brothers. After they sold him into slavery, they had to live with the deception that they all chose. The lies they told went on for over 20 years! They watched their father live in anguish, all because of their deception! They were eventually reunited with Joseph in Egypt but 17 years later we learn that Jacob dies. What do the brothers do? They continue in their deceptive ways. You may recall their fear that once their father died Joseph would pour out his vengeance. This really shows the heart of a malicious person. They can't even comprehend that someone can be gracious and forgiving. But I love Joseph's response. He could have reacted to their further deception by cutting off their heads but instead what does he do? He focuses his attention on God, recognizing that God had a greater purpose in all that happened to him. Wouldn't it be great if when we are wronged or angered by someone that we would be able to look past the incident and look to God to see what His greater plan or purpose might be in the situation? Pastor and Author Max Lucado states it this way; *"We've been given only one piece of life's jigsaw puzzle and only God has the cover to the box!"* I like that thought because it reminds us that everything that happens in our lives has a greater purpose than what is seen on the surface. We need to trust the fact that God is fair and that He sees everything from an eternal perspective. He's always going to do what's right, and just and best for me and for you!

Think about these things – keep studying the Bible – and have a blessed day!

Today's devotional thought from Proverbs 26:27.

27 *If a man digs a pit, he will fall into it;*
if a man rolls a stone, it will roll back on him.

Have you ever been wronged by someone and it seems like they're going to get away with their wrong? This verse tells us two specific things. First, we need to remember that it's not our job to try to see that someone gets justice. Hebrews 10:30 reminds us that vengeance is the Lord's business.

We certainly do need to be careful in our business dealings and when hiring contractors and such. I've heard all too many horror stories of people that have been taken advantage of by unscrupulous people. This verse shows us that the wicked person that digs a pit or plots to take advantage of a righteous man will have God to deal with. They will be doomed by their own crafty folly.

I'm reminded of the great Old Testament book of Esther. If you're not familiar with this amazing story take some time to read the book of Esther today. The evil man named Haman plots to kill the righteous man named Mordecai. Haman is a manipulator from the word go! He spends a great deal of time plotting and planning to have Mordecai hanged on the gallows. But God has another plan and purpose and Mordecai is found to be righteous in the eyes of God and Man and the evil Haman is uncovered as the ruthless and ungodly plotter. His plans are foiled and the stone that he planned to roll on Haman was rolled back on him. The stone in this story came in the form of the hangman's noose. So what's the application for me and you? God knows it all. He never says, *"I didn't see that coming."*

We need to trust that God is watching over us and He will guard us and guide us through each day. Our responsibility is to live a godly life and leave the rest to Him.

Think about these things – keep studying the Bible – and have a blessed day!

Today's devotional thought from Proverbs 26:1-28.

This devotional is a bit unique in that I'm using the entire chapter instead of a specific verse(s). Solomon seems to have picked three recurring topics that he wants to drill into us in a deeper way. In the past I've commented that I wish I could have been a fly on the wall in Solomon's palace. His wise sayings had to have come from listening to the amazing circumstances that would be presented to him from citizens, as well as conversations he heard directly from those he would always have around him. In Chapter 26, I can almost imagine that he just witnessed three striking circumstances that crystallized in his mind why these three personality traits are to be avoided.

The first theme, found in the first 12 verses is that of foolishness. Let's look at Verse 1 here and you can read the rest on your own:

1 *Like snow in summer or rain in harvest,*
    honor is not fitting for a fool.

The meaning here is obvious. Snow would never be good in the summer and too much rain could ruin a good crop. In the same way that honor or prestige or important positions of responsibility should never be wasted on fools. Read through Verse 12 on your own to see the depth of thought on this topic.

The second theme found in Verses 13 through 19 have to do with laziness. I print Verse 13 here to help capture the thought, and you can read the rest on your own:

13 *The sluggard says, "There is a lion in the road,*
    a fierce lion roaming the streets!"

In reality, this lazy individual is using an outrageous assumption to avoid going outside. By stating 'outside' the author seems to be suggesting that going outside would mean going to work or some similar responsibility he or she just doesn't want to do. Read through Verse 19 on your own to see the depth of thought on this topic. The final theme detailed is that of gossips, found in Verses 20 through the end of the chapter.

I'll add verse 20 here, and you can read the rest on your own:

20 *Without wood a fire goes out;*
    without gossip a quarrel dies down.

So here we see that gossip has many bad side effects, one of them the ability for gossip to lead to quarrelling. The balance of the verses in this chapter confirm the very strong point Solomon is conveying . . . and that is that gossip is always wrong and always has negative consequences. Avoid gossip at all costs! You'll be glad you did! So what's the application for you and me? Foolishness, laziness and gossip are all things that Solomon, the wisest man that ever lived is telling us to avoid. It was true then and it is just as true today. Are you struggling in any of these areas? Cry out to God and confess your struggles to Him!

1 John 1:9 carries with it an awesome promise:

9 If we confess our sins, he is faithful and just and will forgive us our sins and purify us from all unrighteousness.

Think about these things – keep studying the Bible – and have a blessed day!

Proverbs 26 NOTES

Proverbs 26 NOTES

Proverbs 27

M any chapters in the Book of Proverbs follow a particular theme or group of themes. In the case of this chapter, the 27 verses are really 27 separate thoughts. You need to take your time reading each verse as a stand-alone. I hope you are taking time to journal your personal thoughts at the end of each chapter.

Today's devotional thought from Proverbs 27:1.

1 *Do not boast about tomorrow,*
    for you do not know what a day may bring forth.

When I first sat down to read Proverbs 27, and to write this devotional, I didn't get very far. I didn't get past Verse 1 and that's because of a number of very recent events that have become a vivid reminder to me that none of us are promised a tomorrow! We all make the mistake of assuming we have plenty of time! Plenty of time to live and plenty of time to save and plenty of time to forgive and plenty of time to be forgiven. The fact is none of us know how much or how little time we have left. A night barely goes by that we don't watch the news or read a paper about some tragic and unforeseen death of someone far too young. I have had to see friends suffer the agony of losing a child and it's always horribly painful and numbing.

If you're like me then you have a few things on a bucket list, like children or parents you want to spend more time with or any number of things you are meaning to get to. If you're a Christian then you understand better than most that time may be short. For you what is most important is knowing you are right where God wants you to be.

In Ezekiel 1 and the last part of Verse 3, we read these words: *"There the hand of the Lord was upon him".* Wow! How great it is when we know that God's hand is upon us and that we are right where He wants us to be. If you can't read these words with confidence that you're right where God wants you to be then I encourage you to make that a prayer of your heart. I'm reminded more and more with each passing year the importance of being where God wants me and seeing how he orchestrates divine opportunities for me.

There is another statement found in Judges 16, at the end of Verse 20 when Samson loses his strength by sinning against God. There we read these words: *"but he did not know that the Lord had left him".* When I read these words, it sends cold chills down my spine. Can we so neglect God's plan and purpose for our lives that we lose the opportunity to be used by Him in His plan of salvation for the lost? Absolutely! I believe my life and your life will be miserable, especially if we have tasted and seen that the Lord is good and then we proceed to 'boast about tomorrow', assuming we have plenty of time to get serious about our walk.

Why not make today the day you rededicate your life to the Lord. No turning back, fully surrendered, ready to be used by Him! If you aren't a Christian and you're reading this then I urge you to make today your day of salvation. If you know you need to accept this free gift then call out to God right now. Confess you are a sinner and acknowledge that Jesus paid the penalty for your sin. Accept Him as your savior. Do it now! Don't wait until tomorrow because tomorrow may be too late.

Think about these things – keep studying the Bible – and have a blessed day!

Today's devotional thought from Proverbs 27:2.

2 *Let another praise you, and not your own mouth;*
   someone else, and not your own lips.

There's much to learn from this verse and I advise you to spend some time contemplating its meaning. We know as Christians we are to be salt and light, but it's important that we make sure that the light is shining out - for others to see. It's another thing entirely if that light becomes more like a spotlight directed at you or me! We want to be reflecting off of ourselves and on to Jesus!

In Matthew 5:16 we read:

[16] In the same way, let your light shine before men, that they may see your good deeds and praise your Father in heaven.

Proverbs 27:2 is a verse that cautions us about the temptation associated with commending ourselves for talents and abilities that we wouldn't even have if God didn't give them to us. There's always the temptation to take credit for our talents and abilities, forgetting that the credit should go to God. We're sometimes even tempted to take credit for things that should go to others. We rarely accomplish things completely on our own. Aren't we all in some way the sum total of everyone who has ever poured wisdom and knowledge into our lives?

Have you ever stopped to think about what you have learned over the years and the number of individuals that helped shape you into the person you have become? The other point to this verse is the aspect of allowing someone else to be the one to praise you. If we're being proper light reflectors, always seeking God's wisdom in prayer and Bible study, it's likely that we will be commended at some point for a gift or ability that we possess from God. Receive the commendation gladly and be grateful that whatever talent and ability we possess has blessed others in some way.

The challenge is to receive it and then forget it, because there's always the risk that a praise will cause us to see ourselves and not the collective knowledge of all we have learned from others. On the flip side I think we do a poor job of telling folks nice things we see in them. I know there have been times in my life when an encouraging word has come to me at just the right time. The enemy of our souls is always trying to condemn us and make us think we don't matter, aren't needed, aren't loved or even noticed by others. This is a lie from the devil, so don't believe it for a minute. God loves you and He has a wonderful plan for your life. You are uniquely created. You are one of a kind. And you can be a blessing to others the way no one else can be!

This verse in no way implies that we as individuals can't encourage someone for some nice trait or ability or gift they have that has blessed us in some way. But we do have to be careful of our motives for what we say. Never compliment someone in hopes of getting something in return.

Hebrews 10:24-25:

And let us consider how we may spur one another on toward love and good deeds. Let us not give up meeting together, as some are in the habit of doing, but let us encourage one another—and all the more as you see the Day approaching.

Think about these things – keep studying the Bible – and have a blessed day!

Today's devotional thought from Proverbs 27:6.

6 *Wounds from a friend can be trusted,*
but an enemy multiplies kisses.

This is a short verse that's long on meaning! Let's take a look at the first part, this comment about wounds from a friend. It's often been said that friends can correct us like no other. You see a true friend is someone we can go to for anything. A true friend is one that won't just tickle our ears and say nice things to make us feel better. They'll give it to us straight! The best thing that can ever happen to you is to find this type of friendship. I jokingly refer to this person as the one that will tell me when I have food in my teeth or if I need a breath mint! But even more than that, this friend will risk the friendship to tell me something that may be very hard for me to hear. A true friend, one you really care about, and who really cares about you, should be able to say whatever needs to be said. The good, the bad and even the ugly!

We learn from this verse that it's not easy to hear the truth and that sometimes it can really hurt. Here's the good news! This is a wound that carries with it temporary pain, but long term healing! A friend that tells it like they see it is a faithful friend indeed. Wouldn't it be far worse if a friend observed a blind spot in your life that you're not seeing and says nothing? Give your close friends permission to be honest with you.

The second part of this verse tells us that the kisses of an enemy are profuse. The thought expressed here is that there are those that will come into our lives that do not have our best interests at heart. This is the person that will say or do things that are clearly deceptive. The idea of many kisses suggests that these kisses, whether they come in the form of lies, hurtful words, intentional gossip or outright harm to you, they are often subtle. This requires great wisdom and discernment on your part. Your best interests may not always be what people have in mind.

271

Two vivid examples in the Bible come to mind when kisses were nothing more than a cover for evil intentions. The first is found in 2 Samuel 20, when Joab pretends to embrace and kiss Amasa, when his real purpose was to plunge a dagger into his belly and kill him. The second is found in Mark 14, when Judas walks up to Jesus in the Garden of Gethsemane and kisses him. We know this kiss was the betrayer's signal to arrest the one he kissed. So what's the application for you and me? Give a few very close friends permission to be brutally honest with you. Risk some temporary pain or discomfort for long term good. And lastly, be wise! Exercise discernment in your work or business dealings and the same with your personal relationships.

Think about these things – keep studying the Bible – and have a blessed day!

Today's devotional thought from Proverbs 27:9-10.

9 *Perfume and incense bring joy to the heart,*
  and the pleasantness of one's friend springs from his earnest counsel.

10 *Do not forsake your friend and the friend of your father,*
  and do not go to your brother's house when disaster strikes you—
  better a neighbor nearby than a brother far away.

The main thought being conveyed in these two great verses of scripture is the blessings that can come from our friendships. I was reminiscing recently with one of my brothers. We were recalling that when we were kids, it was quite normal for our neighbors to stop in for a visit with our mother. The door was always unlocked and always open. The open door was a form of non-verbal communication, an invitation to feel free to stop by. Times have changed and for many different reasons our neighbor-hoods don't seem to maintain this same open door policy.

This just makes it more important than ever before to make sure we are not living a life of isolation from others we may be able to influence in a godly direction.

Just as perfume or incense are pleasant aromas, so too are our friend-ships, or with some concerted effort on our part, can be! Solomon shares a number of Proverbs that deal with the good that can come from having a few close friends. I fear we don't take the time to develop these important relationships. How come? Because they take time to develop and there's risk involved. Having said that, I think the rewards outweigh the risks.

There are at least two very godly reasons to take the time to develop several close friendships. The first reason is based on what we can give to our friends. And the second reason is what our friends can give to us. Whether the givers or the recipients, this verse reminds us that there will come a time in everyone's life when a friend is going to be critical to our spiritual well-being. This verse tells us that there are times when we can give or receive earnest counsel, and it's going to be with a friend. The only way to develop a friendship that can reach to this stage is to work hard at it! This verse tells us that friendships and the counsel we may ultimately give or receive is often the type of counsel that we can't even go to a family member with. So what's the application for me and you? Friendships need to be cultivated! Friendships require regular contact! Friendships can be critical during times of crisis! And lastly, because friendships are good for the heart!

Are you thinking about someone right now that you would like to develop a deeper friendship with? Why not give them a call? Start today to kindle a few friendships that can benefit each other. See what God does as you earnestly pray about this and start working on your friendships!

Think about these things – keep studying the Bible – and have a blessed day!

Today's devotional thought from Proverbs 27:17.

17 *As iron sharpens iron,*
So a man sharpens the countenance of his friend.

I've had the privilege of being part of a number of men's Bible studies over the years. There's something very special about getting together with men, all with open Bible's and desiring to study the Word of God. The important thing for men is to get past the normal conversations we have like *"how's business?"* or *"did you watch the game last night?"* You get the idea. By the way, I'm not ignoring the women today, I just know that men have a much harder time with this then the ladies do. But if you are a woman reading this and it applies, then that's great!

I was recently challenged by a pastor to make it a priority to go deeper with the men that are part of my sphere of influence. Many men are not going to voluntarily tell you about struggles they may be having. They need to be asked those deeper questions, like *"how are you really doing?"* Of course, the question needs to be sincere and we need to earn the right to ask it. This means we need to get to know a few men more deeply.

This verse expresses in a great way the benefits derived from these deeper friendships. You can almost picture the blade being applied to the sharpening stone making the edge of the blade sharper and sharper. This is what happens when we are willing to invest our time and talents into other men. Hebrews 10:24 states:

And let us consider how we may spur one another on toward love and good deeds.

Men are sharpened by meaningful discussions with other men. If you're a man reading today's devotional and you've never participated in a men's Bible study then let me encourage you to find one and give it a try. You may need to give it a few visits to feel like you can fit in, but I'm confident that you'll find the long term benefits worth the effort.

Why not take the challenge I'm presenting. Start with expressing this desire to God in prayer and then don't be surprised if you find someone mentioning a men's group to you or in some way finding out about one. You see, God is aware that you are reading this devotional! You have to believe and understand that He is that involved in your daily life. He knows my heart and yours. He desires nothing more than to help us in our daily walk. He's given us His Holy Spirit, to guide us to men that can sharpen us through His Word. Friend, God has a wonderful plan for your life. Pray bold prayers to Him right now, and watch what He does!

Think about these things – keep studying the Bible – and have a blessed day!

Today's devotional thought from Proverbs 27:19.

19 *As water reflects a face,*
so a man's heart reflects the man.

This verse catches my attention every month I read it. It's taken me quite a few attempts to write a devotional on this verse. I suspect it's because I realize all too often how poor I am at reflecting Jesus to others. This idea of reflection Is both internal and external. It means that if I doubt the power of God to use me today to tell others about Jesus, I'm most likely going to miss the opportunities that God sends my way to tell others about Him. Here's what James 1:23-25 says on this topic;

[23] *Anyone who listens to the word but does not do what it says is like someone who looks at his face in a mirror* [24] *and, after looking at himself, goes away and immediately forgets what he looks like.* [25] *But whoever looks intently into the*

perfect law that gives freedom, and continues in it—not forgetting what they have heard, but doing it—they will be blessed in what they do.

The message God is giving us here couldn't be clearer, yet all too often I chicken out on opportunities to tell others about Him. When I do seize opportunities, I sit back in awe of how God orchestrates the divine appointment. I have concluded that He presents me with open doors in direct proportion to the days I ask God to fill me with His Holy Spirit. When I'm not filled with His Spirit and yielded to His plan and purpose for my life, I just become another selfish slob who is too worried about myself to be thinking about others. A pastor friend refers to this as the trinity of stupidity, which is my tendency to focus on: me, myself and I!

The question I have to ask myself each day and with each encounter with others is "who am I reflecting in this conversation? Is it me or God living in me?

I have spent over four decades in sales and marketing. I have attended more seminars and heard more motivational speakers than I can count. What I have learned most in all this is that:

You can't be 'taught' boldness.

You can't be 'taught' loving kindness.

You can't be 'taught' how to have a tender heart.

These are things that can only be imparted by the Holy Spirit, and only to those with a humble and yielded heart!

2 Timothy 1:7 states:

For the Spirit God gave us does not make us timid, but gives us power, love and self-discipline.

Brothers and sisters, when we are yielded to God and putting Him first, others second and ourselves third, it is amazing to see what He can do!

Let me close with these verses in Hebrews 10:22-25:

[22] let us draw near to God with a sincere heart in full assurance of faith, having our hearts sprinkled to cleanse us from a guilty conscience and having our bodies washed with pure water. [23] Let us hold unswervingly to the hope we profess, for he who promised is faithful. [24] And let us consider how we may spur one another on toward love and good deeds. [25] Let us not give up meeting together, as some

are in the habit of doing, but let us encourage one another—and all the more as you see the Day approaching.

Let me suggest you make this your prayer today!

Think about these things – keep studying the Bible – and have a blessed day!

Proverbs 27 NOTES

Proverbs 27 NOTES

Proverbs 28

*P*roverbs 28 touches on many subjects that include: wickedness, rebellion, greed and ungodliness. These same verses
offer wisdom to avoid and overcome these things. Read the following six
devotionals with a pen in hand. Take a few minutes to pray, and ask God
to reveal the truths He wants you to glean from this chapter.

Today's devotional thought from Proverbs 28:6.

6 *Better a poor man whose walk is blameless
than a rich man whose ways are perverse.*

I love the principle behind this simple verse. I guess I like it most because
it's such a contradiction to what this world recognizes as something to
respect. Several thoughts come to mind. First, Solomon isn't speaking
here about homeless people living on a park bench. His reference to a
poor man whose walk is blameless describes a person that has made
a conscious decision to live a life without moral compromise. A person
viewed as poor, or poor in what this world deems important, might be
tempted to steal, or cheat on their taxes, or cut legal corners in how they
run their small business. But instead, they resist this temptation and
choose instead to walk a blameless life before God. They refuse to allow
worldly traps to cause them to forsake the opportunity to do well in this
world. There are many different ways a person might choose less to actually gain more! A husband and father that refuses a promotion because it
will require him to be away from his wife and children too many weeks in
a year. A Mom who decides to skip a few lunches with her girlfriends each

month so she can afford to give her daughter piano lessons. A single man or woman decides to keep their old car another year so they can help a family experiencing hard times with their mortgage payment. There are many examples of ways men and women make decisions every day that the world would say are foolish choices. After all, the world would say you only go around once so go for the gusto! Or, the one who dies with the most toys wins! Really? If wealth mattered so much, why do we read about wealthy and famous people committing suicide, divorcing or going into drug rehabs?

Why not live this life for God first, others second and ourselves third? Remember, if you're a Christian then this world is not your home. We're just passing through for a brief time and then we'll spend eternity with Jesus! Contrast this with the rich man whose ways are perverse. The world has great difficulty placing value on the honest, godly, poor man vs. the wicked, ungodly, rich man. The world tends to overlook the ungodly compromises of the rich man, especially if he or she does a community some good from time–to–time. A community might be tempted to overlook a person's unscrupulous business dealings because they write a large check each year to the county fair. So what's the application for you and me? Great wealth has its advantages, but sometimes the more wealth we have, the less time or ability we have to do much good for the Kingdom. And sometimes, once someone has tasted of great wealth, there's a temptation to compromise in order to keep it. I think the verse speaks for itself. It is not condemning wealth, but the verse does state that to be poor and blameless before God and man is far better than to be rich in the things of this world if that wealth causes us to forsake godly living.

Think about these things – keep studying the Bible – and have a blessed day!

Today's devotional thought from Proverbs 28:9.

9 *If anyone turns a deaf ear to the law,*
even his prayers are detestable.

These are strong words from Solomon regarding ungodliness and its effects on prayer. Let me start by explaining that when the author speaks of turning a deaf ear to the law he is referring to the 10 Commandments. The person turning a deaf ear means they are willfully ignoring God's divine commands. We know from reading many verses throughout the Bible that the commandments have a long subset of meaning. For instance the seventh commandment is *"You shall not commit adultery."*

But Jesus teaches us that if we even look at someone lustfully, we have sinned.

What's the application for you and me? Have you ever looked at someone of the opposite sex and had a sinful thought? Have you ever lied, even just once, regardless of how innocent the lie was? These questions are asked for the simple purpose of showing that we can't possibly keep the 10 Commandments. The moment we sin it is God who turns a deaf ear to our prayers! Make a note to read Isaiah 1 on your own, but let's look at Verse 15 now because it addresses my thoughts well for today's devotional.

Isaiah 1:15 states in part: *(note that this is God speaking here!)*

15 *When you spread out your hands in prayer,*
   I will hide my eyes from you;
   even if you offer many prayers,
   *I **will not** listen.*

By this standard, my friends, we're all doomed! And that is exactly what Isaiah is trying to tell us. Unless we can be spiritually cleansed, we are doomed! The scriptures are so clear on this point, yet man continues to try to please God through rituals, offerings and ceremonies. We believe that the more incense we burn and the more robotic prayers we pray, that somehow this will cause the scale to tip in our favor.

Guess what? There is no scale in Heaven. God isn't measuring our good deeds against the bad. God doesn't want our empty rituals. But He hasn't left us without hope! He made provision for us to be cleansed from our sin. He gave us a substitute, one who would take upon himself "our" sin. God sent Jesus, His only begotten Son to die in our place. You see friends it's through Christ that we can be eternally forgiven! And then we can once again have fellowship with God! And we can know with complete assurance that He hears your prayers! Here's how Isaiah states it just a few verses later in Isaiah 1:18:

18 *"Come now, let us reason together,"*
   says the LORD.
   "Though your sins are like scarlet,
   they shall be as white as snow;
   though they are red as crimson,
   they shall be like wool.

What a precious promise we have from our heavenly Father! It's never about what we can do to please God but what He has already done for

BRIAN J. RECHTEN

us, if we would just accept His free gift of salvation through Jesus Christ. If you're trusting in Jesus Christ alone for your salvation, then praise God! You can pray with confidence that He hears your prayers and will answer them. If you have never accepted Jesus as your redeemer, then make that the very next prayer you pray.

He is standing at the door of your heart, anxiously, but patiently waiting for you to invite him in. In my nearly 40 years as a Christian, I have never met a single person that has ever regretted giving their heart to Christ. The only regret I ever hear is the regret that they didn't turn to him sooner!

Think about these things – keep studying the Bible – and have a blessed day!

Today's devotional thought from Proverbs 28:13.

14 He who conceals his sins does not prosper, but whoever confesses and renounces them finds mercy.

There's not a lot of mystery behind the meaning of this Proverb. Here's my take on this verse. What was the first thing Adam and Eve did right after eating the forbidden fruit? That's right! They immediately covered *(or concealed)* themselves because they were naked and ashamed.

Anything we do in secret is opening the door to big problems in our walk with God. Not because we're concealing anything from Him because He sees it all and knows it all anyway. By hiding our sin from others, we have opened the door to shame, and ongoing attempts to conceal the sin. Satan will use this in an attempt to condemn us before God. The devil's mission here is to sideline us from effective ministry. If he can convince us we are unworthy, we will become ineffective for Kingdom work.

You've heard the term *"confession is good for the soul",* well that is 100% on the mark! Confession is what makes God's mercy available to us! And believe me when I tell you that you want God's mercy rather than God's justice.

I urge you brothers and sisters to keep a very short account of your sin. Don't conceal it! That's a trap, and the longer you go without confession, the harder it is for you to repent. 1 John 1:8 states:

"If we claim to be without sin, we deceive ourselves and the truth is not in us"

From God's perspective, you can confess a sin from yesterday or a hidden sin from 10 years ago! He is waiting for you to confess! And ready, willing and able to forgive you and cleanse you from all unrighteousness. When we bring our sin before God in sincere repentance, then we have the promise of 1 John 9 which states:

"If we confess our sins, He is faithful and just and will forgive us our sins and purify us from all unrighteousness."

What a wonderful promise! God is so faithful! Please don't ever doubt that! There is never a better time to make things right with God. If you've been holding onto a sin that is keeping you from a closer walk with God, right now is the best time to take care of this with Him. He is waiting to hear from you! Make today the day you seek God's mercy. You'll be glad you did.

Think about these things – keep studying the Bible – and have a blessed day!

Today's devotional thought from Proverbs 28:20.

20 *A faithful man will be richly blessed,*
    but one eager to get rich will not go unpunished.

Well friends, here we have one of the secrets to happiness and it's no secret at all! The way to be truly happy is to be holy and honest! A man or woman faithful to God and to others will surely be blessed of the Lord! There's such a clever play on words in this verse. The first man, by living a godly life, will be richly blessed. The other man that is doing everything in his power to get rich will have a rough go of it. The verse suggests that in the second man's eagerness to get rich, he is most likely climbing over others and perhaps even doing unscrupulous things in his attempt to get there!

Also note that the first man's rich blessings are not necessarily financial, though God may choose that kind of blessing. Here's the bigger point; our primary goal should be an eagerness to live holy lives, not eager to get rich.

Life is so much more than what we accumulate. Riches like silver and gold, and the accumulation of great possessions are more likely to bring misery than happiness. I'm not advocating a life of poverty here and I'm not saying that being rich is universally a bad idea. What I am saying is that one who races through life, chasing after wealth, may in the process run over or around others to get what he or she wants. The people that might get hurt in the process are people that matter to God. If you are wealthy, thank God for the blessing, and look for ways to be generous with what you have been given!

Chasing after wealth distracts us from all the greater, more everlasting things God has planned for us during our time on earth. Remember brothers and sisters, if you're a Christian, this isn't your home! We're just passing through, sojourners walking along the path to the Celestial City, that wonderful place called Heaven.

Riches might bring you temporary happiness on earth, but it can also blind you to the life God has planned for you. Jesus said it Himself in Matthew 19:23:

"I tell you the truth; it's hard for a rich man to enter the kingdom of heaven."

The end result of chasing after riches in this life may be that you are blinded to seeing your need for a Savior. Even if you've trusted in Jesus, if material wealth is all you're after, you will have missed much! I want more and more to live for others and trust God for the rest. I've tasted and seen the blessings that come from *'others centered'* living. It's such a joy to invest in other people and then to watch and see what God does in their lives. I remember the first time my wife and I had the privilege of having a spiritual conversation with a husband and wife that resulted in them praying with us to receive Christ as their Lord and Savior. Because this couple started attending the same church we attended, we were able to share with them over the next weeks and months, share meals together, and pour into their lives the principles for godly living. Many years later this couple still attend church and are seeking God's blessing in their marriage. Investing in lives of others is far more precious and far more long-lasting than anything I can accumulate in this world!

Think about these things – keep studying the Bible – and have a blessed day!

Today's devotional thought from Proverbs 28:23.

23 *He who rebukes a man will in the end gain more favor*
than he who has a flattering tongue.

Here's a great verse that carries a wonderful life lesson. It may seem a bit ironic that there could be someone in your life that rebukes you, meaning they challenge you about something in or about your life that makes you very uncomfortable, but upon further thought, you determine that what they said was spot on (though painful to hear) and you come full circle and find yourself grateful for their rebuke!

In the same way, you may find yourself really liking someone because they are so flattering in their comments to you, but upon further thought you realize the flattery was false, as is all flattery. The word flattery is defined as excessive and insincere praise.

Here's the point . . .

A faithful friend will be the only type of friend that will *'give it to you straight'*. You're not going to like this *'straight talk'* and you may even have a few choice words with this friend . . . but in the end you'll be thanking them for being willing to risk their friendship to offer you this correction. You'll come to respect and appreciate your friend's wisdom and faithfulness.

Proverbs 27:6 states: *Faithful are the wounds of a friend.*

We all need someone in our life that will *'tell it like it is'*, especially if you're in a position of leadership. You need to give others close to you permission to *'speak the truth in love'* and then not punish them for it!

Now, back to the flatterer! This individual is a sly fox! The flatterer always has something else up their sleeve. Remember the dictionary definition is that flattery is always insincere. The flatterer always has an ulterior motive for what they say and you'd be wise to learn how to spot flattery early on. I've mentioned this in prior devotionals, that the Devil wears camouflage! He's never who he appears to be. Can he influence someone to give you false flattery that could lead down a path of destruction? You bet! I've known many good people that have fallen into sin because of false flattery. So what's the application for you and me? Learn to discern between a positive and sincere compliment by a friend, and similar words from a false flatterer. The difference can be subtle but with time and practice is still discernable. And along the way, try to be a good friend. Be the best friend you can be to someone. Don't go out of your way to point out a fault, but prayerfully consider if a corrective comment is appropriate from time to time. In the end a true friend will thank you for it!

Think about these things – keep studying the Bible – and have a blessed day!

Today's devotional thought from Proverbs 28:26.

26 *He who trusts in himself is a fool,*
   but he who walks in wisdom is kept safe.

Note the first part of this verse states that he who trusts in himself is a fool.

It's not a coincidence that the word '*self*' is contained in the word '*himself*'. It seems that '*self*' is the real problem here! It's often '*self*' that attempts to live the Christian life and therein lies the problem. If '*self*' is doing the work then it's doomed to fail. Only when we're yielding our lives to God and allowing Him to develop godly wisdom in us, will we succeed. You see this in the second part of this verse; he who walks in wisdom is kept safe! What we know from scripture is that wisdom comes from God so we can read this verse as '*he who walks in God is kept safe*'!

The problem that comes with trusting in ourselves is that we make a poor substitute for God. We think too highly of ourselves! We're moody, we're selfish, we're critical, we're unyielding . . . I can go on but I think you get the idea.

Walking in wisdom requires dying to ourselves. Dying to ourselves will seem at first glance like something that makes us miserable but in reality, it's exactly the opposite! It's actually our determined refusal to die to ourselves that often makes us quite miserable! The more we die to ourselves, the more we'll see God working through us. When we begin to see how God can use us to bless others we begin to experience the true joy God has planned for our lives.

When we are able to live our life in a God-centered way vs. a self-centered way we begin to see how our lives can be used to impact the lives of those we come in contact with. The more '*others focused*' we become, the happier we will be. It's easy to focus on ourselves, it's our nature, something we're pre-disposed to do. Focusing on others is contrary to our natural tendencies, hence we require '*supernatural*' assistance . . . and this is what only God can do. Brothers and sisters, there is safety in Jesus. He has a wonderful plan for your life. We just need to let go, and let God have His way with us.

Think about these things – keep studying the Bible – and have a blessed day!

Proverbs 28 NOTES

Proverbs 28 NOTES

Proverbs 29

*H*ere's another great chapter with 27 thoughts to ponder and then apply to your daily life. Reading a chapter every day will cause you to consider the many different thoughts and ideas being expressed by God. My hope for you is that this book will cause you to spend more time studying God's Word, right here in the Book of Proverbs, as well as the other 65 books of the Bible! Enjoy!

Today's devotional thought from Proverbs 29:5.

5 *"Whoever flatters his neighbor is spreading a net for his feet."*

There might be some misunderstanding of this word 'flattery'. A woman will often say to another woman that their clothing flatters them, and in this they are being complimentary, however the word flattery is a word that actually expresses a negative or insincere praise. A synonym for flattery is pandering, if this helps to convey its meaning. I often speak to others about the importance of expressing kind words of encouragement or praise when appropriate. This is both good and necessary, but should never be done with insincere motives. A classic book that I refer to often is Pilgrim's Progress. In this great book, one of the men that Christian runs into on his journey to Celestial City is a character named Flatterer. It's interesting to note that Flatterer approaches Christian and his companion, Hopeful, with 'flattering' words but then he leads them down a path that literally lands them in a net. Flatterer is described as a dark man clothed in white, a false Apostle masquerading as an angel of light. You've heard me say this in the past, that the devil wears camouflage.

He is never what he appears to be and he's had thousands of years to perfect the use of flattery to get our eyes and our hearts off God and onto ourselves. The two-fold warning is to be careful about being led the wrong way by flattering words and be careful, too, that our words spoken to others have a proper purpose and intent.

I'm reminded of the fable of 'The Emperors New Clothes'. You may recall the story of how a king was deceived into believing that these two men had a magical thread that could make the most magnificent clothes that could ever be worn by a King. If you know the story then you know that these two con men had no such magical thread. In fact the King was naked. Yet they did such a fine job of flattering the King by telling him only the wisest of individuals could see the magical outfit. It turns out that no one in the King's court had the courage to tell him he was naked. It wasn't until the King marched through his kingdom that one young boy stated; "The King has no clothes". Only then were the King and all the people willing to see that he was in fact, naked!

What's the point to this story? We can easily be fooled by false flattery if we're not seeking our self-worth from God's vantage point. If our goal is to please God, then what people say to us, good or bad, gets filtered through that lens. This is a far better way to go through life as a Christian than being tossed back and forth by what other people say about us. Remember this, you are precious in God's sight. He loves you so much that He sent His only begotten son Jesus to die for you. If you're trusting in Jesus alone for your salvation you have God's assurance that He loves you. If you have never trusted in Him, settle it today!

Think about these things – keep studying the Bible – and have a blessed day!

Today's devotional thought from Proverbs 29:6.

6 *An evil man is snared by his own sin,*
    but a righteous one can sing and be glad.

This verse starts negative but ends positive and that describes well how the Word of God has application in our daily lives. The Bible tells us that man is wicked and that's simply the reality of our lives in a fallen world!

So a faithful expositor of the Word of God is going to give you the scriptures with straight talk. The good, the bad and the ugly. If all you ever here is the good, then how will you ever learn to discern the difference? And how will you ever grow into a mature Christian unless you are learning all that the Bible teaches? I encourage you to seek a church and Bible teachers that *"say it the way God wrote it."*

Okay, back to Proverbs 29:6. It states here that the evil man is snared by his own sin. The idea of a snare is an interesting choice of the word as it is used here. A snare doesn't just trap you, it entangles you! The idea here is that one sin leads to another and another until your entire life is trapped and you can't even tell right from wrong. It's not a pretty picture.

I love the second part of this verse. The righteous one can sing and be glad! What a beautiful word picture that should encourage us to live a life of holiness! The person living in obedience to God is not as prone to these types of snares. It doesn't mean you won't sin, but it does mean you have more spiritual sensitivity to discern right from wrong. The person living in obedience finds themselves in places of safety, far from the snares of the enemy.

Brothers and sisters, if we've trusted in Christ for our salvation then we're spending eternity with Him in Heaven! While we're on this earth, we need to live as ambassadors for Christ! We need to live our lives in such a way that others will want to know about Jesus!

What is it you do for a living? Are you a doctor? An accountant? A truck driver or a plumber? Maybe you're a secretary or office worker, or maybe you work for a radio station! Well guess what? That's just your disguise! If you're a Christian, you're actually an ambassador for Christ, and you're here to glorify God and to tell others about Him. Now that's something to sing and be glad about!

Think about these things – keep studying the Bible – and have a blessed day!

Today's devotional thought from Proverbs 29:18.

18 *Where there is no revelation, the people cast off restraint;*
     but blessed is he who keeps the law.

It's been said that if you don't believe in something you'll believe in anything. That's why it's so important that believers in Christ boldly proclaim the truth that transforms lives and saves souls. We have to think about what a Christless eternity would be like. We need to share our faith boldly, knowing that God offers eternal life to those that believe in Him.

I've lived long enough to know many people. I've known many during their BC (Before Christ) years as well as their AC (After Christ) years! I've observed many who seemed about as far away from God as a person could possibly be. Then one day, God speaks to their heart and they decide to put their faith in Jesus for Salvation. Yet just days prior they were still cursing God and hating people. My own brother who at one time got great satisfaction out of mocking my faith is now a follower of Christ!

I think the point I want to make about this verse . . . is that spiritual darkness is a horrible place for one to be. I believe most people without faith are actually desperate for it, they just don't know it. I've seen so many over the years, mocking Jesus one week and praising Him the next. The Apostle Paul is a good reminder how a single encounter with the Savior can change a man's heart. But then this verse goes even deeper . . . and touches on the importance of growing in our knowledge of God . . . and His wonderful plan for our lives. Satan will try to keep one from coming to faith right up until the moment a sinner repents. Once a believer, the enemy of our souls will try the next best thing . . . and that's to keep us ineffective for Kingdom work. Satan will try to marginalize us or cause us to think "Okay, I'm a Christian now . . . all is good . . . I'm going to Heaven." And that may be true but there is so much more that God has for us! A wonderful plan and purpose and the more we learn of Him, the more we'll understand. There are so many dying to a Christless eternity that we should want to grow and understand all that God has done for us . . . so we can tell others about the hope that is within us.

Jesus Himself set the example in Mark 6:34:

When Jesus landed and saw a large crowd, he had compassion on them, because they were like sheep without a shepherd. So he began teaching them many things.

Note the emphasis on teaching them! We need to be thankful for knowing the truth and be eager in telling the truth to others!

Think about these things – keep studying the Bible – and have a blessed day!

Today's devotional thought from Proverbs 29:23.

23 *A man's pride brings him low,
    but a man of lowly spirit gains honor.*

Well . . . I confess that this subject of pride and humility is apparently a life-long study for me, and maybe for you, too. Maybe it's because I spent 30 years in sales. I had a wall of plaques identifying my sales accomplishments and all too often I foolishly took credit for these accomplishments, forgetting that it is God who gives me my next breath, let alone every talent or ability I possess. The older I get and the more I learn of God, the more I realize it's all about Him. I have been proud and boastful in years past and it's apparent as I look back. Hindsight is a good teacher but the word of God is far better. Verses like Proverbs 29:23 and others are there for all to see and learn and apply. Like I said, it's a life-long process and I want more and more to just be where God wants me to be. Not trailing behind or running ahead. I love the parable Jesus tells in Luke 18:10-14. It's the parable of the Pharisee and the Tax Collector:

10 "Two men went up to the temple to pray, one a Pharisee and the other a tax collector. 11 The Pharisee stood up and prayed about himself: 'God, I thank you that I am not like other men—robbers, evildoers, adulterers—or even like this tax collector. 12 I fast twice a week and give a tenth of all I get.' 13 "But the tax collector stood at a distance. He would not even look up to heaven, but beat his breast and said, 'God, have mercy on me, a sinner.' 14 "I tell you that this man, rather than the other, went home justified before God. For everyone who exalts himself will be humbled, and he who humbles himself will be exalted."

There are three traps you and I can fall into when bringing honor onto ourselves. The first trap is that it makes us proud. The second trap is that it makes us live with contempt for others. The third trap is that it creates self-righteousness within us. Four other times in Proverbs alone we learn that pride brings arrogance, disgrace, quarrels and destruction. This list alone should cause us to seek God in humility and to ask for forgiveness. Someone once told me that it's far better to learn about humility then to actually have to be humbled by God. Jesus uses a little child in Mathew 18 to make the point that we should be like little children, and our humility we be our honor.

Remember . . . it's all about God anyway!

Think about these things – keep studying the Bible – and have a blessed day!

Proverbs 29 NOTES

Proverbs 29 NOTES

Proverbs 30

$\mathcal{P}$roverbs 30 is unique in that the chapter was not written by Solomon, but instead by a man named Agur. He was very likely a friend or possibly even a servant of Solomon. This chapter is often referred to as the *Book of Agur* or *Sayings of Agur*. Regardless of the exact identity of this man, the thoughts expressed will be beneficial to all who read them.

Today's devotional thought from Proverbs 30:1-6.

1 *The sayings of Agur son of Jakeh—an oracle:*
   This man declared to Ithiel,
      to Ithiel and to Ucal:

2 *"I am the most ignorant of men;*
   I do not have a man's understanding.

3 *I have not learned wisdom,*
      nor have I knowledge of the Holy One.

4 *Who has gone up to heaven and come down?*
      Who has gathered up the wind in the hollow of his hands?
      Who has wrapped up the waters in his cloak?
      Who has established all the ends of the earth?
      What is his name, and the name of his son? Tell me if you know!

5 *"Every word of God is flawless;*
      he is a shield to those who take refuge in him.

6 *Do not add to his words,*
   or he will rebuke you and prove you a liar.

I feel a bit inadequate to thoroughly explain the manifold richness of these verses so instead I will attempt to show you just one or two key life applications from these verses. First, let me state that this is a departure from the normal writings of Solomon. Some believe that Agur was a servant of Solomon or even a friend that knew Solomon and was inspired to write the kind of thoughts and ideas similar to what Solomon often did. Ithiel and Ucal were most likely his pupils or servants and they actually penned what he was speaking. Agur is never mentioned again in scripture so what we see is what we get. And what we see is a man of enormous humility and who had come to a point of complete surrender to his heavenly father. Verse 2 and 3 show the degree of humility found in this man. You simultaneously sense he is an incredibly wise man yet at the same time has come to a realization that he knows very little about the ways of God and why God even bothers to use men like him to accomplish His will in this world. He proceeds to outline a testimony to the amazing holiness and wisdom of God! I am personally humbled and even convicted when I read these words, seeing in myself an amazing shortsightedness of the might and majesty of God. I'm amazed at my own ignorance of who God is. When I think of how amazing God is, I wonder why I spend so much time doing things in my own feeble strength rather than 'letting go and letting God'! So what's the application for you and me? First, I would encourage you to read the entire chapter and read it slowly. Ponder the words as you read them and allow God to penetrate your heart, and reveal just a bit more of who He is. Then ask Him to reveal a little bit more of the perfect plan He has for your life. Matthew 7:7-8 reminds us to:

7*"Ask and it will be given to you; seek and you will find; knock and the door will be opened to you.* 8*For everyone who asks receives; he who seeks finds; and to him who knocks, the door will be opened.*

Think about these things – keep studying the Bible – and have a blessed day!

Today's devotional thought from Proverbs 30:7-9.

7 *"Two things I ask of you, O LORD;*
   do not refuse me before I die:

8 *Keep falsehood and lies far from me;*
   give me neither poverty nor riches,

but give me only my daily bread.

9 *Otherwise, I may have too much and disown you*
and say, 'Who is the LORD ?'
Or I may become poor and steal,
and so dishonor the name of my God.

I have to say that these are some of my favorite verses in all of Proverbs. I have always loved the simplicity of this sincere request a man is making to God. It's interesting to note that the writer devotes one sentence to his prayer that God would help him to be a man of integrity, yet he apparently saw a need to expand on his prayer regarding poverty and riches. I think this is because it's such a difficult thing for man, and it has been for thousands of years.

When it comes to money, we never seem to have enough. Some people will resort to ungodly methods in an attempt to get or keep more money. At a minimum, many will waste far too much time acquiring wealth instead of being content with what God blesses us with. Contentment and money never seem to go well together for too many of us! Here's the simple truth. Most of us already have too much and we still seem to want more. And this tends to cause our eyes to shift away from God and on to *'things'*.

The same temptations that caused Adam to sin still plague us; the lust of the eyes (what we see), the lust of the flesh (what we want) and the pride of life (what we think we deserve).

The place we need to get to in this life is the humble request for our *'daily bread'* mentioned in Verse 8. It's this simple reminder that we need to seek God every day for all our needs, not our wants. The same way bread becomes stale, so too our walk with God when we start to think that we can make it on our own without a daily dependence on Him for all things. God has given us so many examples of why He wants us to seek Him daily. Take the nation of Israel during their wilderness experience. Do you recall the manna from Heaven provided by God? What happened to the manna when the Israelites tried to keep it for the next day? The manna became full of maggots and began to smell. This tells me that it's about surrender! It's about being willing to pray, and mean it, when we ask God for neither poverty nor riches but for what He thinks is best for us, and then trust His answer! Brothers and sisters, it's all His anyway! God has a plan for your life that is far better than your plan or my plan. My plan will inevitably be full of me! I need more and more to want to live my life with God as my rudder, guiding and directing in a way that He knows is best.

Our prayer needs to be this same prayer:

...give me neither poverty nor riches,
> *but give me only my daily bread. Otherwise, I may have too much and*
> *disown you and say, 'Who is the LORD? Or I may become poor and steal,*
> *and so dishonor the name of my God.*

Think about these things – keep studying the Bible – and have a blessed day!

Today's devotional thought from Proverbs 30:15-16.

15 *"The leech has two daughters.*
> *'Give! Give!' they cry.*

"There are three things that are never satisfied,
> *four that never say, 'Enough!'*
16 *the grave, the barren womb,*
> *land, which is never satisfied with water,*
> *and fire, which never says, 'Enough!'*

There is much to learn from these two verses. What we're being shown here in rather graphic terms is the simple fact that the things of this earth will never satisfy us. Everything derived from this world is only going to bring temporary peace, never soul satisfying peace that can only come from God.

If fame and wealth satisfied, why do we read continuous headlines that speak of the famous and wealthy dying of drug overdoses, or going in or back into rehab, or getting divorced for the second, third or fourth time, or getting arrested and even committing suicide? You see my point? It would seem that the more we attain in this world, the more apparent it becomes that these things can't bring happiness in and of themselves.

There are two interesting things we can learn about leeches, mentioned here in Verse 15. First, they will attach themselves to man or animal, and they won't stop sucking blood until they are engorged and can't suck any more. Second, they actually shoot an anesthetic into the host's body, so they can't even feel that the leech is attached! Isn't this a perfect picture of what happens to the Christian when they give in to temptation?

We might feel guilty for a short while, but then we begin to get comfortable in our sin and we stop listening to our inward voice that is telling us what we're doing is harmful to us and others. Verse 16 lists four things that are never satisfied, the grave, the barren womb, thirsty land and fire, which never says enough.

The word picture God is showing us is that nothing this world has to offer is ever good enough. We will always want more because it's our human nature. But God in his infinite love and mercy has provided us with a better way, and that's a life submitted to and yielded to Jesus Christ. He promises us that He can fill that empty void, that sense of dissatisfaction, that feeling like there must be more to life. God has a wonderful plan and purpose for your life and mine. Please believe that today. Ask Him to come into your life and be your Lord and Savior. Confess you are a sinner in need of His forgiveness. For the Christian that has fallen away, or not fully yielded, it's the same prayer! Just confess your sin and your desire for God to take control of your life and watch what He will do!

Think about these things – keep studying the Bible – and have a blessed day!

Today's devotional thought from Proverbs 30:24-28.

24 *"Four things on earth are small,*
yet they are extremely wise:

25 *Ants are creatures of little strength,*
yet they store up their food in the summer;

26 *coney's are creatures of little power,*
yet they make their home in the crags;

27 *locusts have no king,*
yet they advance together in ranks;

28 *a lizard can be caught with the hand,*
yet it is found in kings' palaces.

Here we see a list of creatures, all created by God. The greater teaching to be found here are the principles God wants us to understand about Him and His creation. In these verses we see all these very small and seemingly insignificant creatures yet each offers us a glimpse into how involved God is in His creation. First we read about the ant. This little creature is actually quite fascinating! Did you know that an ant can carry something on its back that is 20 times its own body weight? Putting this in human terms it would be like a 200 pound man being able to carry a 4000 pound backpack! It's small and insignificant but an ant colony will never die of starvation. They spend their entire lifespan finding and storing food for the next generation in their colony. Even strong and giant animals like lions and elephants die of starvation in the wild every year because they only eat when hungry and make no provision for droughts or other natural disasters. God is so intimately involved in His creation that He even has a plan for the ant! Second . . . we have Coney's (also known as rock badgers). If you ever go to Israel you'll find these little creatures anywhere you find lots of large rocks. Why? Because they're not very strong creatures so they find great safety in the crevices of rocks, where other creatures have trouble getting into.

I find it fascinating that God is referred to as the rock throughout the Bible and in particular in Psalms. And it was God Himself that hid Moses in the cleft of the rock, protecting him from seeing God's glory! Third we have the locust. They have no King, meaning no leader of the locusts the way bees have their Queen. Yet they travel in ranks as if trained by a King's army. I see this as such a beautiful picture of Jesus as our teacher and guide. We learn from Him, then we go out together throughout the world proclaiming Him as King!

Lastly, we have the lizard, or spider in some translations. The point being conveyed here, whether lizard or spider is that as insignificant in man's eyes as these creatures are, they're found in King's palaces. One day those that have trusted in Christ for salvation will also reside in the *Kings* glorious palace, our home for eternity, in Heaven with King Jesus! If God cares so much for the least of His creation then how much more for you and I, who He intentionally created in His own image!

Think about these things – keep studying the Bible – and have a blessed day!

Today's devotional thought from Proverbs 30:32-33.

32 *"If you have played the fool and exalted yourself,*
or if you have planned evil,
clap your hand over your mouth!

33 *For as churning the milk produces butter,*
and as twisting the nose produces blood,
so stirring up anger produces strife."

Here we have two verses that deal specifically with our words. One topic that is mentioned as much as any other in Proverbs is the topic of the tongue. The tongue! What we say, how we say it and when we say it! It's all related to the tongue. We've all heard the expression of 'putting your foot in your mouth'. We use this term when we realize we've said something that would have been better left unsaid. This verse goes so far as to recommend we walk around with our hand over our mouths. Verse 32 gives a very good word picture of what happens when we unnecessarily stir up emotions and anger with our words.

What's the application for you and me?

I think there are enough lessons in Proverbs, in addition to the great wisdom found in James 3 to remind us how important it is that we learn how to tame our tongues. I heard a great suggestion once . . . the idea of fasting from words! I know we often think of fasting from food but a fast can involve anything that causes us to focus on God in prayer. An interesting exercise would be fasting for an hour, or several hours, or even a day . . . from speaking. This exercise would most likely cause us to spend more time in prayer, or we might sit down and write a note card or two to someone we've been meaning to reach out to. Think about this for a moment. Are there words that we speak that we would never put on paper? Do we ever say something to someone that we wouldn't want to write to them for fear they could copy and share with others? If we wouldn't want to see our words in a newspaper headline, then they are words we should never speak. Let's make today a day where we choose to edify and build others up with our words instead of tearing them down.

Proverbs 16:24 states:

24 *Pleasant words are a honeycomb,*
    sweet to the soul and healing to the bones.

What can be better than that?

Think about these things – keep studying the Bible – and have a blessed day!

Proverbs 30 NOTES

Proverbs 30 NOTES

Proverbs 31

*P*roverbs 31 is broken into 2 sections. The first is Verses 2-9 and is referred to as the wise King. The second section is perhaps the most widely known of all the Proverbs, the Excellent Wife or the Wife of Noble Character. Adding to the mystery is the fact that the authorship is attributed to King Lemuel. Many believe that this was a pen name for Solomon or perhaps an actual title given to him. Either way, the words from this chapter have been inspiring readers for generations! I have dedicated the final devotional of this book, Proverbs 31:10-31 to my beautiful bride of 40 years. She has been my best friend and love of my life since the day we met. I attribute every good and godly aspect of my life to her love, support and prayers for me! I am truly a blessed man!

Today's devotional thought from Proverbs 31:1.

1 The sayings of King Lemuel—an utterance his mother taught him.

I'll start today's devotional with this question. Who's speaking the loudest into your heart today? King Lemuel seems to have had a loving and nurturing mother that poured godly truths into his heart every day. As I sat down to prepare a devotional for this 31st day of the month, a thought came to mind. There are no months with 32 days, so tomorrow is the first day of a new month! In a sense, tomorrow is a fresh start! For those of us that read a chapter of Proverbs each day, we *'start over'* in Proverbs 1 tomorrow.

This idea of fresh starts is one that the believer in Christ needs to embrace. Think about this; when we're at our lowest points in life, when we're feeling defeated and bewildered by all the chaos and noise of life that surrounds us, convinced that we're doomed to mediocrity in our Christian walk, guess what? God is attracted to our weakness! He has a soft spot for those of us that would humbly and honestly confess our weaknesses to Him! Only when we are empty of ourselves, can He fill us with His Holy Spirit! So let me offer you a word of encouragement! God isn't done with you yet! In fact He's barely gotten started, especially if you've been giving in to the whispers of the enemy that you're not good enough to be used by Him.

If you're convinced that there's no way in Heaven that you can bring anything worthwhile to the Kingdom, then guess what! You are exactly where you need to be for God to use you! You see, it's in our weakness that He becomes strong. I've been a Christian for nearly four decades now, and for too many of those years I managed to believe that God was fortunate to have me on His team. I foolishly thought I had great talents that God could put to good use. It was only when I realized that I had nothing to offer God except a broken and contrite heart, that He was able to use me.

So today . . . with this thought on our minds of new beginnings and fresh starts, why not stop right now and pray! Ask God to empty you . . . of YOU! And fill you with His Holy Spirit! Confess your need for Him to be on the throne of your life, and yield your life to Him completely. Be the clay that the Potter can use! Let Him mold you and make you into the man or woman or child He wants you to be!

Think about these things – keep studying the Bible – and have a blessed day!

Today's devotional thought from Proverbs 31:1-4.

1 *The sayings of King Lemuel—an inspired utterance his mother taught him.*

2 *Listen, my son! Listen, son of my womb!*
   Listen, my son, the answer to my prayers!

3 *Do not spend your strength on women,*
   your vigor on those who ruin kings.

4 It is not for kings, Lemuel—
it is not for kings to drink wine,
not for rulers to crave beer,

Most of the attention in Proverbs 31 is paid to the account of the prov- erbs woman found in Verses 10-31, and these are important verses to be sure. But the real story here is the account given by the writer who is most likely Solomon, but possibly someone else. It's the author's account of his mother's reminder of what it will take for a man to find the right wife, and the significant role a wife plays in the making of a man of God.

What is being expressed here are the traps and pitfalls that cause so many men to miss out on God's wonderful plan for their lives. God has a way He wants men to find a wife, but sinful man often allows his lusts to get the better of him, which can interrupt God's plan. The lustful man pursues *women* instead of *a woman*, and he often pursues her for all the wrong reasons. In many circumstances, alcohol accompanies a man's poor choices. To be clear, men aren't the only ones susceptible to poor choices when under the influence of alcohol. I recall reading a survey that confirmed that alcohol played a leading role in the vast majority of unwanted pregnancies.

Alcohol is a mind-altering drug that impairs our ability to make decisions. We are prone to do and say things when we have been drinking that we would never do or say otherwise. The writer reminds us how these pur- suits can blind us to the wonderful plan God has for us.

How I hope and pray that some will heed the tender call of Proverbs 31 to seek a spouse God's way. The application applies to all of us equally, men and women, younger or older.

Although sexual relationships outside of marriage are not specifically mentioned here, it's certainly implied. God designed sex to be between a husband and wife, period, and end of subject. Sexual relationships outside of marriage, coupled with the abuse of alcohol will not only ruin kings, it will ruin you and me. If you've already made a mess of things in these areas, then I have good news for you! God loves to give second chances! Confess your sin and ask God to forgive you, then rededicate your life to Him.

Listen to the words of Jeremiah in Lamentations 3:22-26:

22 Because of the LORD's great love we are not consumed,
for his compassions never fail.

23 They are new every morning;
great is your faithfulness.

24 I say to myself, "The LORD is my portion;
therefore I will wait for him."

25 The LORD is good to those whose hope is in him,
to the one who seeks him;

26 it is good to wait quietly
for the salvation of the LORD.

These words certainly seem to capture the fact that God is ready, willing and able to grant you a fresh start. He can take whatever mess we've made of our lives . . . and turn our lives around in amazing ways. All you have to do is ask!

Think about these things – keep studying the Bible – and have a blessed day!

Today's devotional thought from Proverbs 31:8-9.

8 "Speak up for those who cannot speak for themselves,
for the rights of all who are destitute.

9 Speak up and judge fairly;
defend the rights of the poor and needy."

The first nine verses are written as practical advice for rulers and in particular for anyone in a position of leadership. But theses verses also offer sage advice for me and you. I often think of the employer/employee relationship and the government/citizen relationship in the context of these verses. We can observe both positive and negative aspects in the text before us.

On the positive side, we would hope and pray that employers or government leaders would look out for the best interests of those under their care. An employer should be concerned for his or her employees, their work conditions, their safety and fairness in their compensation. Our hope would be for a governmental leader to lead with their citizen's well-being in mind.

Conversely, an unjust employer would not be concerned with the welfare of those under them just as an unjust governmental leader would put his or her self-interests in mind over the interests of the citizens in their care.

What should our response be to verses like this? I think we have an obligation to speak up and defend those that can't defend themselves. I think of the needs of the unborn and the elderly when I read these verses. Regardless of what our government takes as a position in these areas, we have a higher authority that should govern our lives. In the case of the unborn, it should be apparent that they are at the mercy of others to make it out of the womb. It's an atrocious thought that one so vulnerable would actually be faced with their own destruction before their first breath.

For the Christian, it would seem to be a non-negotiable that the unborn and the elderly and those living with special needs would be assured of our love and protection as citizens and as children of God. When Jesus told the parable of the sheep and the goats in Matthew 25, He tells us very clearly that what we do for the least of those around us, we do it for Him.

It's never too late to right this wrong of our generation.

James 1:27 states:

[27] Religion that God our Father accepts as pure and faultless is this: to look after orphans and widows in their distress and to keep oneself from being polluted by the world.

My admonishment is to defend the unborn, the elderly and those with physical and mental disabilities because it's the right thing to do!

Think about these things – keep studying the Bible – and have a blessed day!

Today's devotional thought from Proverbs 31:1-9.

1 The sayings of King Lemuel—an oracle his mother taught him:

2 "O my son, O son of my womb,
O son of my vows,

3 do not spend your strength on women,
your vigor on those who ruin kings.

4 "It is not for kings, O Lemuel—
   not for kings to drink wine,
   not for rulers to crave beer,

5 lest they drink and forget what the law decrees,
   and deprive all the oppressed of their rights.

6 Give beer to those who are perishing,
   wine to those who are in anguish;

7 let them drink and forget their poverty
   and remember their misery no more.

8 "Speak up for those who cannot speak for themselves,
   for the rights of all who are destitute.

9 Speak up and judge fairly;
   defend the rights of the poor and needy."

Most commentators believe Lemuel is actually Solomon. The name means *'devoted to God'* and most believe that it was an endearing name Solomon's mother used to call him. Regardless of who the author is, there's no disagreement that it was written by a man reminiscing about his early years and pondering the wise council of his mother.

To be clear, not all of us were raised by godly mothers and some reading this aren't raising children, and some are right in the midst of raising one or more. So what's the application for all of us? I think we can all benefit from this Proverb in the same way. And that's to be willing to recognize and apply godly wisdom wherever and from whomever it comes! This advice applies equally to men, women, young or old, single or married, which means it applies to you and me!

None of us should be spending our strength on anything that would distract us from living for Jesus! And I've lived long enough to know that there are many things that can distract from the real meaning and purpose for our lives. Most of the things we will spend our time on are not ungodly things. But that doesn't always make them right things! Let me explain what I mean. I was given wise council many years ago that's been very helpful. I was told that there are really only two types of decisions we make every day. MORAL decisions and PRIORITY decisions! Moral decisions are the easy ones. These are decisions between right and wrong! They're very black and white, meaning this is a right thing to do or this is a wrong thing to do. This doesn't mean that you can't or won't make morally poor choices. You will! But there's a remedy for that and it's called repentance. Priority decisions are much harder to discern because a priority decision is between a right thing and another right thing! This is where the wisdom described in today's verses comes in handy.

Using one of the topics addressed in today's verses, a man can hang around night after night with many different women and do nothing immoral in any way and still be making a poor decision! Wouldn't it be better for a young man to be spending time studying God's word, or sitting at the feet of older and wiser men, or going to school or learning a trade, or exercising? These are priority decisions. If I've used a good analogy here, you can see how these can often be the harder decisions to make. Today's text is about a mother's godly council to a man that might one day be a king.

Today's text is showing us how to live as children of *the King!* The challenge before us brothers and sisters are the daily choices we'll have to make that are not just right or wrong choices, but choices between right and right and knowing which one is the better choice!

Think about these things – keep studying the Bible – and have a blessed day!

Today's devotional thought from Proverbs 31:10-31.

10 *A wife of noble character who can find?*
She is worth far more than rubies.
11 *Her husband has full confidence in her*
and lacks nothing of value.
12 *She brings him good, not harm,*
all the days of her life.
13 *She selects wool and flax*
and works with eager hands.
14 *She is like the merchant ships,*
bringing her food from afar.
15 *She gets up while it is still night;*
she provides food for her family
and portions for her female servants.
16 *She considers a field and buys it;*
out of her earnings she plants a vineyard.
17 *She sets about her work vigorously;*
her arms are strong for her tasks.
18 *She sees that her trading is profitable,*
and her lamp does not go out at night.

19 *In her hand she holds the distaff*
and grasps the spindle with her fingers.
20 *She opens her arms to the poor*
and extends her hands to the needy.
21 *When it snows, she has no fear for her household;*
for all of them are clothed in scarlet.
22 *She makes coverings for her bed;*
she is clothed in fine linen and purple.
23 *Her husband is respected at the city gate,*
where he takes his seat among the elders of the land.
24 *She makes linen garments and sells them,*
and supplies the merchants with sashes.
25 *She is clothed with strength and dignity;*
she can laugh at the days to come.
26 *She speaks with wisdom,*
and faithful instruction is on her tongue.
27 *She watches over the affairs of her household*
and does not eat the bread of idleness.
28 *Her children arise and call her blessed;*
her husband also, and he praises her:
29 *"Many women do noble things,*
but you surpass them all."
30 *Charm is deceptive, and beauty is fleeting;*
but a woman who fears the LORD is to be praised.
31 *Honor her for all that her hands have done,*
and let her works bring her praise at the city gate.

Being a happily married man for over 40 years, this devotional is dedicated to my amazing wife, Patti.

Verse 10 states: *"A wife of noble character who can find? She is worth far more than rubies."*

Well, I can't resist the urge to say that my wife costs me more than a few rubies pretty regularly, but before this statement gets me in trouble, let me be very quick to state that she's worth it!

To the married men reading this, let's face the facts. Most of us would be a mess without a godly wife at our side. God is certainly the one that chisels all our rough edges but it's our wives that help by holding the chisel! Sometimes our wives might prefer holding the hammer, so they can apply it to our thick and stubborn heads! All jokes aside, I have to say that in my case, I have an amazing and godly wife that spends time in the morning, after I leave for work, praying to our Heavenly Father and asking Him to mold me and make me into the godly man He wants me to be. And because God is omniscient, He can already see me as He planned me! Lord, help me to be humble enough to allow You; '*God the Potter'* to mold me, *'the clay'*, into the man you want me to be.

I cherish my wife for her commitment to pray for me, and for all she brings into my life and for all she has meant to me these past 40 years.

The chapter ends with these 3 verses:

29 *"Many women do noble things,*

   but you surpass them all."

30 *Charm is deceptive, and beauty is fleeting;*
   but a woman who fears the LORD is to be praised.

31 *Give her the reward she has earned,*
   and let her works bring her praise at the city gate.

So, to my bride and joy . . . thanks for being my wife, my best friend and the one I can count on to lift me in prayer before our Heavenly Father and to support me in all I do!

Now I realize that this devotional may end up in the hands of some that aren't married, wish they were married, or are divorced, and even some that have made a choice to remain single. I still believe these verses have application for you as well. There are principles presented in these verses that have meaning outside the context of marriage. These verses deal with proper priorities, time management, financial matters and much more. In all these areas of life, including marriage, I suggest you pray and ask God for direction in your life. The Bible tells us to *"make your requests known to God."* He hears your heart. He answers every prayer! Sometimes He answers with a yes, sometimes with a no and sometimes with wait! But He is always faithful to answer.

Think about these things – keep studying the Bible – and have a blessed day!

Author Bio:

*B*rian J. Rechten resides in Northern California with his wife Patti. They have been married for over 40 years. They have 2 grown children and 2 precious grandsons. Brian has been an entrepreneur since he was 10 years old! Brian started a paper route that became one of the largest in that part on NJ. He routinely won 'new subscriber' contests and once was awarded a new bicycle for the largest number of new subscribers in a year! Brian has won numerous awards for outstanding sales achievement and creativity. Brian has served on regional and national Boards of many not-for-profit organizations. Brian owned his own business for 25 years which he sold in 2007. Brian started a new career in radio in 2008 and has held the roles of Senior Account Executive, Local Ministry Director, Director of Sales and General Manager. Brian completed a 2 year 'School of Ministry' program in 2008. Brian & Patti have traveled the world extensively. Hobbies include; Travel, Reading and Golf. Brian and Patti have been Bible study leaders for four decades. They currently host a married couple's life group through their local church. Brian enjoys public speaking and teaching. Brian can be reached at brian.rechten@gmail.com